SIMPLY
CONFUSING OR
CONFUSINGLY
SIMPLE

SIMPLY CONFUSING OR CONFUSINGLY SIMPLE

The Weight Loss Equation

CHRISTOPHER BARKER

CONTENTS

FOREWORD

Weight loss is a topic that has become seemingly more convoluted the more we have learned about nutrition and the human body. Why has something on the face of it so simple become, in practice, so hard for the growing majority of our population? In my day-to-day work as a Clinical Nutritionist, I am constantly hit with some variation of the below statements from new clients:

'I think it's my genes'.

'I've tried every diet; they don't work for me'.

'I think my metabolism is slow'.

'I can lose weight, but I always put it back on'.

Suppose we take a quick look at the advice from alleged experts on social media. In that case, we are hit with any number of so-called revolutionary techniques, from intermittent fasting to keto, carnivore, blood type, or even body type diets. It is no real surprise, given that the demand for products, services, and education has made the weight loss industry worth an incredible $3.4 billion in 2023 in the US alone.

I think this is part of the problem—we have long known how to achieve weight loss; however, most people are looking for alternative/faster/more straightforward ways to lose weight, and therefore, selling or merely telling people the truth is usually a lot less appealing than if I pretend I have come up with a ground-breaking way for you to eat what you want and get the results in half the time. Unfortunately, when money comes into the equation, everything gets a little complicated, and what was a relatively simple issue becomes increasingly distorted.

Dieting also takes on religious-like characteristics where people will defend their point even in the face of undeniable facts. For example, we know from research that ketogenic/high-fat diets are not superior for weight loss when calories and protein are equated, but there are people out there who will defend this diet (smelly breath and all) till they die.[1] If you try to show them the evidence, they inevitably throw their buttered coffee at you or discarded bits of liver meat.

Because there are thousands of conflicting expert advice out there, I guess we shouldn't be too surprised that many people have given up in their attempts to lose weight, blaming hormones, genetics, or the Conservative Party (I don't know, but I feel like we enjoy blaming them for most things). There is no reason someone can't lose weight when given the correct advice; however, such advice seems to have been so diluted by the many self-proclaimed gurus online that what tends to reach the consumer is quite different and, in most cases, far from helpful. One of the tools that has made us more learned as a society has also diluted the truth and, in so doing, made us worse off in many ways. Don't get me wrong, I think the internet and social media are tools for the good, but even the best tools in the wrong hands can become dangerous ones.

By the end of this book, I aim to have unravelled much of the confusion on this topic, along with giving you actionable steps when it comes to creating your diet to achieve your weight loss goals.

Before I start, it is worth pondering that question again: "Why has something seemingly so simple become, in practice, so hard for the growing majority of our population?" Is there any evidence that the rise in knowledge and understanding of the human body has helped our understanding of the obesity crisis? Judging by the continued rising figures for obesity, I would suggest not.

In the book, *Psychology of Money*, Morgan Housel postulates the same problem concerning our finances, "Through collective trial and error over the years, we learned how to become better farmers, skilled plumbers, and advanced chemists. But has trial and error taught us to become better with our personal finances? Are we less likely to bury ourselves in debt? More likely to save for a rainy day? Prepare for retirement? I've seen no compelling evidence". You can see the correlation between our weight loss problem and the financial situation he writes about. The main reason I bring this up is his conclusion beautifully matches my own and highlights what will outline this book. He writes, "Most of the reason why, I believe, is that we think about and are taught about money in ways that are too much like physics (with rules and laws) and not enough like psychology (with emotions and nuance)".

You see, much of the literature and what is taught about weight loss, as well as how doctors approach weight loss, only focuses on one dimension of the puzzle. Like with finance, the focus has always been around the rules and laws. In our case, the rules that govern fat storage. Don't get me wrong, I will go into detail about these as they are integral to understanding the problem, and in going through them, I will hopefully unravel some of the confusion within the scientific literature; however, once the laws are explained and set out, I will then move onto the psychology of weight loss as this is just as essential to understanding the obesity crisis.

Strap in, prepare for some foul language, some non-PC quips, and hopefully, a lot of helpful information to take away. Whatever your reason behind purchasing and reading this book, I want to thank you and remind you that if you find anything offensive within these pages, in the words of Ricky Gervais, "Just because you're offended, doesn't mean you're right".

INTRODUCTION

My journey into the world of nutrition and fitness started in my early teens. Like so many young men, I first witnessed the great Arnold Schwarzenegger grace our television screens as Conan. With one look at those massive chesticles and ripped abs, I was hooked (as gay as that sounds, I'd like to think it was the effect Arnold's muscles seemed to have on the women around him that made me go, "I want that!"). I immediately joined my school gym as soon as I was old enough (15) to do so, and a year later, I was downing rather chalk-like protein shakes (safe to say these have come a long way since the first time I tried one, although tell that to some of the vegan versions on the market today).

The first book I read (other than the fantastic *Harry Potter* books) was Arnold's *Encyclopedia of Bodybuilding* (yes, I was a strange kid). It was safe to say I was hooked. At that time, while the World Wide Web was a lot less accessible and rudimentary, this was almost a blessing as I was then subject to a lot less fad diet advice and misinformation. It did, however, mean I had to rely on the questionable advice from the older and bigger guys at the gym who probably wouldn't have known what good nutrition looked like if it slapped them in the face. Weight loss, or I should say fat loss back then, looked like cutting carbohydrates and increasing low steady-state cardio (walking on a treadmill) in a fasted state.

If you think parents know best, this may be true for something like the choice of school or how best to fold your clothes… this does not, however, hold true for nutrition. I remember returning from school one day and my mother asked me what I wanted for dinner. I wondered if we had any chicken or anything high in protein. She returned with, "We've got lots of cheese! And that's high in protein". Apparently, when something is said with enough conviction, and we don't have enough education to know better, we will blindly follow. No wonder my abs didn't make an appearance that year as I chowed my way through wheel upon wheel of cheese, only to later discover my diet was now 70% fat.

Over the years that followed, it is safe to say I explored (or rather was suckered into trying) many of the new fad diets that came along. Intermittent fasting, Atkins, carb backloading, and even the alkaline diet are just some of the ones that remain imprinted in my memory. There may have been worse ones, but I have likely blocked these out because of the trauma of them (I, like many men, choose to use the old faithful technique of pushing down negative emotions or memories until they boil up to the surface into uncontrolled rage or chronic illness… the latter of which did befall me). Thankfully, even I wasn't stupid enough or willing to try the keto diet or think for a second that adding butter to my coffee would make me lose weight. However, millions of people have, and maybe this is a sign of the desperate measures many are willing to go to in order to try and achieve their goal of fat loss. At this point, it is worth quoting a modern Marmite figure, Jordan Peterson, who said, "In order to be able to think, you have to risk being offensive". While I will make some brash comments throughout this book, know that I am trying to educate, and nothing I say should be taken personally.

In the UK, it's estimated that around 1 in every 4 adults and approximately 1 in every 5 children (aged 10 to 11) are living with obesity. Isn't it a strange state of affairs when you think we now know more than ever about nutrition and the causes of obesity, yet these figures seem to be increasing? The UK isn't even the worst offender of this. It begs the question, where are we going wrong? Is there something we are still missing from the weight loss puzzle? I think this question embodies our main problem; therefore, the aim of this book is to help navigate you through all confusion so that, hopefully, as you finish reading this, you can better understand where you have been going wrong and what to do.

You see, the reality is, we know why people put on weight... no matter what you have read, weight gain does not work outside the realms of an energy balance. And neither does weight loss (unless you have liposuction or lose a limb). We will put on weight when our energy input exceeds the rate of our energy expenditure... FACT.

Energy in vs. Energy out = Weight gain or Weight loss

While the problem is simple at its core, there is so much more going on in the body that will impact this

7

simple equation. It is these variables that people inevitably latch onto and then try to argue that this means energy balance doesn't apply or work or these variables are packaged up and sold to you as a new shiny approach to quicker weight loss (people are always in a rush, so promising quicker results is a good sale to the desperate). I think our attraction to these variables is also part of the problem. You see, many people who have struggled with weight loss are searching for a reason that excuses or explains their failed attempts. Therefore, they are willing/ want to ignore the simple fact that weight loss is governed by one simple principle, and any system claiming to work against this principle is a bit like me trying to argue that I have developed a new type of gravity.

Every single diet works by creating an energy deficit. If you don't believe me, Keto Zealots, try eating 10,000 calories from fat daily… let's see how the miracle of ketosis stops you from putting on any weight. At the same time, please feel free to purchase my new type of gravity called Air Light… details are on my website… use discount code KETOCUNT10 to get 10% off your first order.

Most people sit in one of three camps. Camp one is Energy in vs. Energy out. While this method works, and there is no question about that, many believe it neglects some of the variables within the energy balance system and, therefore, falls short (although, when done right, it doesn't ignore these variables at all; they are still all part of the equation). The second camp is more health conscious and does not like the simplicity of this method as it detracts from focusing on the source of our nutrition.

Finally, the camp of people who have tried dieting and failed and, therefore, are convinced that calorie counting doesn't work, so they are looking for any other explanation as to why they failed.

Are you starting to understand why I called this book *"Simply Confusing or Confusingly Simple"*? While I will discuss the confusion surrounding your weight loss journey, it will always come back to energy balance—we can't escape this FACT. And while you may currently sit in the *it's my hormones* camp, or *my metabolism is naturally slow* camp, I will explain why this impacts the equation and how to navigate around this... but it will always be within the realm of this energy balance. Just like we don't start floating away because of gravity (even if you have purchased my Air Light), we can't escape the principle of energy balance whether we agree with it or not. To quote Ricky Gervais again, "Beliefs do not change facts. Facts, if one is rational, should change beliefs".

Now, if you are sitting there thinking, who are you to tell me about weight loss? Let me quickly introduce my credentials so you don't assume I'm just another PT trying to copy the James Smith blueprint of using swear words and blunt honesty to sell a book (worth noting, I am a fan of his approach). I developed an interest and then a passion for nutrition after my own Crohn's diagnosis at the age of 19. I won't lie, it took me a considerable amount of time to get my health under control. The problem I had with going on and coming off different medications (many of these medications I was meant to be on for life to help manage my condition) was that the side effects that usually followed exposed a glaring problem with not only my condition but the health care system and how we view health. You see, most of the time, doctors (and it's not their fault) are taught to treat symptoms, so they prescribe drug X to treat symptom Y. What is missing from this formula? Don't you think it's interesting that, most of the time, we are not attempting to tackle what caused symptom Y. As a society, we are always looking for a quick fix in all aspects, so rather than looking at our habits or lifestyles and figuring out what has potentially caused our poor health, many of us want a pill or a drug to fix the problem. This is the same problem many people face regarding weight loss—we want to blame something other than ourselves for our problems.

Anyway, I got a little off track there, but essentially, after a few rounds of cortical steroids leaving my physical health along with my mental health in tatters, I decided I would start to learn more about Crohn's disease, the implications that diet and lifestyle played on this condition, and finally, learn to listen to my body. Fast forward a few years where, thanks to some lifestyle/nutritional modifications and, thankfully, the care of an amazing gastroenterologist team, I had come off all medication and was in remission (I do still have flare-ups, usually from stress, however, for the most part, although I don't want to jinx it, I have managed to lead a reasonably normal life... although my bathroom breaks are probably longer than most people's). I moved into Personal Training as it seemed to go hand in hand with my passion for learning more about how to help the human body, my love of exercise, and the reward of helping people.

After I made a move to a gym in Chelsea where the clientele could finally pay what I felt my service deserved (Yas Queen), I quickly realised that while I wanted to continue to help people, helping the rich housewives of Chelsea build better bums or sweat out their weekend sins was not why I became a PT. While this could help at least pay my mortgage, I needed a plan and look to the future. In 2019, I started my first qualification as an advanced clinical weight loss practitioner, and from that, my passion grew and evolved. Every new qualification I did breed more interest and more hunger to learn, moving into fertility nutrition, gut health, cancer nutrition (even veganism...), and many others until I eventually became qualified as a Clinical Nutritionist.

This book is a culmination of all my studies, what I have seen during my ten years of working with clients to help them achieve long-lasting weight loss, and probably at least 15 years of reading everything I can find on weight loss so I could selfishly improve my own body composition (I mean, come on... I can't rely on my personality). That meant sifting through all the shit out there with the hope that now I have done so, you don't have to. I have tried to base most of this book on the most up-to-date and the highest quality research (meta-analysis, human-controlled trials) rather than relying on animal studies and anecdotal evidence, which are the go-to tools of the low-carb community or anyone who claims fasting is the miracle cure-all.

Why is weight loss the topic for your first book? The answer to that is relatively simple: weight management is something that affects most people in one shape or another at some point in their lives; it is also one of the most essential aspects from a health perspective. With the growing rates of obesity and the pressure this puts on our healthcare system, it seems daft that this topic is so misunderstood and only getting worse. Weight loss, while simple, actually has an individual complexity to it that makes it interesting from a physical and psychological perspective. As something that can affect all genders (it is hard to keep up with how many there are now) and all ages and races, it seems like a good topic to start on. I'm sure I will do one on gut health and then probably menopause, but for now, let's stick with weight loss.

Hopefully, if you make it to the end of this book (I know our attention spans have got worse, and most people can't sit through even a 10-second reel these days), you will have a (relatively) complete understanding of weight loss and all aspects that usually get confused/ butchered, and will walk away with something a little more helpful than the mantra *eat less, move more* (although I'm not saying that doesn't work).

Enjoy, and thank you for reading.

PART 1: LET US BEGIN

I have gone back and forth on what order this book should be written in, and while I want to go straight into the part where I get to call people idiots, it makes sense to first tackle the governing principles of weight loss. And to do this, we need to understand what makes up our energy balance. This might be old news to many of you, but it is always worth setting the scene as this will help unpack the confusion later on.

Before I do this, I want you to apply (or attempt to) what Daniel Evertt discovered when he was trying to learn the language of the Pirahã (a village at the mouth of the Maici River in the Lowland Amazonia region)... Okay, it's a bit of a random segue, but bear with me. The story goes that the Pirahã are among the oldest inhabitants of the Amazon. Missionaries for over 20 years had tried and failed to learn the language of the Pirahã. When he arrived, it appeared that learning the language was impossible, and his initial attempts using the linguistic tools he had developed all fell short. How was it that the children in the village could pick up the language, but despite his advanced knowledge of linguistics, he just could not? The truth he learnt was this.

What prevents people from learning is not the subject itself, as our capabilities to learn and grow are potentially limitless, but rather the rigid ideas and realities we form. We think we know the answer and develop a level of smugness and superiority on the topic. We close our minds to other possibilities, searching only for those confirming our bias. Children are typically free from these biases; they feel inferior, which helps drive their hunger to learn, which is part of the reason children learn so quickly. He finally cracked their language when he allowed himself to feel inferior and immerse himself in their way of life, becoming reliant/dependent on them rather than studying them. "Chris, where are you going with this story?"

The point of that segue (other than it's just interesting) is that I don't care what you think you know about weight loss; if you have picked up this book to confirm your smugness, you've failed. Clear your mind (it shouldn't be too hard for some of you), and allow yourself to look at the weight loss equation through fresh, child-like eyes for the first time, free from bias and emotion. (This may also help with some immature jokes I make along the way).

CHAPTER 1: ENERGY BALANCE

We are governed by energy balance: Energy In vs. Energy Out.

In order to lose weight, we need to be taking in less energy than we are burning. Simple, right? Arguing against this is like arguing that someone lost all their money because they were saving more than they spent… see, it doesn't make any sense. You can't escape the energy equation, no matter how much you want to blame your parents, whichever God you worship, or if you think the Earth is flat or round. I don't care; just know that if you take in more energy than you are burning, you will put on weight, and if you take in less than you are burning, you will lose weight. (BTW if you still think the Earth is flat, that is a whole different issue and maybe weight loss shouldn't be your primary concern right now but rather getting your brain scanned.)

Now, we have established that we can look at the two parts of this equation.

Part 1: Energy In
Since we are not plants and, therefore, we don't use photosynthesis (the process by which green plants and other

organisms transform light energy into chemical energy), it is safe to say that the *energy in* part of the equation is very simple… it is from the food and drinks we consume. Simples!

Part 2: Energy Out
The *energy out* part of the equation is a little more complicated, but we will quickly go through this now. This is not where most of the confusion arises but where some people start to get a little confused. Let's refer to this part of the equation as "Total Daily Energy Expenditure". You've probably heard of it before, but again, it's worth breaking down for anyone new to this and to just familiarise ourselves with it.

There are four parts to this.

Basal Metabolic Rate: This accounts for roughly 60% of your energy expenditure and is essentially the amount of energy your body requires to run basic processes. It is our basic life-sustaining functions like breathing, blood circulation, controlling body temperature, brain function and cell growth (to name a few). It is sometimes referred to as resting energy expenditure or resting metabolic rate. Your body is always using energy, even at rest, which is why people can still lose weight in a coma (despite not moving at all).

Non-Exercise Activity Thermogenesis (NEAT): This has gained a lot more attention in recent years with slogans like "Neat up 24/7". While I understand the premise of this slogan, and NEAT does make up a very important component of the weight loss equation, it makes little sense to tell someone to increase their NEAT as NEAT is technically the energy you expend doing unconscious movements throughout the day that aren't actually exercising. If you actively look to increase your NEAT, it is no longer considered NEAT... I digress a little, but it's worth just undoing this marketing gimmick. For example, as I type this on my keyboard, my NEAT is increasing by the simple act of me aggressively typing away. When I wake up in the morning and run to the bathroom before my small old-man bladder bursts, this is NEAT. If I go for a walk to intentionally increase my step count, this is no longer unconscious and, therefore, falls into what is called NEPA (non-exercise physical activity). You see, you can't tell someone to fidget more, it just happens. Maybe it should be called "NEPA up 24/7" although decidedly less catchy. NEAT is one part of the equation that is most impacted by dieting, so we will go into this in a later chapter and explain why NEPA is actually a very useful tool when it comes to weight loss.

Exercise: I mean, we all know that exercise burns calories, although I continually preach that we should never view exercise as purely a way to burn calories as I believe this is one of the least important benefits to it. However, it does increase energy expenditure, so it is part of our equation.

Thermic Effect of Food: The last part of the energy equation comes from the foods we eat. Sounds strange but it actually takes energy to extract energy from the food you eat. Different foods have different thermic effects, so they require different amounts of energy to get the energy out of them. If our diet is made up of foods with a higher thermic effect (meaning they require more energy to process/digest), it means our total energy output will be greater.

There you have it... our Total Daily Energy Expenditure is made up of Basal Metabolic Rate (BMR), NEAT (and NEPA), Exercise and the Thermic Effect of Food. We should now have a basic understanding of both the *energy in* and the *energy out* part of our energy equation. This is important as it is this equation that governs our weight loss goals and also helps to explain all the subsequent confusion.

Obviously, our health is more complicated than just how much energy we take in and burn, but for the purposes of this book, I am attempting to break down weight loss for you, which, if you are someone who is overweight or obese, will, in turn, improve most of your health markers as a result. Just a modest reduction of 5%-10% of body weight has been shown to reduce depression, cardiovascular disease risk, and improve mobility and sexual function... just saying. If you take in more energy than you burn, then the energy is stored. First in the liver and then in fat cells.

The principle of energy balance is based on the first law of thermodynamics, which states that energy cannot be created or destroyed—only transferred. Some critics argue that the flaw of this is that the law of thermodynamics requires a closed system, and our bodies clearly aren't a closed system. If our bodies don't operate like a bomb calorimeter (a machine used to determine the calorific values of solid and liquid fuels), then there are clearly inaccuracies to this system and, therefore, it is not all about energy balance. This is the first misunderstanding and actually one that forms the basis of much of the confusion around weight loss. You see, in our energy balance model, as the energy we take into our bodies cannot just disappear, while it is not perfectly conserved in the body, the various components of our *energy out* part of the equations already take into account that the human body is an open system.

This is why when people talk about the various sources of energy we take in having different effects on our weight loss, we aren't disagreeing—it is factored into the *energy out* part of the equation.

Another example might be: "Well, eating more of this food/macronutrient causes me to be hungrier and have more cravings". Again, the energy equation doesn't dismiss this. In this example, if we end up eating more food as a result of these cravings, it will affect the *energy in* part of the equation as a result… but it is still within the scope of our energy balance equation.

You see, you can argue with me, but you can't escape the energy balance. No matter what your dietary preferences are, you are either affecting the in or the out part, but you are still within the bounds of this equation. You can't escape this matrix—sorry, Neo (or Andrew Tate).

Notice, up until this point, I have used the word 'calorie' sparingly as I am only trying to convey the main principles of energy balance and weight loss. As soon as you start talking about calories rather than energy, people become more opinionated, confused or just hangry. You see, energy balance is sometimes referred to as CICO or calories in vs. calories out. While I don't argue against this terminology or this model, I find it is easier at the start to just talk about energy as it seems to keep emotions out of it and allow clearer minds to prevail.

Hopefully you are still with me at this point, and we can agree on energy balance. With that being said, it's time to get into our friend—the calorie—to clear up why this is still the same thing as energy balance.

CHAPTER 2:
THE CALORIE CONUNDRUM

Now, I'm going to assume (probably correctly) that you have heard of our friend, The Calorie, before. What I won't assume is that you actually know what a calorie is, as when I did a quick survey of people in my gym to check, the most common answer was, "It's what food is made up of". Oh, sweet Jesus! I expected better from a luxury gym in one of the more affluent neighbourhoods in London.

Well, simply put, a calorie is a measure of energy. Webster's Dictionary defines it as: "the amount of heat required at a pressure of one atmosphere to raise the temperature of one gram of water one degree Celsius that is equal to about 4.19 joules". MMMMM, sounds tasty, right! After a little deep dive on Google to explore the origin of the calorie, while a surprisingly interesting yet slightly confusing search, it appeared that the word calorie seemed to originate from Paris around early 1819 noted in lectures given by Nicholas Clement (however, he was talking about heat engines and not donuts). The calorie made its way from France into international scientific literature during the 19th century and reached American vocabulary after Wilbur O. Atwater's series of articles in 1887 in Century magazine included a description of the energy content of foods that defined the calorie (kcal) for American audiences.

So, the little calorie started in the study of heat and energy in machines (steam engines) and slowly moved into human machines as part of food and metabolic studies. Come the end of the 1920s, the calorie was now ingrained in American nutrition science and dieting culture... and we haven't looked back since.

Now that we hopefully understand that a calorie is a measurement of energy—and nothing more—we should start to see the flaw in the argument, "Not all calories are equal". This is like me arguing not all kilograms are equal or not all litres are equal. It is an argument that is framed incorrectly. You see, there are other components to food that will have other impacts on our bodies. The macronutrients (whether it is made up of fats, carbs or protein) and the micronutrients (the vitamins and minerals), for example, can affect things like our hunger hormones, which can impact how we subsequently feel and how much more we eat. It would probably be more accurate to say, "Not all foods are equal", but a calorie is just a calorie, I'm afraid. Where we get those calories from can impact our ability to lose weight, but this will be because potentially poor sources of calories may lead to overconsumption of calories, so you end up consuming more, not because the calories are different. We are still governed by an energy balance, and a calorie is still just a calorie, just like a metre is still a metre.

The problem I see with this is people tend to go too far in one direction or the other. So, some people will say calories don't matter, which is clearly not true since we have explained we are governed by an energy balance and calories are the energy we put into our bodies. People can still put on weight even if they only eat organic wholefoods free from anything artificial, sugar or whatever you have chosen to demonise. I have seen many so-called "clean" eaters pack on weight while shopping solely at Whole Foods, and many people who go vegan actually put on weight, so clearly calories matter. Some people claim they don't need to count calories but can lose weight. Well, this is because they have put themselves into a calorie (energy) deficit. Calories still count even if you choose not to count them.

On the other hand, people go, "Well, I could eat just sweets and lose weight". This is true to some extent as we have seen extreme examples of people trying to prove this point, and while I like the flexibility of the whole 'If It Fits Your Macros' approach, there are some limitations to the overall health of these types of diets. However, yes, if we put ourselves into an energy deficit, we will lose weight. If we look at the famous example of Jared Fogle (the Subway diet guy), he managed to lose 245 pounds following a diet that consisted of skipping breakfast, a six-inch turkey sub, bag of crisps and a Diet Coke for lunch, followed by a foot-long veggie sub and Diet Coke for dinner... definitely not a diet I would recommend as a nutritionist, but illustrating that as long as you are in a calorie deficit, you can lose weight.

It is impossible to gain weight in a calorie deficit, just like it is impossible to lose it in a surplus. When clients of mine have ushered the words, "I have been eating in a deficit and gained weight", without being rude, I politely remind them that this is the equivalent of me saying, "I was walking in the desert and drowned". It doesn't make sense. What we tend to find is that people are lying about their calorie intake, or not so much lying but omitting many foods, condiments and drinks from their tracking. Or you have the weekend warriors who are strict five days of the week, eating in a deficit, only to overindulge all weekend. Again, this is a simple numbers game—if you are eating in a 400-calorie deficit every day, by the end of Friday, you will have created a 2,000-calorie deficit (quick maths). Overeating and drinking too much on the weekend can easily accumulate to erase this 2,000-calorie deficit, taking you out of your deficit for the week = no weight loss. There are many other reasons why they may utter this nonsense, but we will address each reason in depth in later chapters.

There are also those who like to argue that calorie counting doesn't work because of the inaccuracies in the act of tracking. I agree that there are inaccuracies but that doesn't mean calorie counting doesn't work. There are clear inaccuracies in weather forecasting, but trust me, if it says it's going to rain in London, I wouldn't bet against it. As we have mentioned, the human body is not a closed system, so it is impossible unless in a metabolic ward to measure accurately our *energy in* and *energy out*, but the act of tracking is a fantastic way of learning more about what is in the food you habitually eat and is a great form of cognitive restraint. Some form of cognitive restraint is the most common trait of people who are able to lose weight and keep it off in the long run.

I'm not saying everyone needs to track, but it is a great way of better understanding how much energy we are putting into our bodies every day. Let's be honest, it also teaches you more about portion control and what one serving size actually is when you have to weigh your food out. People who have never weighed or measured but claim they can eyeball the amount are only lying to themselves. If we as a species could eat intuitively, this book would not exist, and I would probably be writing a satirical piece on bringing up my children as Xe, ZE or Zim. The truth is, our intuition, when it comes to eating, probably died out at the same time that common sense did. And this probably died in a mesmeric blaze of woke politics, heavily processed food alternatives, TikTok dance videos and mumble rap.

If I were given a million pounds every time I came across these two really small examples of why intuitive eating doesn't work, then I would be at least in the same conversation as some premier league footballers when it comes to wealth. The two examples are olive oil and peanut butter, both labelled as "health foods" (I mean, extra virgin olive oil should definitely be a part of most diets, and well, there was definitely a period where peanut butter was the latest health food), but both foods are easy to overconsume. While I am a fan of these, they are rich in fats, which also means they are a rich source of calories.

The difference between 30g of peanut butter and 50g is around 120 calories. Doesn't sound like a lot, but when you learn that your client has been using a tablespoon instead of a teaspoon when adding peanut butter to their morning porridge, just that one mistake was setting them back around 300 calories, which might be the difference between being in an energy deficit or being in a surplus. How many people don't even think about the olive oil they are cooking with or adding to their salads? One tablespoon contains approximately 120 calories, so while you splash it all over your healthy "clean" vegetables or in your salad, just because it is considered healthy doesn't mean it works outside of the realm of our energy balance.

We should be aware that food labels can be up to 20% inaccurate, according to the FDA guidelines. That means, for example, a serving of hummus that claims to contain 100 calories could actually weigh in at 80 calories or 120 calories. I don't even really want to address restaurant calorie calculations as they are usually terribly inaccurate as portion sizes can vary greatly, although, if you are trying to reduce your calorie intake and that causes you to then choose the meal at that restaurant with the lowest calorie option, it is a form of cognitive restraint and has helped you make a better decision regardless of the inaccuracy.

Also, how the food is cooked or processed can change the calorie content. Even the makeup of your gut microbiome can change the number of calories that you are able to extract from the foods you eat. So, yes, there is lots of room for mistakes. Dr. Giles Yeo, author of the book *Why Calories Don't Count*, was recently on the podcast, 'Diary of a CEO', where he made the point that a stick of celery has six calories raw, but if you cook the celery, it becomes 30 calories... not sure anyone has ever got fat from eating cooked celery, but you get his point...

Another example is that almonds have been overestimated in calorie content by about 32%. J. A. Novotny, in 2012, did a study looking at the results of 18 different people when eating almonds. The results varied threefold around the 'average' calorie estimate, with some people being either good or bad metabolizers. This means that some people consuming a handful of almonds a day could unknowingly consume around 700 calories more over the course of a week than others. This highlights one issue of the calorie counting practice. No matter how accurately you track your calories, you are still limited by the premise that everyone can extract the same amount of energy from the same food. We already know metabolic rates vary, but other factors like the length of our intestines and the speed of food in transit can play a major role. Differences in our genes can also play a role. For example, some people can extract more energy from starchy carbohydrates like potatoes or pasta than others as they produce up to three times more starch-digesting enzymes (amylase), which allows them to break down more starch and release more sugar. Along with our genes, our gut microbiome can also impact how much energy is extracted.

BUT all this is doing is confusing accuracy with precision. Just because we aren't 100% accurate doesn't suddenly mean calorie tracking doesn't work or calories don't matter. Remember, calories or *energy in* is half of the weight loss equation. If we are consistently tracking our intake in order to put ourselves in a deficit even without 100% accuracy, we will likely be creating the eating habits that lead to weight loss, and if we aren't losing weight, we just adjust our deficit further to allow for these inaccuracies. The thousands of clients I have helped to lose weight by putting them in an energy deficit is evidence enough for me, but there are hundreds of research articles out there illustrating that calorie tracking works, which I will add now for anyone who likes to read research papers... if not, just take my word for it.[2,3,4,5,6]

Is it a perfect tool? No. Layne Norton, PhD, makes a brilliant point in rebuttal to this, which I will now steal as it works better than any other analogy I can come up with. If you are trying to keep a budget, you can't know exactly every expense or bill that will come out at the start of every month, you also won't know exactly how much the money you earn is worth as things like inflation and interests can fluctuate. So, you can't know exactly how much you are making or how much you are going to spend, but we don't then say that budgeting is worthless. Have you ever budgeted? If you have, let's be honest, have you then gone on to lose money (put on weight)? The answer is no. Just because something is not perfect does not make it worthless (a phrase I like to repeat to myself while standing naked in the mirror... anywho...).

Granted, there are lots of people who don't need to track and are able to maintain a healthy body weight—

this is probably because their basic eating habits are quite healthy, and they have likely never yo-yo dieted before (also because of body fat set point, which we will tackle in Chapter 4). Just because some people are able to maintain their lean physique without tracking does not mean tracking doesn't work. I am also not telling you that you have to track, but again, it is to say it works even with the inaccuracies because self-monitoring our energy intake is a great way to develop the diet that will put us into an energy deficit. A little dive into the literature again shows that calorie tracking is associated with both clinically significant weight loss and is more common in weight loss maintainers. [7,8] It is also important to note that I did find it has been linked to an increase in the development of disordered eating/eating disorders, so I don't advise it for everyone, and sometimes getting a client to track for a week or two is enough to gauge their average intake and teach them more about what they are currently consuming from both a calorie and macronutrient standpoint, without being too triggering.

Now, before we go further into this rabbit hole of weight loss, can we still agree that energy balance is what governs weight loss and that when we talk about *energy in,* this refers to calories consumed? (I will be using energy and calories interchangeably from now on anyway.) If you, for some reason, still don't agree with this, it might be worth putting this book down, hitting yourself in the face with it, and then picking up a book about a unicorn that shits cocaine because that is probably something you can relate to better.

What we should now understand is that in order to lose weight, you need to be in an energy/calorie deficit... and therefore (drum roll please), all diets work through creating a deficit. Whether you are removing carbs to create the deficit, removing breakfast, eating like a rabbit, only drinking juice (don't do this), whatever works for you at this point, I don't care. Okay, I care (hence drafting this book), but I think it's first worth discussing our metabolism and our energy/calorie needs in order to better understand the slight complexities of working out our deficit or maintenance calories.

I want to just drill these two points in before the next chapter:

1. Calorie is a unit of measure – so all calories are equal just like all inches are equal, although my six inches may feel like an eight... yes, penis joke... I'm not above that.
2. Calories count even if you don't count them.

CHAPTER 3:
MY METABOLISM AND ME

Simply put, your metabolism is the process by which the body converts food and drink into energy. It's a complex process that combines calories and oxygen to create and release energy (ATP). We have probably all heard of ATP from our biology classes back in our school days. ATP or Adenosine Triphosphate is essentially our body's energy currency. If we create more ATP than we use, we store this energy in adipose tissue (also known as fat).

There are two types of metabolic reactions—catabolic and anabolic. You may have heard these terms used in the gym by classic gym bros either in reference to the anabolic steroids they are taking or talking about if they aren't eating enough, they run the risk of "going catabolic, bro". Catabolic refers to reactions that involve the breakdown of body compounds, which release energy. Anabolic refers to reactions that require energy, where smaller molecules are put together to build larger ones. Essentially, think catabolic as breaking down and anabolic as building. So, our overall energy balance determines the level of both these reactions.

Your metabolism is the chemical engine that keeps you alive by creating the energy you need from the food you eat. The speed at which it runs obviously varies from person to person. Our basal metabolic rate will vary for a number of different reasons—sex, age, muscle mass, body size, weight, and hormone disorders. Obviously, a 6ft man who weighs 100kg will need more energy at rest than a 5ft woman who weighs 60kg. So, how do we work out our BMR? Well, there are a few different formulas out there and calculators online that you can use. The Harris-Benedict equation or the Muller equation are two examples of ways to calculate your BMR.

(Remember, your BMR makes up about 60%-70% of your TDEE, so it is worth also adding your activity level into this equation to give you an accurate TDEE.)

Any formula used is an estimate based on normal population data. So, if I calculated a client's maintenance calories to be 2,000, this is the predicted level of calories he/she/it would need in order to maintain their current body weight. I want to place emphasis on the "PREDICTED" part of that sentence. You see, despite the equations factoring in differences in genders and age, it can't take into account differences in genetics, daily habits, past dieting experiences, or hormonal imbalances—all of which will have an impact on how many calories your body uses per day.

We often refer to some people as having "fast" metabolisms. What this means is that their body is inefficient at production and usage of ATP, sounds bad but… this means they end up wasting a lot of potential energy, and therefore, burn through more energy in the day, needing more energy (calories) in order to maintain their current weight. People with "slow" metabolisms are likely to have very efficient ATP production, and therefore, need less energy to support their current weight. This wastage of energy is caused by a process called thermogenesis, which refers to the production of heat. Increased thermogenesis means more calories are burned off at a cellular level. Someone who has taken part in lots of previous "crash diets" will probably have been through a process of metabolic adaptation (which we will explain more about), made their production and usage of ATP more efficient, and now have what we call a slow metabolism.

This means that in my client scenario, where I calculated his/her/its maintenance level to be 2,000, if they had participated in multiple crash diets in the past, then their maintenance level might be lower than predicted, causing them to potentially gain weight at this predicted maintenance level.

So, you see, while we know the energy balance is what governs weight loss, it is not always so simple to figure out what our energy intake should be. Whatever your goals are, I usually suggest starting at maintenance and giving it a month to see how your body responds (although this is for someone willing to track).

This should also shed light on what is actually happening when someone says they are eating in a deficit and not losing weight. They may have calculated their deficit wrong, or their metabolism is operating below their predicted level. I have found in my work with female clients that many who have a greater dieting history, or those with conditions like PCOS or reaching their perimenopausal/menopausal years, will have maintenance levels below their predicted level. This is why many either become disillusioned with weight loss in general or turn to even more extreme diets to achieve weight loss and why many assume the act of counting calories is a futile practice. Don't worry. I will address this in more detail later, but again, it helps explain that while there may be reasons why it is harder for some people to lose weight, weight loss is still governed by energy balance.

The next point worth mentioning is that your metabolism (your body) is not a perfectly closed system, so we can't predict exactly what will happen. This also means your metabolism is not an exact set point. For example, if we worked out your maintenance level perfectly, you might think reducing your calories by just 50 would elicit weight loss over time as you are technically eating in a deficit. However, in reality, nothing would happen (even if we were able to track your calorie intake 100% accurately). The truth is that your metabolism is more of a range than an exact number. If my maintenance level is 2,000 calories, it is likely that eating 1,900 calories wouldn't cause any weight loss but neither would 2,100 calories cause any weight gain. Why is this? Well, as I mentioned before, the body is not a closed system, so if we were to eat just a small amount over our maintenance, we would increase the amount of energy waste (thermogenesis) occurring, or we might unknowingly increase the amount of NEAT for the day. And the reverse is true. In a small deficit, our bodies may just become more efficient with our ATP, naturally slowing the metabolic process.

If we go beyond this so-called metabolic range, as it were, so the energy imbalance—either positive or negative—was sensed, then this would elicit a change (weight gain/loss). This is why when we create someone's deficit, we usually recommend a drop of around 20% of total calories. So, if 2,000 was my maintenance, my deficit would be 1,600 calories (400 deficit... quick maths again).

So, there are some limitations to working out our maintenance calories, and therefore, there is room to make mistakes when setting up our calorie intake, and this might be an area where some individuals go wrong. But this again does not change the fact that we are still—yep, you guessed—governed by an energy balance. Also, it hopefully highlights why we should be patient with our weight loss goals and practices as everyone is different. It may take a little time to first understand how our metabolism is currently operating before we launch into our deficit.

Now we understand, at least to some degree, the nature of calculating the 'energy in' part of our equation (remember, food and drink... and don't worry, we will get to the whole carbs vs. fats vs. insulin arguments), it is worth understanding the principle of body fat set point theory before then moving onto explaining metabolic adaptations that cause the inevitable weight loss plateaus that are the bane in most people's dieting lives. Without this understanding, we will constantly be banging our heads against the wall, confused as to why we aren't able to achieve our weight loss goal, or at least why we are unable to maintain it.

CHAPTER 4:
BODY FAT SET POINT

Body fat set point theory (wow, that doesn't roll off the tongue, does it!?) is an integral part of our understanding of why our diets aren't working, and without this understanding, we would run into further confusion. To understand the premise of body fat set point, I think it helps to give you one of my terrible analogies, although not my worst as you will discover later.

Let's pretend you own a hot tub—essentially, large baths which are self-contained units that provide users with somewhere to relax and destress (yes, I googled hot tubs to make sure that my analogy worked). A thermostat is one of the most important parts of a hot tub. It controls the water temperature based on your preordained settings. The thermostat will turn the hot tub's heater on and off to keep the temperature at the level you have set. This means you can peacefully relax and not worry about slow cooking yourself. It has a set way of working, and if it senses any deviation in the water temperature, it will automatically correct itself (I'm not an engineer but logic and Google back me up on this). This is, in part, a negative feedback system in which a sensor connected to a switch keeps the environment within the prescribed parameters. Our body has a number of these systems—take, for example, our own internal thermostat. What happens when we get too hot? We sweat. What happens when we get too cold? We shiver. Another example of a more tightly controlled negative feedback system in the body is that of our hydration system. Both of these systems are tightly controlled and essential for our survival. If our body temperature increases or decreases too much, we risk heat stroke or hypothermia; if we drink too much or too little, we risk death (although, again, this is at the extreme).

Our hydration system is very tightly controlled, the kidneys sense our hydration levels and send out a message via a hormone called renin, telling us to either increase our fluid intake (thirst) or to increase our water output (increased need to pee). It works year-round pretty much perfectly (except in rare cases when idiots drink too much alcohol or play stupid drinking games, or inexperienced athletes overhydrate during an event). We are all bombarded with messages from people like me telling us to drink more (non-alcoholic fluids that is), but have you ever had to track your fluid intake? The answer is no... unless, of course, you are intentionally trying to hit some preordained target. You see, the negative feedback system is so strong that you don't have to track—your body will tell you. Have you ever tried to ignore thirst? It's fucking impossible and a stupid thing to ever try.

Why is this relevant to weight loss? Well, just like our hydration, our body fat is controlled by a negative feedback system. Sounds a bit strange given the obesity crisis but stay with me. Remember I mentioned there are people who are able to stay roughly the same weight for years without ever counting a single calorie. This is because we have sensors and switches in our bodies that govern this negative feedback system. Don't believe me? Let's just quickly look at the rise in obesity. The obesity epidemic emerged in Westernised countries during the 1980s, when the average man consumed roughly 2,000 calories a day (I mean, I have found a few different figures, but I've chosen the average) and weighed 172.2 pounds or 78kg. The most recent research I could find (2017) says that the average American man is now consuming 3,600 calories and weighs 199 pounds or 90kg.

So, during those 37 years, our calorie consumption has increased by 1,600 calories more per day, yet the weight has only increased by 12kg? This is a bit confusing, given that scientists calculated that to gain 1kg of body fat requires an extra 7,700 calories.[9] If we were to look at things from a purely numerical point of view and I were to consume only an excess of 500 calories per day for a year, this would equal (500x365=) 182,500 calories extra in one year. If 7,700 calories is 1kg of body fat, in one year alone, I would gain almost 24kg (#Quickmaths). So, if there was no negative feedback system preventing an infinite weight increase, then we should be, by all definitions, no longer a bipedal species but some species closer resembling that of Jabba the Hutt. Remember that is just for one year of only 500 calories extra. If in 2017 we consumed 1,600 more calories per day, we would gain almost 76kg in that year alone.

This clearly illustrates that something in our bodies is preventing this extra energy intake from being stored. You see, the negative feedback system is designed to protect our bodies; hence, we cannot hoard energy indefinitely. This negative feedback system is what Dr. Andrew Jenkinson, in *Why We Eat Too Much*, refers to as metabology rule number 2 (rule number 1 referring to the energy balance governed by the first law of thermodynamics—we have already covered this). There are actual studies looking at this exact phenomenon. Before the time when ethic committees were quite so strict, there was an amazing study done at the Vermont State Prison in Burlington. In 1967, American scientist Ethan Sims wanted to study what happened to a group of men who deliberately over-ate to increase their body weight by 25% over the period of three months. Sounds like a good deal for someone stuck in prison and probably used to appalling food conditions, but good luck getting this passed through an ethics committee now. Anyway, the men started out by increasing calories from 2,200 to 4,000 per day. The participants steadily gained weight until something unexpected happened. They just stopped, despite not being allowed to exercise and still eating 4,000 calories, they were no longer gaining weight. Calories were then ramped up to 8,000-10,000 per day in order to get the participants' weight up by 25% of their starting weight. This was four times what the scientists had predicted they would need in order to increase body weight. Some of the participants, even at 10,000 calories, were resistant to further weight gain. Unsurprisingly, they noticed that the metabolic rates of these previously normal-weight subjects sped up in response to their increased caloric consumption as if to defend their initial lower weights. Also, the men had difficulty maintaining weight gain, and most shed all the weight they had gained relatively easily once their calorie intake returned to normal.

In 1995, the overfeeding studies done at the Rockefeller University Hospital investigated the effects of a 10% weight gain on two different groups. One group was of normal-weight participants, and one group was obese. One really interesting point to make here is that the metabolic rates of the obese group were higher than predicted. You see when overweight people like to blame their "slow" metabolism on their inability to lose weight, the irony is that, for the most part, they will have a much faster metabolism on average than someone smaller who they deem to have a "fast" metabolism. The results of this study showed that when participants had a 10% weight gain, their basal metabolic rate increased by over 600 cals per day in the normal weight group and 800 cals per day in the obese group.

When we look at the evidence, we can see that our bodies will fight to keep our weight below a certain level. Interestingly, none of the Vermont prison study participants had to follow any type of diet protocol to get back to their normal pre-study weight.

Why is this so important? Well, if our bodies fight against excess weight gain, then the same must be true for weight loss, right? Think it's time to introduce why we plateau next—the other half of the body fat set point.

CHAPTER 5: WHY WE PLATEAU

We as a species have evolved, adapted and gone on to create amazing new technologies. If you had told someone 60 years ago that we would all walk around with a device not much bigger than a wallet in our pockets that could contact other people anywhere in the world, access the World Wide Web, take pictures and videos, and have access to live television, it would be safe to assume they might think you are crazy.

Our lives have changed drastically but some of our inherent genetics/evolutionary/biological traits have not. Our bodies, hormones, and inherent drivers for survival are still what they were hundreds of years ago. When we put ourselves into an energy deficit, we know why we are doing this. For most people, it is likely to get more "summer body ready" or whatever health or aesthetic reason you may have. We have the ability to come out of the energy deficit when we feel we have reached our goal or when our willpower to diet comes to an end.

While we know this, our body is not so well informed, so when it senses the energy deficit, it assumes famine. You see, there was a time when food was seasonal and, at times, scarce (and we didn't have the means of storing and preserving it like we do now). If our bodies could not adapt to these times of scarcity, we would inevitably die. So, our bodies have an inherent "self-defence mechanism". Layne Norton, PhD, in his book *Fat Loss Forever*, talks about this system as a three-pronged system:

1. Defend
2. Restore
3. Prevent

The idea is that when food/energy is scarce, the body needs to defend its energy stores (fat). Then, the next time food is available, it will do its absolute best to capture as much of the energy intake as possible and store it to lower the potential for starvation in the future. Finally, the body will then defend its restored energy stores by making it harder to deplete them again, usually by increasing the efficiency of energy use so that less is required for daily use.

This system makes no sense for a world in which I can sit on my ass and get a single ice cream delivered to my door by using my phone, without so much as having to leave the comfort of my home.

Let's go into this in a little more depth so you can better understand the mechanisms involved in these three prongs and how they pertain to our energy balance. This also should help highlight the dangers of crash dieting.

Defend refers to a process called metabolic adaptation, which, in essence, is a series of biological adaptations to energy restriction. It's basically your body's way of creating an energy balance again by reducing your overall total daily energy expenditure (your metabolism) in order to slow down/prevent more weight loss. How does it do this? Well, if you remember what makes up the *energy out* part of our equation, you will remember our BMR or basal metabolic rate. To not overcomplicate this, I will go for the more layman's terms approach (any science nerds out there or those of you who know more about this topic, don't hate on me. I understand it better than most, but for a mass book, it seems unnecessary to go too deep).

Essentially, one reason for a decline in our BMR is due to our reduction in weight. In essence, it will take less energy to carry around your reduced body mass and fat, and to a larger extent, muscle is metabolically active tissue (which is why it is important to hold onto as much muscle when dieting as possible). Seems obvious that it probably requires more energy for a 100kg man just to get out of a seat and walk downstairs than it does a 50kg man. You see, as I have previously mentioned, ironically, a fatter person technically has a faster metabolism than a skinnier man—that's why the notion of fast/slow metabolism can be a bit misleading.

Next up, NEAT or non-exercise activity thermogenesis. This is an area of the *energy out* part of the equation that is most affected by dieting. Research has shown that individuals who lost at least 10% of their body weight while dieting had a reduction in their NEAT by up to 400 calories per day.[10] Remember, this refers to non-conscious movements. Apparently, when we are in an energy deficit, our body senses this and reduces our non-voluntary movements such as fidgeting. I myself competed years ago in a bodybuilding show and remember towards the end of my diet that even walking to the shops was laborious. As a result, I definitely moved a lot less, even if I didn't realise it at the time.

This is one of the reasons why I suggest that my clients keep an eye on their normal daily step count. While this refers more to NEPA than NEAT, it is a great way of helping to slow down/offset the metabolic adaptation taking place. If my client walks 10k steps a day on average (not tracking) and we have started a dieting phase, I will tell her to keep an eye on it. If she notices that her step count naturally starts to decline below this, it is then worth putting into place a step goal to make a conscious effort to fight against the body's attempts to conserve energy.

In terms of exercise, our bodies become more efficient the more we do—this isn't necessarily in a deficit, but in general. This is one reason why fitness trackers calculating your calories are hugely inaccurate, and even more so the calorie readouts that the cardio equipment at the gym gives you. Obviously, when we are dieting and energy sources are reduced, our performance may naturally decline, which may reduce the energy we expend from exercise anyway. It is super important to focus on the benefits of exercise outside of calorie burn as exercise actually only makes up a small portion of our TDEE, and viewing it as a way to purely burn calories creates an unhealthy relationship with it and is more likely to reduce your adherence over time. Making sure we have some resistance training in our routines will help improve bone density, mental health, but most importantly, in a deficit, it will help maintain our muscle mass, which is more metabolically active tissue and, therefore, the more we can hold onto, we can usually blunt the amount/speed of metabolic adaptation. Exercise can help with weight loss, but it should not be the focus—it should be part of your lifestyle regardless of your weight goals.

This is one area that I find too many people become heavily focused on, throwing hours and hours of cardio into the mix to increase their deficit. This creates a number of problems (including the risk of losing muscle mass), but if we just look at it simply, if you are having to do four hours of cardio every week to drop weight, what happens when you reach your weight goals and then decide to stop doing all this cardio? It can't be of any real surprise that if you continue to eat the same calories but are now no longer doing the excessive cardio, you will inevitably regain the weight lost. Also, let's be honest, people normally stop their diet at the same time, so they actually increase their calories and reduce their exercise at the same time. Maybe we are just becoming fatter as a society because common sense is no longer common.

There are other mechanisms going on within our bodies that are all working to help reduce the energy deficit. Our bodies annoyingly seem to want to be balanced—apparently, a trait that most people don't seem to understand when it comes to nutrition, but more on that later. Herman Pontzer, an evolutionary anthropologist, explained that our metabolism responds to changes in exercise and diet in ways that thwart our efforts to shed pounds. Using the Hadza tribe of Tanzania as an example, he measured the number of calories they expended (burned) every day. They are a lot more physically active than the average American—the men, for example, were walking 14 kilometres daily while the women were walking 8 kilometres on top of all the other physical work they did, which amounts to a daily step count more than the average American's weekly step count. So, you'd expect them to expend a lot more calories every day. However, he found that their calorie expenditure was roughly the same as most Westerners, and some even burned 10% less than average. The Hadza tribe had adjusted to their environment, so their metabolism became more efficient as a result. Your body adjusts how it spends its energy to keep the total calories burned every day within a relatively narrow range. This makes sense from an evolutionary perspective. If your metabolism continued to burn hot due to increased activity levels but your food stores/food intake could not keep up, you would inevitably starve and die out. Our bodies are clever; however, that depends on who you are asking because there are a lot of overweight people who would strongly disagree with this.

In another study by Herman Pontzer, he looked at understanding the impacts of activity on energy balance, noting that increasing levels of activity may bring diminishing returns in energy expenditure due to the compensatory responses in non-activity energy expenditure. In the study, it was found that if you were to burn an extra 100 calories through exercise, only 72 of these calories would represent a net increase in calorie expenditure, so

28 calories were lost/compensated for by the reduction in non-activity energy expenditure.[11] To reduce our weight or to help fix the obesity crisis, we need to understand the adaptive nature of our metabolism.

Herman Pontzer: *"Our metabolic engines were not crafted by millions of years of evolution to guarantee a beach-ready bikini body".*

Now, what's everyone's favourite seven-letter word that they like to use when looking for an excuse as to why they can't lose weight? The word you are looking for is HORMONE(s). Yep, there are many people out there who love to blame hormones for their struggles, and I'm not saying you are wrong for doing so, but hormones just affect the energy balance… it doesn't make it impossible to lose weight. I will go into this again more in detail and more specifically in later chapters, but in the case of our weight plateauing, there are a few different hormones that change in order to slow our weight loss.

Losing weight can reduce your output of thyroid hormone and raise thyroid stimulating hormone, which can contribute to a slowing of our metabolic rates. The main hormone I want to talk about though refers to leptin, the satiety hormone, which is actually produced by our body's fat cells.

High levels of leptin tell your brain that you've stored enough fat, so you don't need to eat more, and you can burn calories at a normal rate (normal metabolic function). This is essentially the fat controller part of our body's fat thermostat. The more fat you have, the more leptin there is in your blood. Leptin is the signal that tells the hypothalamus how much fat you are carrying. It is a bit like the petrol gauge in your car telling you how much energy you have in the tank. When we lose weight during a diet, our fat cells shrink, and therefore, our levels of leptin usually decrease. Leptin plays a big role in metabolic rate, and when our levels decrease, this tells your body (brain) that you are starving and, therefore, move less, eat more food and burn few calories at rest. At the same time, we will also get an increase in our ghrelin levels, nicknamed the "hunger hormone". I don't think you need to guess what effect this has on our bodies.

So, with a reduction in leptin, the hormone that usually reduces appetite, and an increase in ghrelin, the one that increases appetite, it is no wonder that hunger levels tend to rise when we are dieting. This is part of the 'restore' prong of our body's self-defence system. It's a bit like Vegas, where the house always wins, but instead of the house, it's our body's desire for homeostasis in terms of our energy balance. It will be sending incredibly powerful signals to restore your energy balance, and trust me, these signals are powerful.

Have you ever heard of the Minnesota Starvation Experiment? A brilliant, although painful bit of research done back in 1944, which demonstrated the effects that extreme energy deficits have on our bodies. Physiologist, Ancel Keys, and psychologist, Josef Brozek, sought to explore how individuals would be affected physiologically and psychologically by a limited diet. They wanted to identify how they could best help these individuals in the refeeding process.

For the experiment, they recruited healthy young men (healthy both physically and mentally) and the study fell into a few different phases. Phase 1 (first 12 weeks) was a control period, phase 2 was a 24-week calorie restriction, and phase 3 (last 12 weeks) involved controlled rehabilitation/re-nourishment. For the dieting/starvation phase, the men had their calories cut by 50% down to 1570 calories (to reflect the conditions of war). They lost approximately 25% of their weight (yes, we can conclude that starvation mode isn't a thing).

The reason I bring this experiment up is three-fold. Firstly, the scientists noted that the participants' metabolisms were reduced by more than would be explained by the reduction in body weight alone. Their BMRs decreased by 50% on average of their starting value—only half of this was explained by the 25% reduction in weight. The hormonal adaptation was clear: the body was reducing energy expenditure as much as it could to reduce further weight loss.

Secondly, during the dieting phase, they noticed psychological changes as well as physiological ones. Participants became obsessed with food, from talking about food more to daydreaming about food, and this even extended into their habits as some started reading cookbooks or collecting recipes. This change was also reflected in their eating practices, with participants becoming possessive over their food, guarding their food and licking their plates clean at meals. Some tried to navigate their cravings by stealing food, and some chugged water, seeking fullness. Some took up smoking to help fight off hunger and others chewed packs and packs of gum a day until the laboratory banned it.

Granted, a 50% reduction of calories is quite dramatic, but this helps illustrate that while I can talk all about hormones and the chemical/biological drivers of the body to try and make you regain weight, we can see what this translates to into actual behaviour. One subject (and remember, they were all screened and deemed healthy both physically and mentally before starting) even tried/ succeeded in chopping off his own fingers with an axe (I found some reports that he chopped off one or three fingers, or he tried... either way, that's fucked up). He reported being "unsure" of whether or not he did it on purpose. Demonstrating the real power that these biological drivers have on us.

Finally, a small group of subjects stayed for an additional eight weeks and were fed an unrestricted diet. During those first two weeks of the unrestricted diet, each participant was allowed to choose their own meals. Any idea what happened? Well, when left to now choose their own meals, they subsequently ate between 7,000-10,000 calories per day! Yup... more evidence that the body will win in the inevitable war to restore its energy balance and increase future reserves. One of the participants remembered being taken to the hospital to have his stomach pumped because he "just simply overdid it" during a refeed meal. Another was sick on the bus on the way back from one of his many binges, stating he couldn't satisfy his craving for food. And one other described his eating behaviour afterwards as a "year-long cavity" that needed to be filled.

You see, when people talk about a lack of willpower, they are really underestimating the power that these hormones or biological and psychological drivers have on us. I remember reading about this the first time and feeling almost bad for having always looked at overweight people as lazy or gluttonous. Yes, it probably does play a role for most, so again, I'm not trying to excuse it, but the complexities of the weight loss equation can help us understand why there should be an individualised process when trying to tackle overweight/obese people's eating patterns and behaviours. Yes, we are still working to create an energy deficit, but if we fail to take into account the individual differences in people, we are likely setting them up for failure.

The hormonal changes that are part of the defence system also work to create the perfect environment for weight regain so that when we come out of our deficit or stop our diet as it were, we not only regain the weight we have lost but increase our weight beyond that of our previous pre-dieting weight.

Imagine your fat like a wet towel (stay with me here)... when the towel is wet, our fat stores/energy stores are full. During the diet, we are slowly ringing the water out of the towel. At the start of the diet, it is quite easy to squeeze water out of the towel (weight loss), but the further into the diet we get, the drier the towel gets and the harder it is to get more water (weight) out of it. The drier the towel is, the more absorbent it becomes again, so if we were to drop a bit of water (calories) into it, it would easily recapture this water (energy) and hold it. It is more efficient at recapturing this water the drier it gets.

You see, the drop in leptin usually slows our metabolic rate and reduces our satiety, increasing our hunger. If we then increase calories, which is likely given our increasing hunger levels, the body is in a state where it is looking to recapture the available energy and has increased its efficiency at doing this.

It also makes a lot of sense that if you go back to eating at your pre-diet levels, of course you will go back to your pre-diet weight—remember Einstein's classic definition of insanity: "Doing the same thing over and over again and expecting different results". This perfectly illustrates what people are doing by yo-yo dieting. Why we think we can escape this probably perfectly illustrates the stupidity of anyone who has tried a diet and failed (myself included). Think about it, honestly... if you fit into a size 16 dress when you were eating 3,000 calories a day, then dieted down and now fit into a size 12 dress (men can wear dresses too apparently, so this is a gender-fluid example), if you go back to eating 3,000 calories again, at the end of your diet, why do we think this won't result in us at least returning back to that size 16 dress size again? It's actually mental when you think about it. How are we still getting this wrong? This is why actually looking at a diet as a temporary fix is immediately setting yourself up for failure. The only way a diet will work is if you can stick to it for the long term. Ask yourself honestly, "Do I see myself on this diet in six months' time, in a year, in five years?" If the answer is no, then it is not right for you. This doesn't mean you need to be in a deficit for the rest of your life, but we need to have a plan when we come to the end of our deficit phase (I will explain more about this later). Hopefully, understanding this should immediately explain why diets like the keto diet, which remove whole food groups, are usually set up for failure unless you think you will be okay never eating carbohydrates again (in which case... what is wrong with you?).

This doesn't even take into account the final part of the body's defence system—prevent. This refers to a process called fat cell hyperplasia. Sounds scary, right? The idea is that (again, in layman's terms) if/when you regain fat too quickly in the post-diet window, we can actually gain new fat cells. You see, normally, when we lose a little weight and add a little weight, our fat cells shrink and expand, but the number of them remains the same. Obesity researcher, Paul Maclean, first noted this formation of new small fat cells produced by a process called pre-adipocyte differentiation. Usually, the number of fat cells we have is under fairly tight regulation, however, this can be overridden in certain circumstances. Maclean noted that during the post-diet period where we have this hormonal environment that favours weight regain, it also favours the creation of new fat cells. You see, in order to prevent our energy stores being depleted again, it makes sense to increase our energy stores, making future weight loss harder. This is sometimes referred to as body fat overshooting. If we go back to my terrible analogy of the wet towel, just imagine us having a bigger towel... we would be able to absorb and hold more water (energy). Okay, I will leave the analogy alone, but it worked in my head and, hopefully, made some sense.

If we look at the Minnesota Starvation study again and the participants who then went to two weeks of the unrestricted diet, each subsequently ate between 7,000-10,000 calories per day—that's not a small increase, is it? The body is desperate to restore its depleted energy stores but is also doing what it can to create new energy stores so that future weight loss is harder.

Hopefully, you should start to understand the body fat set point. You see, our energy storage is too important to be left to free will. Our bodies want to defend a pre-set point. As Dr. Andrew Jenkinson wrote: *"Suggesting that energy storage is under conscious control because we can deliberately stop eating for a period of time is like suggesting breathing is under conscious control because we have an ability to hold our breath. We don't have to remember to breathe- our subconscious brain does that for us. If we change environments and live on a mountain with thin air, we don't have to tell our brain that we need to breathe more quickly or deeply- the subconscious brain will sense the environment change and breathe more deeply for us".*

This body fat set point basically rules over metabology rule 1 (energy balance) and rule 2 (negative feedback system). If you lose weight below your set point, then the negative feedback system (rule 2) will kick in, increasing your appetite and slowing your metabolic rate. The slowing of your metabolic rate and an increase in food intake will lead your weight back up (rule 1).

If you suffer from obesity, you may wonder, "Well, what the fuck has happened to my body's fucking internal thermostat? Can I get a refund?" Unfortunately, there are a few reasons why our body fat set point may be stuck at a higher point. One of the main reasons should have become obvious.

In the last decade of working with thousands of people to help them achieve their weight loss goals, there is one type of client I come across more than any other who perfectly embodies the results of the body's self-defence system, and in essence, represents the failure of our dieting culture.

Introducing the yo-yo dieter—typically a woman (although it can affect any gender) in her mid-20s to early 30s. Usually focused on losing weight for an occasion (say birthday, holiday, wedding), she goes into a deficit in order to lose the weight and adds shit loads of cardio. At the end of the deficit period, she goes straight into a period of overindulgence. A few of these cycles in her early 20s have now left her in a position where the deficit she used to use no longer works, and she is left consuming fewer calories while maintaining her current heavier bodyweight.

How many of you read that and were like, "Oh, fuck… that's me"? The other question to ask now is how many of you can spot two of the key mistakes she made?

1. Short-term goal, short-term mindset leading to short-term results.
2. No plan at the end of the diet. The old saying, "Failure to plan is planning to fail".

After the body has gone through its self-defence system a few times (yo-yo-ing up and down), you are left with a heavier body weight yet with a slower metabolic rate than predicted. This is the creation of what I think people refer to when they talk about a broken or slowing metabolism, and it perfectly illustrates one of the ways in which we have pushed our body fat set points up. This is why people who run more diets during their lifetime are more likely to gain more body fat over time instead of losing it, which I'm guessing is the aim.

You see, the secret of successful and sustainable weight loss is, therefore, understanding how we regulate this set point. Yes, energy balance governs weight loss, but it is not as simple as energy in and energy out.

PART 2: TELL ME WHY

Why are we as a population getting fatter? (I can still say that, right? Or do I have to say becoming more overweight/obese?) It can't be purely because we are just greedier, right? The World Obesity Federation's 2023 atlas predicts that 51% of the world, or more than 4 billion people, will be obese or overweight within the next 12 years. That is a terrifying thought, although for someone who makes money off helping people lose weight, I guess there won't be a shortage of potential clients (remember, try and always see the positives in life). Clearly, our diets and lifestyles are failing us. You may have heard the statistic that 95% of all diets fail. I don't want to focus on this as it was taken from a single 1959 study looking at 100 people where participants were given a diet and sent on their way. This statistic has been reinforced by other clinical studies, which also showed people with discouraging results. However, as Dr. Kelly D. Brownell, the director of the Yale Centre for Eating and Weight Disorders, wrote: "Unless we can prove they're typical, the data cannot be generalised".

I feel while this statistic appropriately highlights a particularly important problem in our weight loss puzzle, it is a bit outdated and reductive. What is also important is that it makes people believe they can't lose weight, which simply isn't true. What is actually true is that we don't have so much of a weight loss problem but more of a weight loss maintenance problem. Six out of every seven people who are overweight will lose a significant amount of weight in their lifetime. However, within one year of weight loss, nearly 80% will have relapsed to their pre-diet weight.[12] While in the last chapter I explained why our weight plateaus, this doesn't fully explain the obesity epidemic. Every overweight person surely didn't get that way from yo-yo dieting.

There are other factors at play and that's why a look into obesity needs to take into account all things from psychological to sociological to physiological factors. Ask yourself now why you think we are seeing an increase in obesity. What contributes to someone's sensitivity to developing obesity?

Is it just a lack of willpower and greed?

Is it their genetics?

Is it your parent's fault because of your home environment and how you were raised?

Are carbohydrates to blame?

Are fats to blame? Maybe we can blame artificial sweeteners or seed oils... I mean, if we listened to some of these Bio Hackers (made-up job title) and nutritionists online, we would all be wandering around bare-footed with blue tongues, blaming evil companies like Coca-Cola for making us fat.

Honestly, while it would be easy to blame our parents

(genetics) for everything (like we do for most of our youth), it would unfortunately be a lie. I think the quote that best sums this up came from Dr. Mehmet Oz, who said, "Your genetics load the gun. Your lifestyle pulls the trigger".

Yes, energy balance governs our ability to put on weight, but overeating/overconsumption is driven by so much more than just greed.

I think, at this point, it is worth tackling the old *blame the genetics* game that has been around for years, before getting onto the other arguments for why we are seeing a rise in obesity.

CHAPTER 6: I HAVE FAT GENES

Look, I'm here for blaming our parents for all our troubles. Trust me, as someone living with inflammatory bowel disease, I love to blame my mum and dad for my shortcomings (even when there is only weak evidence of a genetic link to developing IBD, I still tried). Unfortunately, I also liked to tease my parents when they were behaving embarrassingly that I was adopted. My dad rightfully called me out on this and was like, "Chris, pick… it's either our fault or not, but you can't blame us and be adopted at the same time". I then tried some convoluted take on the old nature vs. nurture argument. Anyway, it does pose a good question… are our genetics to blame?

Why can one person eat all the foods we can only dream of eating and stay lean year-round when we may just sniff that chocolate bar and put on weight? Some of these differences must be down to our genes, which can influence both our appetite and our eventual weight.

I am not arguing that it's not part of the puzzle, however, it is unlikely that it is the main driver. Why do I say this? Well, large-scale changes in genetics take many generations, but obesity essentially became a crisis in less than a generation. It is, therefore, unlikely that most obese people are obese because of "bad genes".

Tim Spector's studies of twins in the UK (The Twins-UK study) found that twins are much more similar to each other in body weight and fat than fraternal twins. Since twins are essentially genetic clones and share the same DNA, it shows the importance of genetic factors. He noted that "On average, identical adult twins are less than 1 kilo different in weight. These gene-influenced similarities extend to other related characteristics… such as the percentages of total body muscle and fat, and exactly where fat is deposited in or on the body. Habits related to eating are also influenced by genes, such as food likes and dislikes, and even how often people like to exercise or have meals".

Since identical twins have the same upbringing as their sibling, this may also say more about the home environment than necessarily their genetics. Well, another study done on twins by Jane Wardle looked at pairs of identical twins who had been separated at birth and adopted into different homes. Looking at over 2,000 pairs of twins and comparing their BMIs, they hoped to show whether the home environment was a more powerful driver than genetics alone. The study found that there was a 75% consistency in the level of obesity between identical twins when they became adults, despite lifelong separation. So, we can potentially exonerate our parents in terms of what they got us to eat growing up, but it doesn't excuse the genes they provided us with.

Now, before you all jump to any conclusions about this, in the words of Tim Spector, "Just because a trait is 60% or 70% genetic doesn't mean it is predestined". Someone can be more at risk for obesity, but their body won't suddenly start storing rays from the sun as fat, it will still require them to eat in a calorie surplus. There are also many identical twins with different waistlines despite having identical genes, so again, while we can't fully blame genes, it is worth knowing that they may make someone's fat loss journey harder, and therefore, the simple *eat less, move more* mantra—while not incorrect—doesn't fully grasp the difficulties many people face.

I think one of the most interesting parts of these arguments can come from looking at the populations with the highest levels of obesity. The Pacific Island nations of Nauru, Cook Islands, and Palau have the highest rates of obesity, with over 30% of their populations being classified as obese. Nauru is the most obese country in the world, with 61% of its population being obese. Can we just take a second to let that sink in. According to recent evidence I found online, 90% of the adult population has a body mass index over the world average—approximately 40% of the population suffers from type II diabetes, and rates of heart and kidney disease are high. Not exactly a glowing Trip Advisor review.

Why is this relevant though? Well, Nauru was first settled by Micronesian and Polynesian explorers approximately 3,000 years ago. The journey to settle on the island would have been long and dangerous, and unsurprisingly, many who attempted the long journeys at that time died as food and water ran out on the way. Quite often, the people who were able to survive the voyages

67

were those who had enough fat reserves before the journey or had efficient metabolism (slow metabolisms) that allowed them to survive, or both of these traits. There was, therefore, automatically a huge selection bias for anyone settled there.

This is sort of what farmers have done over the years. By using essentially artificially induced natural selection, they select the cows that put down fat deposits within their muscles to give the eventual meat the tasty marbling effect, and these ones are used to breed for the next generation. Any skinny ones will not be selected, and their 'skinny genes' will be lost to the next generation of cows. Continuing with this unnatural selection generation after generation, you end up with a herd of cows that grow quicker, get bigger and fatter. Essentially, the gene pool has been manipulated to produce the farmers' desired result. Now, obviously, this is not what the population of Nauru did, but as only those with so-called 'slow or efficient' metabolisms were able to survive the colonisation process, the subsequent generations of the population were more than likely to have had a greater genetic propensity for obesity.

Did this mean they have always been fatter? No. Just because you have the genes that may predispose you to obesity doesn't mean you come out of the womb in full obese mode. In fact, if we look at the Nauru accounts back in 1917, it was described as a place where one 'very seldom see[s] a badly proportioned man or woman', and the inhabitants were of fine physique'.[13] Obesity didn't rear its head until the second half of the 20th century.

The recorded prevalence of diabetes in the Nauruan population rose from 2% to over 30% during a 15-year period in the 1960s and 1970s.[14] So, despite the original settlers probably having the so-called thrifty genes, they didn't just suddenly get fat. The rapid rise in obesity came a lot later and is more likely a shift in farming, cooking, cuisine practices and lifestyle changes... but we will get into that more in later chapters.

Another great example of this natural selection can be found in the slave trade between West Africa and America. The transatlantic journey took, on average, two months where slaves were subjected to unsurprisingly horrendous conditions. Despite them usually only selecting the younger, fitter slaves to embark on the journey, it was common for many to not survive it. In fact, it is estimated that between the 16th and 19th centuries, approximately 2 million enslaved Africans died during the journey to America. Those that survived were more likely again to carry the "fat genes". Now, America as we know it is one of the fattest countries and contains within it a large ethnic diversity. Currently, all Americans are subjected to horrendous fast food Western diets. If genetics were a major player in the obesity equation, we would, therefore, expect to see differences between ethnic groups and obesity rates (I want to caveat this and say economic positioning will also play into it, so I'm not suggesting genetics are the only thing to note). Interestingly, we do see a much higher rate of obesity in the Black population than in the White/Caucasian group. In fact, in 2021, the obesity rates in adults were 31.5% for Whites and 43.9%

for Blacks. The obesity rate for Black women living in America is a whopping 57%.

Can we just blame women for our fat genes? Strange statement to make, I know, but before all you feminists get angry, I am just teasing. Although, at the same time, since you are the only ones who are able to give birth, the reproductive fitness hypothesis does kind of make sense, and in so doing... yup, it puts the blame a little bit on you guys. You see, if you were a woman with these 'fat genes' as it were, and possibly holding onto more body fat at a time when food was less readily available, you were more likely to have remained fertile in times of food shortage. We know that a lack of calories and nutrition can cause fertility issues (hypothalamic amenorrhea, for example). So, women with inadequate fat reserves (those skinny bitches) would not have been able to pass their skinny genes onto the next generation. These fat genes were, therefore, passed on not necessarily by physical survival but purely as a result of greater fertility in those with the 'fat genes'. I feel like this is a set-up for the worst *your mother is fat* joke ever, but that's where my mind just went.

Again, I think this quote from Dr. Mehmet Oz perfectly illustrates the obesity angle: "Genetics loads the gun, lifestyle pulls the trigger". While the population of Nauru—through a variation of natural selection—has a genetic propensity for obesity, it wasn't until significant changes in their lifestyle pulled the trigger for them to become the most obese population in the world. Also, Nauru is just one of the examples. Most of the top 10 list of obese populations in the world are made up of similar islands where the original settlers would have had to survive perilous voyages to get there. Also, those living on small islands hundreds of years ago were at the mercy of severe famines (hard to imagine life before supermarkets and Deliveroo). These famines again reselected those people who had built up adequate fat reserves to survive, so again, over the years, the population would have continued to reselect the 'fat genes' to be carried onto the next generation. We can start to see the genetics angle in the argument for obesity, however, we can also start to see that genes are only a piece of the puzzle.

While we know that if both of your parents are obese, your likelihood of developing obesity is as high as 80%— this does not mean you have to be obese. Remember, being overweight is down to energy balance. We don't materialise energy out of thin air. Yes, you may have genes that predispose you to obesity, but it doesn't mean you will be. This also brings us neatly into the theory of epigenetics, which is the study of how your environment and lifestyle can cause changes that affect the way your genes work. We can essentially turn genes on and off, so unlike genetic changes, epigenetic changes are reversible and do not change your DNA sequence, but they can change how your body reads a DNA sequence, and these changes don't need generations and generations to take effect. In fact, switching off of some genes takes place while we are still growing in the womb. Due to the baby's environment/nutrition, it is likely that this is preparing the baby for the environment into which it will be born.

Back in 1944-1945, at the end of World War II, the Nazis had cut off food supplies to the western part of the Netherlands in retaliation for the Dutch government supporting the allies. This period of time later became known as the Dutch famine or the Dutch Hunger Winter. It is believed that 20,000 people died and 4.5 million were affected by the direct and indirect consequences of the famine. Strict rationing of available food was introduced, with most of the population rationing 400-800 kcal per day. There were many young women who were pregnant at the time. The tragic circumstances of the Dutch famine created a unique opportunity to assess the effects of pre-natal undernutrition on human health in later life. Introducing the Dutch Famine Study, conducted 30 years after the famine, to investigate the effects of acute maternal undernutrition during the specific stages of gestation on later health, with a particular focus on chronic cardiovascular and metabolic diseases, ageing and mental health.

By looking at the children who had been in utero at the time of the famine against their siblings born before or after the famine, they could identify if there had been any impact on the future health of the child. The children from starving mothers were—as expected—much smaller than normal, however, once grown up, the exposure to famine was associated with a threefold higher risk for earlier onset of coronary heart disease (CHD), a more atherogenic lipid profile, and glucose intolerance.[15] Unsurprisingly, as a result of this glucose intolerance, they found a higher rate of type 2 diabetes in the offspring and a greater level of obesity when compared to their siblings.

While these findings should only work to reinforce our understanding of the importance of correct nutrition for pregnant women, it also helps illustrate how epigenetics can cause changes in our risk factors for obesity.

To confuse you a little bit more, while undernourishment can alter your genes (genetic expression) to make your metabolism hyper-efficient (that sounds sexy, but again, it just means slow metabolism), we can also do the same by overeating during pregnancy (although I might caveat this to overeating on hyperpalatable ultra-processed foods that are micronutrient sparse food—like crisps). There is plenty of evidence to support that maternal overeating can create what is called obesogenic traits in their offspring. One study I found even suggested that intrauterine exposures to maternal diabetes and obesity are strongly associated with the development of type 2 diabetes in youth.[16]

Maternal obesity during pregnancy predicts a two to threefold increase in obesity in the offspring by the time they reach four years of age. So, if your parents are overweight or obese, they are likely passing on the possible genetic traits predisposing you to obesity yourself. Remember, the twin studies showed that genes can have up to a 75% influence on your future weight, then if we add an obesogenic environment during gestation for you, you are now likely to have mutations or epigenetic changes, further enhancing your likelihood for obesity. It's not looking good.

It seems strange that either undernourishment for the foetus or over-nourishment can cause the same risk for obesity. While only a theory, I believe this is likely due to the increase in ultra-processed foods that are low in nutrients in the diets of the mothers that cause the risk for children. So, the foetus in utero is not benefitting from more nutrients just because their mother is carrying more weight. This theory is backed up by many studies by many authors that indicate a higher incidence of food deficiency among people with excessive body weight than in people with normal body weight of the same age and same sex.[17] You see, more calories don't mean more nutrients, and I think this is a concept people forget. Many of these ultra-processed foods (usually of the beige colour) are usually very nutrient-poor, and actually, a diet high in ultra-processed foods is directly associated with an increased risk of micronutrient deficiency.[18] While we will get into the ultra-processed food side of the argument more in the following chapters, this does illustrate a particularly important point. Prenatal nutrition is super important for the growth, development and future health of your child. This is not open for debate and so we should be focused more on educating mothers on proper nutrition as currently, this seems to be an area that is still neglected—or ignored, I guess.

As obesity has become more prevalent since the 1980s, is each subsequent generation suffering as a result of these genetic and epigenetic changes? Have we just been priming each generation to be more at risk for obesity, just like the farmer naturally selecting the fatter cows? Is this why we are seeing an increase in childhood obesity? Hopefully, as you read this, you are starting to see why obesity is more confusing than you may have first thought. If you are reading this thinking, '*Well, my mum is fat* (bit rude…)*, that means I'm fucked',* I want to remind you that while genes may make it harder, they don't guarantee your outcome as demonstrated by the identical twins who ended up different weights. Also, if you remember, through epigenetics, we can turn genes both on and off. This means that with correct nutrition and lifestyle, we may be able to alter how our bodies read our genes (or DNA sequence) for the better.

Genes definitely play a role, there is no doubting that, but as I have mentioned before, we don't just inhale fat into our body, it still comes from an energy imbalance. Going back to the analogy of our internal thermostat, we can see that your genes might predispose you to having a higher body fat set point, but with the right nutrition and lifestyle factors, we can adjust that thermostat/set point down. We have a say. Whether you are willing to do what is needed is another question altogether, but don't worry, I will explain how we can lower our thermostat in the last few chapters. For now, we will continue to look at other reasons why our thermostats might be broken.

CHAPTER 7:
IT'S MY HORMONES... WELL AT LEAST THE ONES THAT REGULATE APPETITE

redominantly, when people try to blame their hormones on their inability to lose weight, they are probably talking about their thyroid hormone. You see, the thyroid hormone is required for normal development as well as regulating metabolism in adults. It has been known for a long time that thyroid hormone status correlates with body weight and energy expenditure. Hyperthyroidism (excess thyroid hormone) promotes a hypermetabolic state characterised by increased resting energy expenditure and weight loss. Conversely, hypothyroidism (reduced thyroid hormone levels) is associated with hypometabolism, characterised by reduced resting energy expenditure and weight gain. So, yes, your thyroid status will 100% impact your ability to lose or gain weight.

While I mention the thyroid hormone, it is actually not the main hormone I want to discuss. Yes, hypothyroidism can cause you to gain weight, but most of the time, this is caught by your doctor, and as a result, you will be prescribed thyroid hormone medicine. A daily dose of levothyroxine (Levoxyl, Synthroid) should work to restore healthy thyroid levels, and with it, your metabolism. It can take some time for you to find the right dose, but once you have, your weight should stabilise, and you shouldn't have any more trouble losing weight than anyone else. You see, hypothyroidism only explains a small amount of obesity, and actually, once correct medication has been prescribed, this should no longer get in the way of your weight loss goals. If we could blame the obesity problem on just our thyroids, we would have such an easy method of eradicating it all together and this book would be a hell of a lot shorter. Unfortunately, this is wishful thinking.

The hormones I am actually talking about are the ones that govern our hunger, appetite and cravings (I guess). There are two signals that drive our food intake—one to start eating (hunger) and one to signal to stop eating (satiety). We have already touched on this a bit back in Chapter 5 while explaining how our body fat thermostat is regulated. These hormones are powerful drivers and can act to change our behaviour without us using our free will to make conscious decisions. The Minnesota Starvation study perfectly illustrated how strong these hormonal signals can be with a man willing to chop his fingers off so that he could escape the pain of hunger.

Let's first discuss two hormones that help dictate this balance, and hopefully, this will also give you more insight into why it can be hard to lose weight, and why questioning someone's lack of willpower is a bit like me questioning your inability to grow two inches taller (without the use of fat insoles in your shoes). Ghrelin, the hunger hormone, was discovered in 1999 and is produced in the upper part of the stomach. Its levels increase in response to food deprivation. Once we have eaten, the level of ghrelin drops. The other hormone I want to discuss in relation to ghrelin is peptide YY, which was discovered in 1980. It is produced by the cells of the small intestine in response to food that is inside the small bowel. Peptide YY is released after eating, circulates in the blood and works by binding to receptors in the brain. Binding of peptide YY to brain receptors decreases appetite and makes people feel full after eating.

So, if/when we attempt to diet (restrict food intake), what happens? Research has shown that in participants who had dieted for six months, at the end of the dieting phase, their ghrelin signals were 24% higher throughout the day compared to their pre-dieting levels.[19] This constant increase in ghrelin, even after eating, left them feeling ravenous throughout the day. If you have ever dieted, you may have experienced this sensation yourself of being unable to quench your appetite. This is the body's attempt to drive your weight back up to your pre-diet weight. In addition to increasing food intake, the increase in ghrelin decreases metabolic rate and the catabolism of fat, thereby affecting all aspects of the system of energy regulation in such a way as to increase body weight.

In another study, they took 50 overweight or obese patients without diabetes and enrolled them in a 10-week weight-loss program. Their levels of ghrelin and peptide YY were measured before the start, at 10 weeks (after program completion), and at 62 weeks.[20] They found the same thing: that ghrelin levels increased after the diet and that the satiety signal provided by peptide YY was significantly lower. So, again, dieters were now hungrier, and when they ate, they experienced more reduced feelings of satiety than they did before the diet. A year after the diet had finished (where most participants had regained all the weight lost), their levels of ghrelin remained higher, and their levels of peptide YY remained lower than pre-diet levels. This gives a clear indication of why our attempts to lose weight can be futile and actually why dieting without the right knowledge can become counterproductive and work to only stimulate more weight gain in the long run.

Now, I'm not suggesting that everyone who is obese or overweight got that way because of failed diets, but it has definitely contributed to the problem and highlights the complexities of losing weight. So, yes, we can blame hormones to an extent.

Now, before moving on, there is more to the hormone story than just ghrelin and peptide YY. Introducing leptin. Leptin is essentially how our fat cells communicate with our subconscious brain. This hormone, as I already mentioned in Chapter 5, is essentially the fat controller part of our body's body fat thermostat. It is the master regulator and works to control both the long-term appetite and satiety drivers as well as our metabolic rate. Leptin is produced and released by our fat cells and acts to maintain homeostatic control of fat mass as the amount of hormone in circulation mirrors the amount of fat that we have available as our energy stores. When fat mass falls, plasma leptin levels fall, stimulating appetite and suppressing energy expenditure until fat mass is restored. When fat mass increases, leptin levels increase, suppressing appetite until weight is lost. This system maintains homeostatic control of adipose tissue mass.

You may wonder how people are able to get fat if we have something controlling our fat mass. Well, in 1994, when Jeffrey Friedman discovered leptin, it was thought that this was the missing puzzle to obesity and that obese people had a mutated gene and, therefore, weren't producing enough leptin. This would explain their ravenous hunger. In 1997, Dr. Sadaf Farooqi and her team checked the level of leptin in two cousins with extreme early onset obesity.[21] They discovered that these two women produced virtually no leptin, despite having large amounts of fat mass! Since they were not producing any leptin, their bodies were essentially sensing critically low energy stores and, therefore, increasing their appetite in order to offset this energy imbalance. Their bodies now had plenty of stored energy but no way of sensing it. You can see why this looked promising from a curing obesity angle. They were given leptin replacement injections and almost immediately, their behaviour changed, their appetite decreased, and they started to lose weight. If this was the case, why are we not just dosing obese people up with leptin or adding it to breakfast cereal like we seem to do with every other vitamin or mineral that conveys health benefits?

Unfortunately, when leptin was trialled in human subjects, only a very small subset of obese people lost weight. Confused? It turns out that the genetic mutation that causes leptin deficiency needs to be transmitted by both your parents. It is very rare and predominantly found as a result of consanguineous (relating to or denoting people descended from the same ancestor) marriages, so more reason not to date your cousin (not that you should need a reason).

It actually turns out that when they studied obese people, they found that most had high levels of leptin in their bodies, but their bodies failed to respond to it. So, rather than leptin deficiency, obesity is usually characterised by too much leptin. So, what has gone wrong with our feedback mechanism? You see, fat cells produce leptin in proportion to their size, so people with obesity also have very high levels of leptin.[22] When the scientists discovered this, they concluded that at high leptin levels, the message to the brain starts to get disrupted. When leptin reaches a certain threshold, you develop what is called leptin resistance. The leptin receptors become desensitised and, therefore, leptin signalling no longer works. The brain is essentially blind to the high leptin signal (and high fat reserves), and instead, the opposite message gets through. Sensing a much lower leptin level, the brain confers this by further increasing appetite, leading to more weight gain. This ends up in a bit of a vicious cycle of more weight gain and even higher leptin levels, leading to greater leptin resistance (giving new meaning to the phrase too much of a good thing).

While it is important to understand this so we recognise why some people are so averse to the simple
prescription of eat less and move more, given that their
bodies are inherently fighting this on a chemical level, we
need to know why it occurs. The problem is, this is quite
a confusing part of the puzzle (trust me, I read some
articles that honestly could have been in Mandarin they
were so confusing), so we have to differentiate between
cause and effect. You see, gaining weight could increase
your risk for leptin resistance, but it might not cause the
weight gain in the first place (I hope that makes sense
because I've been re-reading this page for a while and
it makes sense to me, but I also talk to myself when no
one is around, so I might not necessarily be of sound
mind at times). One paper I read concluded that "obesity
promotes hyperleptinemia, which in turn self-promotes
leptin resistance and further obesity, making leptin resistance both a consequence and cause of obesity". See, it's
confusing—I'm not making it up.[23]

This poses a bit of a dilemma for me because, obviously, I am trying to explain the causes of obesity, not the
consequences of it. The main theory is that it is caused
by a disruption to a part of the brain called the hypothalamus. Leptin works by sending signals to the hypothalamus, and studies suggest that people with obesity have
increased inflammation in this area, which may disrupt
the hormone's communication with the brain[24].

The problem with this is we know that obesity is a
pro-inflammatory condition. Obesity itself causes an
increase in the production of TNF-alpha, which stim-

ulates further inflammation and can affect all organs. There is now evidence emerging that the inflammatory reaction causing obesity can also have a direct effect on the hypothalamus. Hypothalamus inflammation could lead to leptin resistance as the signals are not getting through, so the high leptin levels are not being sensed. When TNF-alpha in the blood increases, it can also act to block the effectiveness of insulin, leading to insulin resistance. So, we end up with more insulin and more leptin, which, combined, will work to attack our body fat set point and push it up. The problem with this is, again, it does not occur without weight gain already taking place, so it is hard to say if it causes the weight gain itself or just works to add to it.

Other theories suggest either elevated fats in the blood stopping leptin from crossing the blood-brain barrier,[25] or genetic differences in LEPR genes, which encode the leptin receptor,[26] and finally, due to changing levels of specific proteins in the brain.[27]

What I would conclude is that whether the consequence or cause or both, it is part of the puzzle and tied up in all the previous chapters and subsequent chapters to come. The interplay between ghrelin, leptin, peptide-YY and even insulin definitely works to govern our eating habits, and when there is an imbalance in these hormones, our weight will change as a result. I'm not sure we can fully blame it for the obesity problem, but it definitely plays a role.

What this should tell us again is that energy balance is still what governs weight gain or weight loss. Yes, hormones impact the *energy in* or *energy out* part of the equation, it still works under this principle. No hormonal imbalance causes weight to just miraculously form out of thin air.

Before finishing this chapter, I just want to take PCOS as another example of hormones impacting weight. PCOS, or Polycystic ovary syndrome, is the most common endocrine and metabolic disorder, impacting more than 20% of females of reproductive age—it is no surprise this is a topic that turns up in my day-to-day life while trying to help women achieve weight loss. The condition is usually characterised by insulin resistance, and research has shown that even women who are 'lean' with PCOS still had significantly greater insulin resistance compared with their BMI-matched non-PCOS counterparts.

Insulin resistance makes weight loss harder, but it can still be achieved by adopting a calorie deficit. Weight loss itself is the strongest predictor of improved insulin sensitivity.[28] In fact, abdominal fat is a key factor for insulin resistance, hyperinsulinemia, hyperglycaemia, type 2 diabetes, and over-secretion of androgens, so losing fat, specifically abdominal fat, has a direct and positive impact on all the major issues in PCOS women.[29] As I said, it is harder but not impossible. You see, research shows that women with PCOS, particularly those with insulin resistance, present a significantly decreased basal metabolic rate[30] (translation—slower metabolism than predicted), so we would need to factor this in when working out their deficit calories. I would also advise adopting a lower GI diet or at least reducing the overall glycaemic load of the diet by increasing protein and fibre with each meal or snack. So, yes, harder but not impossible, so while you can blame your hormones at this point, there is lots we can do to rectify your insulin resistance and weight gain—you will just have to be more diligent than others. Anyway, hopefully we have at least covered the whole hormone argument, and don't worry... all the actionable tips to improving your body fat thermostat will be covered at the end of the book, so keep reading.

CHAPTER 8:
IT'S ACTUALLY A GUT PROBLEM

What isn't a gut problem these days? Ever since we discovered the gut microbiome. It seems that everything, whether good or bad, is linked to our gut health. As someone with Crohn's disease, I'm not going to debate this. I blame my gut for my hair falling out and my parents (although my dad annoyingly still has a full head of hair, but my mum's side of the family were all bald, and apparently, the X or female chromosome carries the primary baldness gene, and men inherit this X chromosome from their mothers. This makes the hereditary factor around baldness most dominant on your mother's side… so fuck you, Mum). Anyway, the human gut microbiota has been suggested to play a critical role in obesity and its comorbidities by affecting adiposity and glucose metabolism. I think this is another case of cause or effect.

We know that obesity has a direct negative consequence on gut health. Obesity has been strongly linked to gastroesophageal reflux disease, wherein stomach contents rise back into the oesophagus, causing heartburn and cell damage. This is probably due to an increase in leptin, more relaxation of the muscles between the stomach and the oesophagus and direct pressure placed on the stomach from visceral fat. Obesity is also involved with a few IBS symptoms like diarrhoea. In a large population-based survey of over 1,900 subjects in Olmsted County, Minnesota, Delgado-Aros and colleagues studied the relationship between BMI and a range of upper and lower GI symptoms. They found there was a significant association between obesity and upper abdominal pain, bloating, and diarrhoea.[31] Most studies show a modest reduction in IBS symptoms like abdominal distention, passage of stools, heartburn, acid regurgitation and insomnia when participants lose weight.

We also know that fat cells increase inflammation by increasing the release of adipokines, which attracts immune cells to the fat cells, which induces inflammation. The inflammation caused by obesity can become systemic, meaning it affects other parts of the body, and not just the adipose tissue itself. This might be working to further damage our gut microbiome by altering the composition of our bacterial species. Studies into Crohn's disease have found that when there is more visceral fat inflammation, there is also increased inflammation in the gut. We know systemic inflammation is something we want/need to avoid, so obviously, we want to promote a healthy weight always. However, so far, I have written the impact obesity has on the gut, but we want to look at how our gut can potentially negatively impact our weight.

There are two main theories that I could find for how dysbiosis (imbalance in our gut microbiome) may lead to obesity. The first theory basically involves certain people (obese people) absorbing more calories from foods due to having a higher number of Firmicutes (a species of bacteria) in their guts. I will add that a lot of the evidence I found was done in mice studies, so let's not jump to conclusions just yet. The Firmicutes are able to break down molecules that are usually poorly digested in the gut and thus extract more calories from the foods we eat. Firmicutes work to increase short-chain fatty acids (SCFAs)—an important energy source. Research supports this as significant differences in SCFA concentrations between lean and obese individuals have been found.

Similarly, overweight/obese women with metabolic disorders had a higher proportion of bacteria belonging to Eubacterium rectale-Clostridium coccoides (name just rolls off the tongue)—a bacterium associated with efficient energy harvest from nutrients in the gut—than overweight/obese women without metabolic disorder and normal weight women.[32] So, certain species of gut bacteria might be increasing our ability to get more calories out of the foods we eat. The problem with this (other than most of the research and evidence being found in animal studies) is that butyrate, the SCFAs, is not generally observed with weight and fat gain. In fact, many studies show the opposite. One paper I found even noted, "Metabolites such as butyrate produced from intestinal microbes may be beneficial for enhancing the metabolism of humans by increasing mitochondrial activity".[33] For some people, there is no connection between butyrate production and weight gain, so there might be something else involved in their obesity risk. Also, even if this theory was correct, it still works in the realms of energy balance as that just means more energy in, but I guess if you were tracking calories, it might be adding to the inaccuracy of it.

The second theory around dysbiosis and obesity is linked to our good friend, leaky gut. You have probably heard this phrase before since every Tom, Dick and Harry on Instagram loves to use this term to try and demonise something new each week with clickbait titles like "X causes leaky gut". Leaky gut itself is not a disease or disorder but is a symptom of damage to the gut, it has been proposed that it is the reason for most gut ailments and the cause of many symptoms which are not related to the gastrointestinal system. This concept has been around since the 1980s, also commonly referred to as 'increased intestinal permeability' or 'intestinal hyperpermeability'. It refers to the gut barrier. When this is functionally well, it selects what may pass in and out of it. When the gut barrier is damaged, the gaps in the barrier widen and materials that normally wouldn't be able to pass through the barrier are able to do so. This is what then causes unwanted health effects and increases low-grade inflammation in the body.

The research (again in mice/rats) suggests that this increase in leaky gut and inflammation is driven, in part, by high-fat diet (HFD) induced alterations in gut bacterial composition. Ding et al. reported an increase in inflammatory mediators in the ileum and colon of mice following HFD feedings. Interestingly, these effects preceded weight gain and obesity and showed strong and significant associations with the progression of obesity and development of insulin resistance.[34] Basically, in mice fed a high-fat diet, they saw changes in gut bacterial species, then increases in gut permeability and inflammation before the onset of obesity, so there is a correlation there. Although, again, in mice, correlation doesn't prove causation. Also, this is still being driven by calories (in this circumstance from a high-fat diet), the mice weren't materialising obesity from water or thin air. I mean, I have condensed hundreds of very complicated and confusing articles into about two pages, so it is a little simplified but that's kind of the point of this book—to try and give you the footnotes of the ridiculous and confusing literature and simplify it.

I think it is also important to note that leptin (you remember the hormone we spoke about in the last chapter... come on, memory can't be that bad) is elevated in obese people. This is important because there are studies suggesting that high leptin levels can negatively impact our gut microbiome. However, depending on the specific balance of gut bacteria, the microbiota can increase or decrease leptin sensitivity. This could help explain part of the reason why obese people have more leptin resistance, but more importantly, it gives us an insight into how we could potentially improve leptin sensitivity and subsequent weight loss attempts. But we will get into that in the final chapter, where I attempt to give you the blueprint for weight loss. But first, we need to have discussed everything involved in why obesity is increasing, and what we can learn from the why.

PART 3:
THE OBESOGENIC ENVIRONMENT

The obesity epidemic appeared in the USA around the 1980s and then spread across Westernised countries. If we look back at life pre-obesity, there are some very obvious differences between society then and now. Farming practices have changed. Where we get our food from and in what form has changed significantly, as have our day-to-day lives in terms of activity levels, job roles and hobbies.

On my short walk to the giant Asda by my house yesterday, I saw the perfect embodiment of today's society. A very large man (my neighbour) who is currently unemployed, so collecting benefits (so spends his days watching Netflix... okay, I guessed that, but it doesn't appear like he's doing anything physical with his day), was coming out of the McDonald's (yep, there is a McDonald's attached to the giant Asda... why not?) with a large bag of fried bliss. Instead of walking the gentle 10-minute walk back to where he lives, he then stepped on one of those fucking stupid electric scooters and proceeded to whiz back home having expended only the energy needed to pay for his burger and chips and whatever minimal core strength it takes to stand on that fucking scooter for all of two minutes. If you compared this to the environment that my parents grew up in, you would think you were watching two different planets or species.

I mean, seriously... the more I think about it, the more I think we can blame hormones, gut health and genetics all we like, but the answer to the question of why we are now living in a world where obesity continues to rise is actually obvious. Over time, we have created an environment that, along with habits and lifestyles, is designed for obesity. The ones who are able to escape this norm are either the genetic outliers with inefficient metabolisms or the ones who have been able to adopt the right habits and avoid the dieting pitfalls that seem to have become common practice. My parents or grandparents knew nothing about counting calories or what their protein intake was. They would never have tracked step count, yet obesity back in the 60s was dramatically lower. This doesn't mean calorie counting doesn't work or that your step count is not important; it just shows you that they were able to maintain, on average, a lot healthier weights due to their environment. There is not one thing that has changed or that we can blame it on; hundreds of things have come together to form the obesogenic environment we now live in. In this chapter, I will attempt to summarise and simplify the obvious areas where things have changed and why this is negatively impacting our waistlines and health. Hopefully, the better we understand this, the more we can understand what we ourselves can do in order to survive in this environment (because it is unlikely that it will be changing any time soon).

Let's start by looking back at how early man survived (prepare yourself for some generalisations and slight layman language, but I don't want this chapter to become an in-depth anthropomorphic evaluation. Also, this topic alone could take up a whole book, so we are summarising it just so you understand where I'm coming from).

CHAPTER 9: EARLY MAN TO THE RISE OF OBESITY

Early man usually split itself into hunter-gatherer tribes, whereby the men would hunt and the women and children would forage and gather. A lot of their day was spent working hard to collect the necessary nutrients in order to survive. For the women and children, food was spread out far and wide, and it took many hours for them to find enough for the evening meal. A lot of the carbohydrate sources at the time came from sources usually hidden in the ground, like tubers, roots and bulbs. Seasonal fruits would also have been available, but again, hard to find so could not be relied on year-round. For the men, hunting different animals required trekking vast distances, which not only carried certain risks for the men but may often not bear any fruits. Once the gathers and hunters were done for the day (having only consumed small snacks like insects, maybe fruits, or honey), the food would be cooked, prepared and eaten together.

If we look at the Hadza tribe, we get a population that still eats a diet that resembles what our distant ancestors ate millennia ago. As a hunter-gatherer tribe, it is probably unsurprising that they do not suffer from an obesity problem. Consuming meats, berries, fruits and tubers, they are eating the same diet that they have been eating for 150,000 years. When you actually examine the weights and sizes of individuals in the tribes, you find a similar pattern to any animal species that is left to consume their natural diet. There are some who are underweight and some who are slightly overweight, but the majority of the population (80%) fall within the normal weight and size range.

Fast forward to around 20,000 BC when, in Egypt, the first farmers began changing the foodscape. Food supply was becoming more predictable than a hunter-gatherer format, which relied on seasonal and unpredictable food sources. This was the beginning of the agricultural age— seeds like buckwheat and spelt could be planted and grown for the first time, animals were now also becoming tamed and domesticated so that herds of cattle and sheep would guarantee an easy year-round supply of meat. This ability to control the food supply started to increase the development of permanent settlements. It also meant that a lot less people needed to spend their days in pursuit of food. As the productivity of food production improved, settlements were able to start trading with other settlements and this increased food variety. Where you lived and the climate dictated your basic food supply. In North Africa, Europe and the Middle East, the staple was predominantly wheat. In India and China, it was rice, and in America, it was originally maize. While sugar production primarily started in Asia, it was only consumed on a local level as they had not yet discovered how to store/process it, so it would not survive long enough to be transported further afield.

After a breakthrough in India around AD 300, farmers discovered that if the sugar cane pulp was squeezed/crushed and left to dry in the sun, then crystals of sugar would form (introducing one of the first forms of processing). This meant sugar could now be transported and traded. After the discovery of the Caribbean islands by Columbus in 1492 (according to my quick Google search and the National Geographic website), early explorers noted that the climate would be ideal for growing sugar cane. The first sugar plantation was established in Cuba in 1501, and with it came the global demand for 'white gold' (no, not cocaine). By the 1800s, sugar was much more available globally; however, due to its price, it was more of a staple for the aristocracy than the everyday working man. This is beautifully portrayed in Victorian times by the poor oral hygiene. What I mean by this is that having black teeth in Victorian times displayed your affluence and ability to afford sugar products and confectionaries. Some accounts I could find also noted that some citizens used to paint their teeth black to emphasise their status (mental when you think of how our culture now sends every Love Island wannabe off to Turkey to get fake gleaming white teeth put in... seriously, how times have changed).

Interestingly, despite this increase in sugar trade, if you remove infant mortality from statistics, then the life expectancy of a poor Victorian was similar to that of today (even without the benefits of modern medicine). Analysis of the mid-Victorian period in the UK done by Dr. Paul Clayton reveals that life expectancy at age five was as good or better than exists today, and the incidence of degenerative disease was 10% of ours.[35] Why is this? Well, the diet of the poor Victorian was low in sugar and refined carbohydrates and high in fresh vegetables, fish and offal (not to be confused with awful... offal is the entrails and internal organs of an animal used as food). Their diet was also all 'organic' as this was before the birth of the 'agro-chemical industry' and the widespread use of artificial pesticides or fertilisers. Also, their levels of exercise were much higher than ours today as most walked a lot more, worked physically demanding jobs and were, in general, much more active (despite there not being a PureGym on every corner or Joe Wicks' home workouts in every home). Obesity was almost non-existent, except for the rich, who were a lot less active and could afford more of the white gold treats. I will come back to this later, but the Victorian analysis gives us a great insight into not only what goes wrong but also what we should do to correct the problem.

Fast forward to the mid-18th century, and we were in the whirlwind of the Industrial Revolution, which went hand in hand with the agricultural revolution. Before this, agriculture workers laboured six days a week, from sunup to sun down. The mechanisation in agriculture reduced labour costs and machines were developed to help with tasks such as planting, harvesting, and processing crops.

This increased efficiency and production and so increased profits. Transport networks became wider and cheaper, and thanks to new farming and processing techniques, food could survive longer trips. Techniques like pasteurisation, canning and freezing were developed along with the innovation of refrigerated transport, which also meant that meat could now be shipped worldwide. Food was no longer available based on where you lived, so seasonal foods were no longer relied on. Britain had moved from being a net exporter of foodstuffs to a net importer. The foodscape was beginning to become unrecognisable, the success of agriculture allowed for the growth in mechanised factories in urban areas, which caused a growth in population, which, in turn, created a greater market for agricultural products, further boosting the farming industry.[36] Food was becoming big business, and where money is concerned, we know innovation and change will follow.

An obesity problem still hadn't materialised though, despite this step forward in processing, access to sugar and farming practices. Unsurprisingly, if we look to the early part of the 19th century, we had two world wars to survive (where food rationing was common practice) and the Great Depression to get through, so we can't be too shocked that we still hadn't hit obesity mode yet. The Great Depression, which started in 1929 and continued into the 1930s, was a time of food scarcity. Practicality outweighed cultural relevance, which led to a diet more about scraping together whatever ingredients were easily accessible and, hopefully, filling. Despite the shortage of food during the Great Depression, it was actually around this time that a lot of the sweets/chocolate bars we enjoy today got their start. The early 1930s saw the rise of candy bars. Some of these chocolate-covered bars were considered affordable meal replacements at the time. You may have heard of one of them—Snickers. Yup, the Mars company has been producing the great Snickers bar since the Great Depression. We started to see the creation of more "cinema-style" snacks at this time; even the creation of Rocky Road ice cream was in 1929. The foodscape was still changing but had not yet tipped the scales.

In 1939, World War II started, and by 1940, food rations were re-introduced. The scheme was designed to ensure fair shares for all at a time of national shortage. Basic foodstuffs such as sugar, meats, bacon and cheese were directly rationed by an allowance of coupons. It was not until the early 1950s that most commodities came 'off the ration'. Meat was the last item to be de-rationed and food rationing ended completely in 1954. Unsurprisingly, there was no "obesity epidemic" at this time as food supply and travel were limited, meaning people ate less and walked more. Interestingly, 1954 is also the date that Ray Kroc signed a franchise agreement with McDonald's, beginning the journey of global domination by McDonald's. Okay, that sounds a bit extreme, but let's rewind a second because I think the rise of fast food is a very important factor to take into consideration when we discuss the obesogenic environment.

CHAPTER 10: FAST FOOD

When we think of fast food, or at least the beginning of fast food, we think of McDonald's and the culture that it spawned. Fast food has actually been around in some sense since Roman times. While ancient Romans wouldn't have enjoyed drive-throughs, they could still buy food in a hurry from places called thermopliums, which translates to "hot shop" (a sort of snack bar/lunch counter). Also called popina, these small stalls offered food that was hot and ready to go or could be quickly warmed up on a stove. From legumes, vegetables, eggs, olives, skewers of meat, fish, cheeses, seasonal or dried fruit, even some focaccia and sweets. Fast food existed, although, let's be honest, it is a far cry from the fast food landscape of today.

There are other examples from early fishing villages offering seafood to go, or town vendors in the Middle Ages offering pies and cooked meats. It wasn't until around 1860, or more precisely, 1863, when England got its first fish and chip shop near Oldham. While these shops started popping up in more and more locations in the 19th century, they were originally small family businesses, growing in number in order to satisfy the needs of the growing industrial population of Great Britain. Interestingly, the wars didn't put a stop to the fish and chip shop trade. In fact, the government ensured that there was a continuous supply of fish and potatoes during WWI and WWII. Not only was fish and chips an enjoyable meal for the population, but it also saved lives in combat zones (according to some articles I managed to find on Google). British troops were known to use the name of the popular dish to identify friendly troops—one would shout, "Fish", and the other would reply, "Chips". Like the fat and slightly riskier version of the game Marco Polo.

Over the pond in the US, the first fast food was an automat type of restaurant that opened in 1912. Imagine a giant version of today's vending machines, but instead of candy bars, there was hot food like pies or macaroni and cheese, to sandwiches and chicken pot pie. Advertised as a "New Method of Lunching", customers could enter the shop, put some money in the giant vending machine, and open the drawer holding their chosen food. Out of sight, kitchen staff worked to quickly refill empty compartments as if by magic. Joe Horn and Frank Hardart's creation was a marvel of efficiency that revolutionised the American food service industry.

The first official hamburger chain, "White Castle" (you may recognise the name from the Harold and Kumar films if you aren't from the States), opened in 1921. This was the first establishment to standardise the production of food, creating the first fast food supply chain that supplied ingredients to all outlets. It was a small menu, but popularity grew, and they are credited for the popularisation of the hamburger (and actually, Walt Anderson, the founder, is credited with the invention of the hamburger bun that we know today). This industry still hadn't fully taken off when brothers, Richard and Maurice McDonald, having failed in the movie business, decided to open a barbecue drive-in in 1940, in the city of San Bernardino, California called McDonald's. In 1948, they streamlined their operation, creating their new 'Speedee Service System', and with it, I believe the true beginnings of the fast food world were formed. As I mentioned, in 1954, Ray Croc signed a franchise agreement with the McDonald's brothers, and from there, McDonald's spread like wildfire. (If you are interested in this and haven't watched 'The Founder', the story of Ray Croc and the McDonald brothers, I would highly recommend it.)

The food landscape from here was beginning to change. Even the way we enjoyed meals had transformed drastically, going from a family affair where we would sit down and enjoy a meal together, now food is having to keep up with the growing speed of our fast-paced lives. Fast food was taking off in large part because of the progresses that the Industrial Revolution had heralded and the highway system that had been developed. Americans started driving more, more people were living in bustling cities than ever before, so the growth of fast food was a natural business response to the on-the-go kind of lifestyle. Despite these changes, obesity rates in the 1950s-60s were still sitting at around 10% in US adults. Our calorie intake had not taken off yet, however, we were definitely seeing shifts in eating habits.

CHAPTER 11: SUPERSIZE ME

Another change, and one that I think highlights one of the bigger problems in our diets today, is portion sizes. Introducing David Wallerstein. I'm guessing you've probably never heard of this man before, but he is largely responsible for at least one of the main flaws of the American diet to this day. David Wallerstein owned a movie theatre in the 1960s. Back then (and if my last few excursions to the cinema have shown me), movie theatres, more often than not, relied on the revenue generated not from the ticket sales but actually from the overpriced concession stand (where you buy your snacks from... I'm not sure if anyone calls it a concession stand anymore).

The problem Wallerstein was having was that despite employing multiple tactics to try and make movie patrons buy more snacks, like a good old two-for-one deal or matinee specials, he couldn't seem to get customers to purchase more than one bag of popcorn or return to the stand to purchase another. While these marketing tactics seemed to work in other industries, it seemed as though there was a social/psychological aversion to these tactics within the cinema. What was this?

Well, if we think about it, the obvious answer is not that people don't understand a good deal because we know value is a great purchase motivator. What is more realistic is that most of us are put off by ordering a second bag out of embarrassment of people judging us for gluttonous behaviour. Leonard Mlodinow, an American theoretical physicist, wrote in his book, "Elastic: Flexible Thinking in a Time of Change", "In the 1960s, people viewed consuming larger amounts of food as unattractive". So, Wallerstein needed to find a way around this problem.

The solution—offer a larger bag of popcorn. And so was born the jumbo size. The results were immediate… popcorn sales shot up overnight. What seems like an obvious answer to the problem was actually a move going against/challenging a very basic assumption of the marketers of the day. The thinking back then had always been that if people wanted more popcorn, then they would just make an additional purchase. They had not realised the socially induced inhibitions of the times against gluttonous behaviour. With the larger bag of popcorn available, people could get more popcorn without feeling the pressure of worrying about gluttonous behaviour.

David Wallerstein had solved his financial problem, and in so doing, had taken the first step of supersizing the American diet. The next step would come in 1970 when—you guessed it—Wallerstein took up a position working for… McDonald's. Using the success of his larger-sized popcorn bags, Wallerstein pitched to the CEO, Ray Kroc, the idea of selling French fries in larger bags. Kroc, who was the mastermind behind the growth of

McDonald's, actually didn't seem to like the idea at first, insisting that if people wanted more fries, they could just buy another portion. McDonald's finally came around to the idea and designed a special red cardboard container to present the large fries as a premium item. And well, I think it's safe to say Wallerstein's method worked again. McDonald's introduced their large fries in 1972, and by 1992, had launched a supersize.

Now, there are many other factors to note, but you can see how one little idea has helped increase the average calorie consumption since the 1980s. Marketers were no longer constrained by nutritional values or needs, it became simple—the more they offered, the more we consumed.

The same story is true for things like soft drinks. Let's take Coca-Cola for example. Born in 1886 by John S Pemberton, it originally began as a tonic for all your 'ailments'. I mean, since it originally contained cocaine and red wine, I can't blame people for thinking it was healing them... okay, it actually contained coca, not full-on cocaine, and the alcohol was removed due to prohibition and was replaced by sugar water instead. The syrup was added to soda water and so was born Coca-Cola. By the early 1900s, annual sales of Coca-Cola hit $1 million and had entered markets outside the United States. Bottling operations expanded to Canada, Cuba, and Panama by 1906. While consumption of Coca-Cola grew in the early 1900s, again, this increase is not reflected in the obesity statistics. To be fair, this was pre-high fructose corn syrup being added to the ingredients but does illustrate that while we can demonise soft drinks nowadays for increasing people's weight, it still works within the realms of energy balance.

Like the supersizing of popcorn and French fries, the same happened with Coca-Cola. In Jack A Bobo's book, *Why Smart People Make Bad Food Choices*, he writes of the interesting story about the struggling 7-Eleven convenience store. In 1967, the store's merchandise manager, Dennis Potts, was approached by Coca-Cola representatives about a new 32-ounce cup design. Potts believed the cups were too big for practical use and felt that they didn't need to adjust the current stock of 12- and 20-ounce cups. He was offered two free cases (containing 500 cups in each), and after less than a week, the store he sent them to had run out. It turned out that the Big Gulp was a hit with Americans (shock), so another element of the American/Western diet was supersized.

Coca-Cola interestingly made the switch to high fructose corn syrup (HFCS) in the late 1970s for economic reasons (the shift from using sucrose to HFCS was encouraged by extensive government subsidies of corn farmers, with a majority of US farm policies focused on promoting increased production of inexpensive corn). While this is a topic of controversy for a few reasons, it is worth noting that in 1970, HFCS represented less than 1% of all caloric sweeteners available for consumption in the United States. This jumped up rapidly in the 1980s, and by 2000, represented 42.0% of all caloric sweeteners. With the rates of obesity jumping up in line with this increased consumption, it is understandable that people demonise sugar-sweetened beverages and HFCS for increasing or even causing the obesity problem. While correlation does not prove causation, it is important to note that there are studies that show that the ingestion of calories via sugar-sweetened beverages does not seem to have the same satiety effect as ingesting the same number of calories from food. Therefore, consumption of sugar-sweetened beverages could lead to increased weight gain as you are likely to increase your overall calorie consumption as a result.[37] This, again, still means we are working within the realms of energy balance in this argument. You could, therefore, consume a soda every day if you wanted to, you would just need to make sure it fit within your calorie budget, but as noted as something that is not very satiating, I would always advise you to limit your intake of sugar-sweetened beverages when trying to maintain your body weight. Currently, soft drinks constitute the leading source of added sugars in the diet—currently approximately 36.2g daily for adolescent girls and 57·7g for boys. These figures approach or exceed the daily limits for total added sugar consumption recommended by the USDA.[38]

Unsurprisingly, while many people like to demonise artificial sweeteners, if you are someone who enjoys sodas and have a sweet tooth, this would be a much better choice for your waistline (assuming you don't then go and eat extra food to reward yourself). Studies comparing artificial sweetened drinks to HFCS-sweetened sodas concluded that "drinking HFCS-sweetened soda for 3 weeks significantly increased the calorie intake and body weight of both sexes. Drinking large volumes of aspartame-sweetened soda, in contrast to drinking HFCS-sweetened soda, reduces sugar intake and thus may facilitate the control of calorie intake and body weight".[39] Before you jump on other arguments like, well, they are linked to cancer or leaky gut, know that there are no studies done in humans to show this, despite what your favourite influencer might say. There are a few studies in humans showing that it can alter your gut microbiome in the short term, but this didn't prove/show whether these were negative or positive changes.

Anyway... sorry, little off topic I know, but I hate people demonising things incorrectly.

It is becoming increasingly clear that soft drink consumption may be an important contributor to the epidemic of obesity, in part through the larger portion sizes of these beverages, helping to increase our overall calorie intake to the fact that they provide very little satiety and, therefore, are easy to overconsume. It has been proposed that fructose, which is digested, absorbed, and metabolised differently, could also be working to increase obesity. Differences in responses of insulin, leptin and ghrelin create circumstances where increased caloric consumption might occur following ingestion of fructose, but not glucose. In particular, the failure of fructose in studies to stimulate insulin production, with subsequent leptin production and suppression of ghrelin, suggested a metabolic situation where increased appetite and subsequent weight gain could occur. While studies in rodents gave us cause for concern (as it increased de novo lipogenesis, the conversion of excess carbohydrates into fatty acids), thanks to research looking at the effect on humans, it found that on a calorie-per-calorie basis, it is not fattening compared to other carbohydrate/sugar sources.[40] Meaning 50 calories from glucose or 50 calories from fructose is still just 50 calories. If you are in an energy deficit, you will still lose weight, and this is shown by the research.

Anyway, back to the supersizing movement. It is not just popcorn, McDonald's and fizzy drinks that have increased their sizes. If we look at the average dinner plate back in the 1950s, it was about nine inches, but if you were presented with that sized plate now, you would assume it was a starter. The average dinner plate now is 12 inches. This might not sound like a big difference, but trust me, those three extra inches can make a big difference... to the number of calories on the plate (get your mind out the gutter). Plate sizes can get even bigger when you eat out at restaurants (The Cheesecake Factory, famous for having large portions, often serves dinners with a 15-inch plate... clearly overcompensating for something).

An increase in plate size means an increase in portion size, which means an increase in calories (no shit, Chris), and while we have satiety signals in the body designed to stop us from overeating, the portion can still appear normal size when it's on a larger plate. While this sounds a bit stupid, it is true. It tricks our brain into thinking we should be able to finish the larger portion as it appears like a normal amount of food. This is why one dieting trick you are often told to try is using smaller plates and bowls to control your portion sizes… remember, a bit like the popcorn, people wouldn't buy two bags for fear of being judged for being gluttonous, it is similar to using a smaller plate as you are less likely to go for a second portion when using a small plate for fear of looking greedy. Also, your brain will think you are eating a bigger portion anyway as it fills up the smaller plate.

There are lots of studies showing that providing people with larger food portions can lead to significant increases in energy intake. This effect has been demonstrated for snacks and a variety of single meals and has been shown to persist over a two-day period. Despite increases in intake, individuals presented with large portions generally do not report or respond to increased levels of fullness, suggesting that hunger and satiety signals are ignored or overridden.[41] So, as portion sizes have got bigger, we have, in turn, started consuming more calories without the subsequent increase in satiety to prevent us from overconsuming more calories later.

Increased portion sizes aren't limited to just restaurants—we see it in packaged goods, at bakeries, cinemas, supermarkets and even in our dinners at home. There are all-you-can-eat buffets now… a concept that would have been laughable during the depression. I mean, we can't be too surprised when eating challenges at restaurants appear on menus and all-you-can-eat buffets are now commonplace that we are finding ways to consume more food. Companies are competing to give you more value, so you end up with jumbo packs of everything. If you compare recipe books to those back in the 1950s, while the recipe may not have changed, the number of servings it provided has. A muffin recipe that usually made 12 muffins would now only produce six to eight muffins in the new roided-up muffin tins. The original burger that was served to Ray Kroc at McDonald's weighed in at 3.9 ounces (this was for the bun, pickle and lettuce), today, it's closer to 12 ounces. A small order of fries today is the same portion size as you would have received in 1970 if you ordered a large. McDonald's isn't anywhere near the worst offender—a large fries from somewhere like Five Guys is 1,314 calories... that's even before you add the burger or milkshake to that order. I feel like we are looking for specific items to blame when, in reality, a lot of the foodscape does point to the obvious—we are just eating more, and it is predominantly coming from more hedonic fast food... (but more on that later).

An interesting study I found looking at portion sizes between 1977-98 found that they increased both inside and outside the home for all categories they measured except pizza. Salty snacks increased by 93 calories, soft drinks by 49 kcal, hamburgers 97 kcal, French fries 68 kcal and Mexican food by 133 kcals.[42] I would dread to think how much they have risen by now, but another worrying point that the research shows is that the largest increases in consumption were observed in the younger (2-18 and 19-39) ages. We are now consuming more food from fast food places than at home, further suggesting that our eating habits and patterns have permanently changed. Quite a far cry from the traditional setting where eating was a time when everyone would come together. So, where we get our food from was starting to change in the late 1990s as were the sizes of the portions, so you can begin to see the foundations of the obesogenic environment developing.

If I think back to when I was growing up (in the late 1990s) when obesity was starting to increase, if we ever wanted a takeaway, it was usually considered a treat and couldn't have happened more than four or five times a year, and when we did, it was a choice between either the Chinese takeaway, the fish and chip shop or maybe the Indian takeaway (although I don't think we ever actually chose the Indian). My point is that we were limited in our choice and actually the takeaway restaurants were quite a drive away, and the selection was very limited. Today, however, if you just go on one of the million apps that offer food delivery, the possibilities are endless. While I have found it hard to find the exact statistics for the growth of fast food restaurants, I found one study which showed that the number of fast food takeaway restaurants in Norfolk (a county in the UK) rose by 45% between 1990 and 2008. What's really interesting about this study is that the largest increase in these fast food restaurants was seen in the most economically deprived areas where the numbers rose from 4.6 to 6.5 outlets per 10,000 people. This is, again, only the statistics from 2008, the growth has only increased, and now, even after a number of closures due to the pandemic, has increased to a massive 46,200 takeaway and fast food restaurants in the UK alone. This highlights the overall changing landscape of where we get our food from now. Statistics from

2016 show that 36% of people eat out on average at least once or twice a week.

It is also important to note that research shows we eat, on average, 15% fewer calories when we sit down and take our time to enjoy our food as opposed to eating on the go. Researchers have explained that this can occur because when we rush a meal or eat while distracted, the parts of your brain that usually sense satiety don't register the strength of the satiety signal, which may cause you to disregard that you have already eaten or cause you to feel hungrier again sooner. I actually have an ex who used to do this. She would say, "I'm starving, I haven't eaten in ages". I then reminded her that she had wolfed down a croissant no more than 45 minutes prior, which was usually met with a reply along the lines of, "That doesn't count", despite most croissants containing upwards of 250 calories.

As I write this, it dawns on me... isn't it a bit ironic that back in Victorian times, being overweight and having black teeth were a sign of affluence. It seems now those two things seem closer correlated to poverty than affluence. Eating "healthier" appears more expensive and a privilege... just an observation (as I think education around nutrition plays a role in this as well), but if you think of the price of organic fruit and veg and the difference in cost of going to your local butchers shop or the local bakery vs. shopping in giant supermarkets like Costco or Lidl or Aldi, we are finding that, yes, for most people, going to the Saver Menu at McDonald's or getting a meal deal in Tesco is a cheaper and more convenient option for lunch. If we look at rates of obesity and socio-economic status, there is definitely a correlation there we can't ignore. The Royal College of Physicians London notes that adults in the most deprived regions have almost double the prevalence of obesity compared with the least deprived (36% compared with 20%). In 2018/19, the prevalence of obesity in children aged 10-11 was 27% in the most deprived areas and 13% in the least deprived areas. This gap is only growing in obesity prevalence between children from the most deprived and least deprived areas, with an increase from 8.5% in 2006/7 to 13.9% in 2018/19.[43]

This supersizing movement has also made its way into our supermarkets as marketing looks to play on this added value angle. Price/value deals can influence the speed of consumption even when the food has already been purchased. Studies have found that people accelerate the consumption of products perceived to have been purchased at a lower price. Citing that this happens because a reduced past price is seen as an indication that it will be potentially discounted again in the future or simply because the reduced cost means that consumers feel they do not have to wait for a special occasion to consume the product as it was cheaper and, therefore, not so special.

Research also suggests that quantity discounts generally lead to stockpiling and increased consumption, especially for overweight consumers. One study found that during weeks in which multi-unit packages were purchased, consumption of orange juice increased by 100% and cookies by 92%.[44] So, we have direct evidence that these supersized value discounts are not only increasing purchasing but directly increasing our consumption. I think this also has something to do with the products that are being discounted since the studies didn't find an increase in consumption of non-edible products. So, just because you buy a discounted bag of toilet paper doesn't mean you will suddenly start wiping your ass more. However, if you buy a jumbo bag of crisps, it is likely you will increase your consumption of crisps by quite a lot.

CHAPTER 12: VARIETY

I t isn't just where we buy our foods from, it is the variety of foods now that has completely exploded in the last 50 years. If we just take one item like Coca-Cola, created in 1886, for many years since its conception, it remained the only option people had. Then, 96 years later, in 1982, they introduced Diet Coke. It took almost 100 years to create another version of their drink. In 2002, Coca-Cola Vanilla was introduced, so just 20 years this time for a new version. Now, there appears to be a new flavour out every year. If I try and count all the versions in my head now, I can note down over 10. And that is just for those called Coca-Cola. Obviously, if we look at the soft drink aisle at the supermarket, you are looking at hundreds of varieties. What about biscuits or crisps? According to a quick Google search, there are 85+ different flavours of Oreo cookies… what the fuck!? I don't think I could even come up with 20 ideas for different cookie flavours if I tried.

A lot of the supermarkets that we now take for granted started their lives as much smaller shops or stalls. Tesco started life in 1919 when Jack Cohen began selling surplus groceries from a stall in the East End of London.

It was 1869 when John James Sainsbury and his wife, Mary Ann, opened the first Sainsbury's store on London's Drury Lane, which started as a retailer of fresh foods and later expanded into packaged groceries such as tea and sugar. Supermarkets are a far cry from what they were 50 years ago. Variety is great, and we should celebrate how far we have come, but there is a downside to this growth. While this increase in variety not only gives people more options, usually in the foods that we probably wouldn't recommend for anyone looking to lose weight, it can also impact our food intake and food choices via two different processes.

The first process is something called 'decision fatigue'. In the 1980s, you would have walked into a grocery store and been faced with one or two decisions to make like which vegetables were in stock, which meat were you cooking for dinner or whether you needed any ketchup. Now you have aisles of condiments, hundreds of varieties of almost everything you can think of, there are even rows of Free From foods where someone has worked out how to make mac and cheese without gluten or dairy in it… this is also before we mention all the different packaging designed to make you think they are healthier for you (more about this later anyway). Not only are there hundreds of different varieties of products, but there are also a variety of different sizes of each product, all designed to make you spend more money by making larger versions that provide more value. Going food shopping is now an obstacle course and a mental challenge that, unless you are well prepared and have blinders on, you will probably fail.

This is where 'decision fatigue' comes in. Coined by social psychologist, Roy F. Baumeister, decision fatigue is the emotional and mental strain resulting from a burden of choices. You see, making decisions about what to eat may not be as complicated as something like filling out your tax return, but our brains are usually bombarded on a daily basis by the very mentally stimulating/exhausting fast-paced world we live in. At the end of a long day of making decisions, our brains will often lean towards whichever feels like the easiest option, which is rarely the one that aligns most with our health goals. If you are tired, have to maybe pick the kids up from school, get petrol, cook, prepare your kids' uniforms (or pack lunches) for tomorrow, do you really think you are going to be reading the calorie content on the pack of the pasta sauce looking for the one with less sugar in it? Are you going to be checking which vegetables are in season? Or are you going to be grabbing the easiest, quickest (and possibly cheapest) option that will hopefully shut your kids up and make your life in the short term easier?

Deborah Cohen, author of *A Big Fat Crisis*: *The Hidden Influences Behind the Obesity Epidemic* — *and How We Can End It*, Writes, "We have a limited thinking capacity, so as we use our brains more and more, our ability to think carefully and calculate and analyse is worn down". Supermarkets are aware of this mental fatigue and, therefore, place things like candy and crisps at the checkout station to increase your impulse purchases of these products while you wait. Let's be honest, the more health-conscious consumers have become, the more savvy food manufacturers have become to make it harder to distinguish between what is good or bad. Even as someone who specialises in nutrition, I can fall foul of their tricks. Who has ever bought something and quickly glanced at the back of the packet to check calorie content? I think most of us have. Well, how many times have you gone on to enjoy that food only to realise that it wasn't listing the calories for the bag but per serving and, actually, the bag contained four servings? That's actually one of the more obvious ones. I find people are always shocked when I explain to them that when companies realised we started to become more health conscious and started to read the ingredient lists looking for how near the top things like sugar was, they then started to split the sugar sources up in the ingredients list in order to reduce how high up sugar was listed. Also, let's be honest, given that there are over 61 different names for sugars, I think it is quite easy that to the average eye, you would miss most of these.

Having to decide between the varieties of foods on display in order to pick the healthier choices is an energy-draining form of decision-making. And as I said... when we are mentally fatigued, we don't make the best decisions. A bit like when we are drunk... but that's a topic for another day. When products seem identical in terms of nutritional value, we will then look at price and weigh up value against our budget. Before you realise it, you could have spent 10 minutes in Tesco and only have got a third of the way down your shopping list, and that is if you were organised enough to make a list. I used to live next to an Aldi and would often find myself walking in there for chicken and leaving with a wet suit, a two-kilo pot of yoghurt, a box of tools, and a family bag of popcorn, only to realise by the time I got home that I forgot the fucking chicken.

There are even studies showing how simple mental fatigue can immediately impact our decision-making when it comes to food choices. One study got people to memorise a two-digit number or a seven-digit number. After memorising the number, participants were then offered the choice between either chocolate cake or fruit salad. The group memorising the longer number was twice as likely to choose the chocolate cake over the fruit salad. Even just memorising a slightly longer number was enough to exhaust our mental reserves enough to affect a simple 50/50 decision.[45]

So, increased variety can lead to decision fatigue, which usually leads us to making worse food choices, or if you are like me, a collection of unnecessary things from Aldi that you have never used and often then gift to family members. The other way variety can impact our waistline is through something called sensory-specific satiety or SSS. This is essentially the desire to eat a food that has already been tasted, which is significantly reduced compared with one that has not; therefore, a greater variety of food offered at a single meal means the more people will subsequently eat. This phenomenon has been studied, although the experiments are slightly longer and less interesting than memorising numbers and choosing between cake and fruit salad, so I will save you from the details. What they have shown is that food variety has indeed repeatedly increased consumption. Both the effect of food variety on meal intake and its influence on the development of SSS showed an increased food intake and attenuated SSS when a variety of foods was consumed.[46] I think a good way to look at this is if you imagine when you eat a lot of something sweet, that taste becomes sickly and you are more likely to want to consume something more savoury next, and the reverse... after something savoury, you are more likely to want something sweet. There are a number of interactions during SSS, whether it is food texture or nutritional profile, everything can play a role. If I tried eating a large pot of yoghurt on its own, I would struggle as the texture and taste are a bit boring, but throw a bit of crunchy granola in there and maybe some berries and I've added differing textures now, some different nutrients, and as a result, I will probably consume more and will increase the caloric load of the meal altogether.

The increased variety we now have when we sit down at meals, whether it is condiments, cooking techniques, or even the herbs or spices used to flavour it will enhance our enjoyment and work to help reduce our satiety and allow us to consume more food. Think of all the varieties of cuisine we now have to choose from as well. Given how multicultural the world has become, we are no longer just stuck with recipes our grandparents passed down to us. Studies of the effects of consumption of monotonous army rations indicate that repeated presentation of some foods can lead to a very persistent decrease in pleasantness of these foods (although I can't imagine the army rations tasted great to begin with).[47] Moreover, it appears that the more hedonic-type foods don't seem to suffer the same fate of a decrease in appeal, the more they are consumed. For example, things like coffee, desserts, sweets, and bread do not seem to lose their appeal even when consumed daily. As a man who enjoys his coffee every morning, this does not come as a surprise, however, we can see that while our taste buds are celebrating our increased variety in cuisine, all the while subconsciously steering our food choices towards the more hedonic foods, it has unsurprisingly had a less than favourable effect on our waistlines.

CHAPTER 13: BLISS POINT AND THE ULTRA-PROCESSED WORLD

Where would a weight loss book be without talking about ultra-processed foods? Earlier, we spoke about the changing farming practices, the Industrial Revolution and the modernization of transport and communications, the emergence of food-processing and food-packaging industries, eventually making it possible to extend food trade on a global scale. From techniques such as tinning and canning food to pasteurisation, it is safe to say food processing has come on leaps and bounds since then. New technologies like freeze drying, different preservatives, emulsifiers, E numbers, artificial sweeteners, ready-made meals, vegan alternatives, inventions like the microwave, food processors and blenders... all of these miracles of technological advancements have served to completely alter the grocery aisles of our now super-sized supermarkets. These changes have also led us to the creation of the so-called "Western Diet", which is not synonymous with health.

Don't get me wrong, some of these advancements are really revolutionary and have allowed for increases in food production, removal of harmful bacteria and toxins, increase in shelf life, and increases in the foods on offer and quantities, meaning that areas of the world that suffered from malnourishment and starvation no longer experience such afflictions or at least to a lesser extent. Studies on the fortification of foods, for example, have shown positive results not only in the control and prevention of micronutrient deficiencies among vulnerable populations, especially women and children, but also along social, economic and environmental dimensions.[48] So, let's not just immediately demonise all processed foods. Also, if we are going by definition, most food in your supermarket has some level of processing these days since we aren't exactly picking things from our garden to eat (thank fuck... because the only thing growing in mine are weeds). By definition, a processed food is simply one that has been altered from its original form, even broccoli when it has just been cut and put into a packet, has technically been processed, but clearly that is not what we are referring to when we talk about ultra-processed food.

I went to find what the definition is for ultra-processed foods (as in I googled "define ultra-processed foods"... yup, research at its finest), and it turns out there is some complexity to the definition as it has changed over the years along with changing food practices, and depending on who you ask, there are very different versions. The most popular of those food classification systems is the NOVA system, which introduced the term "ultra-processed foods" to describe the highest level of food processing. The problem with the NOVA classification system is that it relies largely on categorising foods based on the content of added sugars, saturated fat, and sodium, so it is possible to misclassify some nutrient-rich foods as ultra-processed. Other classification systems have been created to address some of the classification problems within the original NOVA criteria. After finding a PubMed article titled "Ultra-Processed Foods: Definitions and Policy Issues", the most recent definition (2017) I could find is as follows: "Industrial formulations typically with 5 or more and usually many ingredients. Besides salt, sugar, oils, and fats, ingredients of ultra-processed foods include food substances not commonly used in culinary preparations, such as hydrolyzed protein, modified starches, and hydrogenated or interesterified oils, and additives whose purpose is to imitate sensorial qualities of unprocessed or minimally processed foods and their culinary preparations or to disguise undesirable qualities of the final product, such as colourants, flavourings, non-sugar sweeteners, emulsifiers, humectants, sequestrants, and firming, bulking, de-foaming, anticaking, and glazing agents".

I don't want to get too hung up on the definition, although I felt like I should still give you a proper definition—I think most of us can use our common sense when we talk about removing ultra-processed foods from our diet. Oreo cookies from Sainsbury's = ultra-processed. An egg pot from Pret (which is essentially two boiled eggs and a bit of uncooked spinach) = not ultra-processed. Looking at an ingredient list of most foods can give you a good idea of how processed something is or not. Some of the ingredient lists for vegan fake meat alternatives is like trying to read Chinese for the first time (assuming you aren't Chinese). Alternatively, if I purchase something like a nut snack pot from Tesco, I expect the list to read: Cashew nuts… assuming I had purchased the cashew pot.

It is not a surprise that part of the obesity equation is an increase in the consumption of calories from ultra-processed foods. Recent studies have reported that these foods account for a significant percentage of about 50%-60% of the energy content in the usual diet of the average US, Canadian or British consumer,[49] although for certain populations, this might be even higher. Again, I need to point out that the consumption of ultra-processed foods still works within the confines of our energy balance equation. You could eat all your calories from ultra-processed foods, but if you were in a deficit, you would still lose weight. This was clearly demonstrated by Kevin Maginnis, a 57-year-old man from Nashville who ate three meals a day for 100 days from McDonald's (the poster child of ultra-processed foods) and dropped 60lbs… his wife was so impressed with his diet results that she decided to join him, and after 65 days, she was down 18lbs (so it worked for both men and women… just saying). The problem with ultra-processed foods is that they are usually hyperpalatable and easy to overconsume on, so the vast majority of people end up overconsuming calories as a result of these ultra-processed foods being in their diet.

A very good study was done by Kevin Hall looking at how the introduction of ultra-processed foods affected overall energy consumption in weight stable adults. In the study, participants were randomised to receive either ultra-processed or unprocessed diets for two weeks immediately followed by the alternate diet for two weeks. Meals were designed to be matched for presented calories, energy density, macronutrients, sugar, sodium, and fibre. They were instructed to consume as much or as little as desired. In the ultra-processed diet, participants ended up consuming around 500 calories more per day (predominantly from carbohydrates and fats). Unsurprisingly, the participants on the ultra-processed diet gained weight after two weeks (due to their increased calorie consumption) and then lost this during the unprocessed diet (as they then reduced their calorie consumption). He rightly concluded that limiting consumption of ultra-processed foods may be an effective strategy for obesity prevention and treatment. Again, I need to stress this still works in terms of energy balance—ultra-processed foods don't make you magically put on fat... look at the man losing weight on just a McDonald's diet, it is their energy dense nature and their hyperpalatable nature that make them easy to overconsume on, causing you to overeat total calories.

Interestingly, they also found that the appetite-suppressing hormone, PYY, increased during the unprocessed diet as compared with both the ultra-processed diet and baseline. Also, the hunger hormone, ghrelin, was decreased during the unprocessed diet compared to baseline.[50] So, the source of the food was impacting hunger and satiety levels, making it easier to overconsume on the ultra-processed foods.

When we talk about ultra-processed foods leading to an overconsumption of calories, it is important to understand what is termed 'bliss point'. Bliss point refers to how the food industry/food companies have manipulated the taste/ingredients of their products to make them irresistible. This blend of fats, carbs and salt are working to create the perfect balance for maximum appeal, which results in maximum addictiveness. American market researcher and psychophysicist, Howard Moskowitz, termed this the "bliss point"—essentially the point where the levels of saltiness, sweetness, and richness were perceived by the consumer as just right. You then add mouthfeel or crunchiness into the mix and you have a recipe for overconsumption. If we look at one of the most overconsumed snacks—crisps—we can see that this is the blend of fats, sugar and salt.

This is an important point to note because whether you want to demonise sugar or fats or salt, it appears that it is the combination of all three that creates this hyperpalatable nature. If sugar on its own was addictive, why do people not just buy bags of sugar and eat them? It's because the source, as in the food it comes from, matters. Fruit is very high in sugar, but no one ever got fat from just eating fruit.

Yes, the creation of hyperpalatable foods definitely plays a role in the obesity epidemic. Dr Kessler, in his book, *The End of Overeating*, describes that while some people want to blame a lack of willpower on why people overeat, it is a lot more complicated than this and that the seductive and addictive combination of sugar, fat, and salt, which is layered into many foods now found in our supermarkets and food delivery services, have worked to create an environment where our satiety signals are being overridden and our body fat thermostats are rising as a result. Irrelevant of whatever dietary religion you fall into, I don't think anyone would disagree that reducing your overall consumption of ultra-processed foods would improve your health and waistline. The problem is, they are everywhere now. Why? Well, as I mentioned, the food industry is a money-making machine. If companies could find more profit and addiction in broccoli rather than cookies and chips, then we may be looking at a very different population.

Neuroscience originally was meant to unlock the mysteries of the consciousness and the brain, however, wherever there is innovation, there is profit to be made. There is actually a field called neuromarketing! Their aim is to market happiness in a bottle, hamburger or new smartphone. The reality is that companies are working with neuroscience, creating a legal market of mass addiction. The aim is to push pleasure as pleasure results in "this feels good, I want more", which leads to more money for the company. I would like to quote The Notorious B.I.G here and say, "More money, more problems", but it appears the problems are for the consumers and not the companies, so maybe we can just paraphrase it to say, "More calories, more problems", although definitely less catchy. You see, in the brain, pleasure employs dopamine and opiates, both of which operate in short-term bursts. Dopamine = incentive and motivation, and opiate = pleasure and reward.

Neuromarketing is a strategic invasion of human consciousness. The more a product can activate/agitate the dopamine/endorphin functions of the brain, the more we will be driven to buy/eat it. Nothing makes companies turn a blind eye to health issues quicker than profit margins (just look at the Alcohol and Tobacco industry). Food companies use the expertise of scientists along with marketing wizards to find the bliss point in foods where the perfect combination of fat, sugar and salt makes all the brain's pleasure centres dance around, screaming for more and more.

Essentially, our brains were hacked... sounds a bit farfetched but I think it's quite hard to argue against. I'm not saying you aren't in control, but we are living in a society where companies are using our own neurochemistry against us to get us to purchase more.

A report published in the Lancet found that 11 million deaths worldwide in 2017 could be attributed to diets deficient in vegetables, seeds, and nuts but laden with salt, fat and sugar. I guess when we think about killing for money, our minds turn to burglary, mugging or maybe a dramatized bank heist rather than looking at companies like Coca-Cola and the potential damage that policymaking and profit is having on our society. I'm not placing all the blame at the feet of the food industry because as someone who tries to eat a nutritious diet, I still like to believe we have free will. That being said, the cost of free will (good nutrition) seems to be slowly pricing many lower economic groups out of this luxury/necessity.

Again, important to note that this is all still governed by energy balance. Hopefully, you are starting to understand that there are many elements involved in why we overeat/overconsume calories, making most of our weights jump up, but this still just involves overconsumption and nothing more. People online will probably use words like inflammation or demonise a single ingredient, but the reality is much simpler—we are overeating calories and it's not from a single nutrient source.

CHAPTER 14: CHANGING OUR EATING AND SHOPPING HABITS

Hopefully, by now you can see how our environment since the 1900s has definitely been a leading driver for obesity. Again, still working within the equation of energy balance but it has been driving our calorie intake up, and we can say that without blaming it on a single macronutrient. If we think about it, how different is the food and how we consume it compared to the 1960s and 70s? We consume food on the go, made up of highly processed foods—food is eaten on public transport, while watching a movie, while out shopping, at work in between meetings, in the car park... let's face it, are there any spheres where food is no longer consumed? I mean, I see people walking around the gym chomping down a protein bar in between sets. Okay, maybe people aren't eating in public bathrooms, but I know women who take snacks with them to enjoy in the bath! We are eating literally everywhere (my mum used to grab something from the pastry section of Sainsbury's and eat it while going around the supermarket, only to pay for the wrapper at the checkout... mental, although she did pay for it so at least not criminal... sorry, Mum) and eating more variety of foods, some of which are about as natural as Katie Price. We have moved away from home cooking, family meals and meal times. It can't really be any shock that this has led to an increase in calorie consumption for the vast majority of us, and unsurprisingly, it has not come with an increase in fruit and vegetable consumption but rather fat, sugar, and salt.

Snacking is now common practice, caused by a prevalence in food availability. If I think of the options my parents had available to them growing up, they would have probably had the option of fruit or maybe a bourbon biscuit if their parents were in a good mood, whereas if you hit the snack aisle in my local supermarket, there are likely more options than there are brain cells in the average fitness influencer. A six-year longitudinal study published in the Clinical Nutrition Journal showed that frequent eating and or/between meal snacking is associated with significant weight gain and an increased risk of obesity.[51] Despite some people recommending mini meals/grazing as a way of reducing overeating, it appears that grazing can be a habit that leads to weight gain, especially in those with a tendency to overeat, particularly because these individuals tend to be more sensitive to food rewards.

Now, you don't even need to go grocery shopping; you can just order your groceries online and have them delivered to your door. Not that going around a grocery store was very physically demanding, but now people aren't even doing that. The Nielsen Global E-commerce and the New Retail Survey of 30,000 people in 60 countries found that, worldwide, Millennials and—shock horror—Generation Z are the most frequent users of online grocery shopping. It is unsurprising that this industry is only continuing to grow, but is it having a positive effect on our shopping habits?

Doing your grocery shopping online COULD, if used correctly, be a tool for improving your consumption of healthier foods. For example, I sometimes get my clients to prepare their online grocery shop a week in advance, and this removes some of the decision fatigue we discussed earlier. Also, since you aren't getting stuck in the checkout, you are avoiding those impulse decisions made around the till. By having better control over our food purchasing, we can then better control our home environment, which is so important when it comes to improving overall diet quality. That being said, research actually suggests that online grocery shopping might be making things worse. Realistically, if people are getting decision fatigue in an actual store, what do you think will happen when presented with potentially thousands of varieties online? Also, think how much the power of value comes into our thinking… 50% off on an ultra-jumbo size of Rice Krispies… yes please. You are no longer limited by what you can fit in your basket or what you can carry. The online platform will suggest things for you based on your other purchases, and deals will be pushed into your line of sight, tempting you into buying foods you may never have stumbled on in your usual shopping trips.

Imagine this scenario… you are doing your online grocery shop, it's Friday evening, you want to get your order in now so you can relax on the weekend and not have to worry about hitting the grocery store when it's busy on Saturday or Sunday, and actually, you need this weekend to just unwind. This is a good idea because your boss has got you pitching a big project on Monday, and between that and the kids going back to school, you are running yourself a little thin. You get your shopping list out and as you are searching for each item on your healthy shopping list, you begin to tire as you are searching for your normal no added sugar almond milk. As you tire, you start to crave something sweet to give you a bit of energy. As you find the almond milk you were looking for, the site says, "Because you purchased this, you may like… this sticky toffee pudding". Normally, you wouldn't, but you are tired and start to salivate at the thought of that sticky toffee pudding. You add it to your basket, telling yourself you will have earned it come Monday night when it's delivered. Doesn't sound like the end of the world, does it? Well, Monday comes along, the presentation goes well, and you celebrate with your sticky toffee reward. Happy days. Next Friday rolls around and you go back online to do your grocery shop again. As you shop, the online store shows you your previously purchased items, and there at the top of the list is that sticky toffee pudding again. You are reminded of how great that was and how you felt eating it and after. As you begin to salivate, you notice that it is currently on offer 'buy one get one half price'… You are sold. Next week, you end up consuming both (on separate occasions, you aren't an animal). A bit long-winded, I know, but you can see how in this little scenario, you have not only been led to alter your normal food purchases BUT are now forming a new unhealthy habit as a result. Think of the compounding damage—the more you purchase that pudding, the more it will probably suggest other hyperpalatable foods for you to try, and the more deals will be thrown at you to purchase more.

Yes, we have free will, and online grocery shopping won't suddenly make you overweight, but you can see how we can easily be influenced where an unhealthy 'once in a while' treat becomes a prompt for more frequent purchases. In addition, the ease of online grocery shopping could lead to over-purchasing and, subsequently, overconsumption.[52]

I also personally think unless you are using a delivery service like Hello Fresh or Oddbox, most people are likely using online grocery shopping for predominantly ultra-processed foods, as fruits and vegetables make up only a small part of these online grocery shops, and actually, most people would rather pick out their own vegetables (if they eat any) rather than relying on the shop to pick the best ones for them (I've done it in the past and ended up with some very green bananas and some very questionable strawberries). I also found this was supported by the evidence as two studies concluded, "Shoppers are hesitant to purchase perishable items via online grocery shopping and preferred to purchase fresh, perishable items in store".

Also, if we go back to the whole idea of social restriction or social judgement potentially altering our food choices, like the scenario of not going back up to buy a second bag of popcorn for fear of being judged, if we think of online shopping, it's discreet—you don't need to worry about someone looking in your basket and judging you. Seems ridiculous but that can have an impact on what you purchase (I mean, very useful if you want to buy things like condoms or lube, so you don't have to try and hide it in your basket with a few packets of crisps and some broccoli, only for the lady behind the checkout to judge you hard when she scans them). But if it means people are able to do their food shop without fear of judgement, I can imagine this won't be improving most people's food choices. Have you ever noticed if you go out as a group to a restaurant (I usually find this is a lot more common in women groups) that the larger of the members of the group will often be most insecure about food choices and order a salad out of fear for being judged? Just an observation, but it is clear they didn't get that way from eating just salad, so there is an element of secret eating involved. I'm not saying shopping in person is good because we can shame overweight people out of buying ice cream, but you can see there is definitely an element of online grocery shopping that can affect societal judgement behind food purchases.

Interestingly, due to Covid, we ended up with populations of people forced into online grocery shopping. While I don't want to put too much weight on blaming only this for an increase in obesity and weight in these population groups, it is worth noting because it definitely changed many people's eating habits and not for the better.[53] The irony is, most people blame a lot of their poor food choices on having to eat out and eat on the go during the busy week, or because of the dinners and drinks out on the weekends, or hosting clients. We were then forced into a situation where we now had full control of our diet (assuming the supermarket hadn't run out of what we wanted... although that was usually just toilet paper), and yet instead of people losing weight, the opposite was true for many. In fact, according to reports in the UK, more than 40% of adults in England gained weight during the pandemic, with the average gain being just over 3kg.

The Public Health England (PHE) surveyed 5,000 people, and it was clear that the Covid lockdown disrupted daily routines and made it more challenging for people to eat healthy and keep fit. Yes, increased stress leading to comfort eating, a reduction in general activity levels, and poor sleep all played their part in increasing our waistlines during this period. But you see, even when we had the chance to have even more control over our dietary food intake, this didn't result in better decision-making. We can't really blame eating out when we had months of being forced to eat in, and this didn't help—although, yes, thanks to apps like Deliveroo and Just Eat, many people still hadn't discovered the art of cooking just yet. I don't want to point to one factor for the Covid weight gain (apart from some of the women I knew, it was due to a dramatic increase in alcohol consumption... not naming anyone, don't worry). We can see that online grocery shopping can change our common eating habits, which may negatively impact our weight.

CHAPTER 15:
MARKETING MANIPULATION

One of the biggest changes we have seen, and I believe one of the biggest drivers of the obesogenic environment, actually is from the media and the food industry itself. Food is big business, and since the rise of the obesity epidemic and growing health concerns, companies have had to become smarter with their advertising and labelling. Before I go further into it, just think about how bombarded you are on a daily basis with adverts for different foods. Food companies, whether they are big/small/new/niche/artisan, are all vying for our attention. Commercials are on buses, taxis, the sides of buildings, on TV, during movies, and on social media. There are pop-up ads, targeted ads... I doubt it will be too long before they can start sending ads out in our minds as we sleep. Think about how many different cooking shows there are online. We are bombarded on a daily basis. Even on Instagram, you probably follow some food pages, influencers who are always posting delicious-looking food, or you are just hit with #foodporn. Our appetites are being whetted from every angle. It can't be that surprising that as we are bombarded with adverts for all manner of food and coupled with now the ability to get food absolutely everywhere, that actually, we are doing just that, and this is working to—shock horror—increase our calorie intake.

Did you know that, on average, each day we make 227 decisions about food! 95% of these decisions are non-conscious. Interestingly, obese people tend to make around 100 more food decisions than their overweight counterparts. As I said, we are unaware of most of these decisions, but just because we are unaware of them doesn't mean these can't be influenced. Our decisions can be affected by any number of things, whether it is through visual cues being impacted by social or educational manipulation, what about olfactory cues (smell), your levels of stress, or sleep? What about your internal values, ethics, or need for conformity? All of these elements can be played on to get you to purchase something, unbeknown to you.

I would say that probably not the most surprising element is the effect this has on the younger generations. If we think that today's children between the ages of 8 to 18 are ingesting multiple types of media a day, spending a shocking 44.5 hours per week in front of some form of screen (television, computer, games console), this is probably more than any other activity they are doing, probably even more than they are sleeping, then it should be no surprise that there is a strong association between increases in advertising for non-nutritious foods and rates of childhood obesity. Just a single commercial exposure can increase product preference, and this is only repeated with frequent exposure. Unfortunately, there aren't big marketing drives for eating fruit or vegetables, rather for allegedly healthy snacks, or cereals with funny cartoons plastered all over the front of them to make them more desirable and child-friendly. This affects children's product purchase requests, and these requests influence parents' purchasing decisions (shock horror). I am not blaming the parents... I remember complaining to my mum that I wanted to buy some Haribo, only to be told I could only purchase sweets with my own money (this led me to go into my dad's tennis racket bag, where I knew I would find some loose change lying around... yup, when deprived of the sweet treats I craved as a child, I turned to a life of petty crime). So, my parents were clever enough to say no; however, this didn't actually make it better, so I can't say depriving kids of these foods is any better (sorry, Dad, feels good to get that off my chest).

If we look at the tobacco industry as an example of the dangers of marketing, we can see that in the 1940s, tobacco companies hired doctors and dentists to endorse their cigarettes to help reduce public health concerns. Do you remember slogans like, "Just What the Doctor Ordered", and, "More Doctors Smoke Camels"? It's actually mental when you think about it. They also turned to celebrities and advertising to portray cigarettes as manly and independent or sexy and feminine—you try watching a film from the 1960s without craving a cigarette after, their product placement was highly effective. They even tried to make cigarettes more kid-friendly with characters like the cartoon camel that smoked. In 1964, the US

Surgeon General released the first report on the health effects of smoking. Having reviewed more than 7,000 articles in the medical literature, the Surgeon General concluded that smoking caused lung cancer and bronchitis. Okay, well then, surely all advertising would be stopped, right? Well, it wasn't until 1971 that a ban on advertising cigarettes on TV and radio came into effect; however, they were still able to advertise in magazines, newspapers, billboards, and transits. It wasn't until 1998 that new rules were brought in banning advertising on transit and billboard advertisements, paid brand product placement, cartoons, tobacco brand sponsorships of sporting events and concerts, as well as advertising and marketing practices that targeted individuals under 18. That's 34 years after we knew it caused cancer!

While I could expand more on this, I think that serves the purpose of showing how the sphere of marketing and advertising isn't exactly an ethically sound field. I'm not saying that the food advertised today is as bad as smoking is for your health, but you can still find adverts on TV for processed meats, which actually joins smoking as a type 1 carcinogen, so it's not far off. Also, if we think of the true impact that the obesity epidemic is having on our society, health care systems and overall health, especially given the rates of childhood obesity and type 2 diabetes, I don't think I would be so wrong if I did say it was just as criminal in a way (although less direct).

Going off of the research, there are a number of ways that marketing and advertising have impacted our food decisions. If we quickly look at just television consumption, it doesn't take a genius to figure that our increased consumption of television and screen time is linked to more sedentary lives, an increased consumption of unhealthy snacks (higher calorie snacks, I should say), and a reduction in satiety. Since we are distracted while eating, this slows awareness of satiety, leaving us with greater risk of overconsumption. These are all factors before we even mention all the adverts affecting your food choices. Some experimental studies have shown that TV advertising can have a direct effect on kids' snacks and food choices. In one study, two weeks of daily exposure to televised food and beverage messages at a summer camp altered five to eight-year-old children's afternoon snack choices. Children who viewed candy commercials picked significantly more candy over fruit as snacks. Eliminating the candy commercials proved as effective in encouraging the selection of fruit as did exposing the children to fruit commercials or nutritional public service announcements.[54]

In another study, children were tested on two occasions separated by two weeks. One condition involved the children viewing food advertisements followed by a cartoon, and in the other condition, the children viewed non-food adverts followed by the same cartoon. Following the cartoon, their food intake and choice were assessed. The results showed that exposure to food adverts produced substantial and significant increases in energy intake in all children. The increase in intake was largest in the obese children, but all children increased their consumption of high-fat and/or sweet energy-dense snacks in response to the advert.[55] So, yes, TV doesn't just appear bad for our waistline because we are sitting on our asses doing less than ever before, it is also directly impacting our food/snack choices.

It is worth noting that while we have already discussed bliss point and the food industry manipulating the taste profiles of foods to make them more addictive, this is also driven by marketing and advertising. For example, advances in market research can correct the fact that some people may not like a given amount of sweetness. When Coke first launched its "New Coke", it was a train wreck, and after just 77 days, the previous version of Coke was brought back as "Coca-Cola Classic". This doesn't just stop with taste—certain colours are associated with certain foods, therefore, marketers have long used colour to improve taste expectations. Colours with a strong flavour expectation can influence the perceived sweetness of food and will inevitably impact consumers' purchasing decisions.

Marketing manipulation doesn't just exist in adverts and on billboards, our shopping experiences are all designed to increase consumer purchases. Even just the layout of certain shops can manipulate you into purchasing more. One study I want to discuss is the one done by Anne Thorndike, a primary care physician at Massachusetts General Hospital in Boston. She had the idea that she could improve the eating habits of thousands of hospital staff and visitors without changing their willpower or motivation. Sounds a bit too good to be true, right? Thorndike designed a six-month study to alter the "choice architecture" of the hospital cafeteria. They started by changing how drinks were arranged in the room. Normally, the refrigerators located right next to the cash registers were filled with only soda, so they added water to these as an option. Additionally, they also placed baskets of bottled water next to the food stations throughout the room. What do you think happened?

Over the next three months, the number of soda sales dropped by 11.4%, meanwhile, bottled water sales increased by 25.8%. You see, people often choose products not because of what they are but because of where they are. Think how many times you've been standing in a queue waiting to check out and have been drawn to the bright packaging of one of those little shelves right next to the counter and ended up leaving with a chocolate bar you had no intention of buying or a fizzy drink you didn't really want (it even works on things other than food... I mean, I'm pretty sure I've left Primark with some bath salts and Christmas socks before because I was stuck in the queue long enough staring at discounted items calling out to me).

You see, self-control is a bit of an illusion. Recent research shows that when scientists analyse people who appear to have tremendous self-control, these individuals aren't all that different from those who are struggling. Instead, "disciplined" people are better at structuring their lives in a way that does not require heroic willpower or self-control. The easiest way to practise self-restraint is by creating an environment when you don't have to use it very often. For example, if I have a sweet tooth and always have sweets on my kitchen counter, I will have to practise self-restraint every time I walk past them. Eventually, I will walk past it tired or angry (whatever cue is needed) and I will indulge in those sweets. My self-restraint could only take so much. Now, imagine I don't keep sweets in my house, but instead, there is a beautiful fruit bowl on top of my kitchen counter. Now, my self-restraint is not activated every day when I walk through my kitchen, and when I'm tired, I'm more likely to reach for an apple or banana first.

Don't believe me? This was actually studied (well, sort of). Researchers photographed and catalogued 210 households in Syracuse, New York, and measured the occupants' height and weight. They found that the presence of fruit on the counter was associated with lower BMI in the household, but the presence of foods such as candy, cereal and soft drinks were associated with weight differences that ranged from 9.4-4.4kg more. So, by having unhealthy food choices in direct sight in the kitchen, families were more likely to be heavier (cereal 20lbs more, cookies 8lbs more, Coke 26lbs more).

The more obviously available a product is, the more likely you are to try it. People don't drink Starbucks because it's the best coffee, it's because they are everywhere (I mean, they obviously have good marketing too). We like to think we are in control of our decisions. If we chose water, it's because we wanted water, right? And not because that was the obvious choice presented to us because of our environment. The truth is, many of the actions we take each day are shaped not by purposeful drive and choice but by the most obvious option.

This is only touching on product placement, there are so many other ways in which shops will manipulate you. We have already spoken about the power of "added value", and who can say they aren't drawn to a good deal? But there is another manipulation I discovered on my own by chance the other week. I have already mentioned I live next to a giant Asda, well since I go into it probably four or five times a week, I know the layout like the back of my hand. I am a man of routine and will fly around the store purchasing exactly what I need within minutes. The other day, I walked in to find that they had decided to rearrange the entire store. As I was picking my chicken up from the butchery section (luckily, this hadn't been moved), I asked the lady who always saves me the best bits of chicken why the fuck they had moved everything, seemed like a lot of work for their staff and it didn't seem like it had improved the feel of the store at all.

The reason, she said, was simple—it was to make sure customers like me wander around the shop more looking for their items. Not knowing where things are will make you discover items you weren't looking for in the first place and, therefore, lead you to make additional purchases that were not on your grocery lists to begin with. Well, it worked. I left with a new flavour of rice cakes I had definitely not planned to purchase and will subsequently be buying again since they were fantastic. Such an easy little change, but so effective. Even the size of the aisles can play a role. What about where items are positioned? According to some research, shoppers looked at the brands positioned in the centre of the shelf nine times more than those placed in the corners.[56]

These aren't even the best ways... what about smells, scents, temperature, lighting and even using different sounds to make you purchase more? Sounds far-fetched but this is actually a thing!

For example, temperature may have a direct physiological effect on consumers. Studies have shown that people consume more energy when the ambient temperature is outside the thermal neutral zone (defined as the range of ambient temperatures where the body can maintain its core temperature solely through regulating dry heat loss). For example, consumption increases more during prolonged cold temperatures than in hot temperatures because of the body's need to regulate its core temperature. Supermarkets are naturally cold to help keep the produce fresh, but this air conditioning might be further impacting your purchasing choices.

What about lighting? Well, it appears that harsh lighting makes people eat faster and reduces the time they stay in a restaurant, that's why you will normally find most restaurants have dimmed lighting, so customers are likely to relax more and are more likely to stay and order both a starter and a dessert.

The presence of background music can even change your eating habits and choices. In one study of 78 college students, it appeared that the presence of music is associated with higher food intake.[57] In the context of restaurants, research seems to suggest that gentle soft music usually created an environment in which diners spent longer, and therefore, ordered more food and spent more money.[58] The same is true for retail shopping, where slower tempo music increases shopping duration. Really makes you think, how much are we being manipulated? I haven't even mentioned that there is research suggesting that seafood rated better tasting when accompanied by sounds of the ocean playing in the background, or ice cream tastes better when the sounds of a park can be heard... (not sure which park the researchers were in because some of the ones in London are usually accompanied with the whine of ambulance or police sirens and people protesting whatever is currently filling the woke agenda's itch for that month). This means next time you are serving fish at a dinner party, just stick on some background noises of whales or something marine-like and hopefully your guests won't notice your average to poor cooking skills (can't say this book hasn't provided you with some useful tips, eh!?).

In terms of smell, shops will often use the aroma of things like chocolate to increase sales. Net Cost supermarket in Brooklyn, N.Y., installed machines on the walls to infuse the store with aromas of foods that would attract customers. The smell of grapefruit in the produce section, and chocolate in the candy aisle. They reported sales went up at least 7% since they were installed. And a convenience store that started pumping the smell of fresh-brewed coffee at a gas station increased coffee sales by 300%. Turns out smell is a very powerful driver... have you ever gone past a supermarket and all you can smell is fresh baked bread? This isn't by accident, even companies like Cinnabon intentionally place their ovens toward the front of the stores so that the delicious scent of cinnamon can call out to potential customers like the sirens calling out to the sailors of old.

It seems like there is no limit to what isn't being influenced by this obesogenic environment, although, by realising this, hopefully we can start to understand the obesity puzzle in better light and begin to formulate better ways of navigating through it.

PART 4:
MISTAKES WE HAVE MADE

I think one element that might not often be spoken about when we talk about the growing obesity epidemic actually comes in the form of nutritionists, doctors, governments and then social media promoting the wrong solutions when looking to tackle the growing obesity problem. I am talking about the changing narratives that began coming out back when obesity first started to be noticed as not only a growing concern but a genuine threat to human health.

Unfortunately, the food industry, as well as the diet and supplement industries, are big businesses, so changes in narrative can have huge economic impacts. Just like the tobacco industry spending millions on lobbying and marketing to pretend their product wasn't resulting in an increase in cancer, we have to assume that while I want to talk about how the policies that came into place to tackle obesity had obvious health consequences, it definitely had financial ramifications as well. Money talks, so if the sugar industry or dairy industry wanted to keep its profits up, you can imagine pockets were being lined to change the narrative to demonise something other than their product. Also, let's be honest, large sections of the food industry just bought early into what was going to be the next big industry—the diet industry—so they were going to profit off of the problem either way. Some of it is genius if I think about it, they were creating the ultimate oxymoron of diet foods, creating one of the most profitable cycles. People pay good money to buy the fat-free version of something like a yoghurt sold as diet-friendly without realising it was pumped full of more sugar than the original version and just as many calories, so they don't lose any weight and the problem only gets worse.

Now, I'm not going to go down some conspiracy theory rabbit hole. My point is that money talks and it is always worth remembering this when we try and understand the logic behind some of the original policies and I guess mistakes that we have made. Yes, some of it is also probably just from floored logic, poor research and a lack of understanding of metabology. But the problem is, and I will discuss in length that these decisions, narratives and misinformation have helped shape our internal biases and knowledge surrounding nutrition, only working to increase the obesity problem still to this day. How many people do you know that still demonise fat or sugar? See, what started off in policy decades ago, with poor understanding of metabology, is still rife in our beliefs and internal biases.

If you had been paying attention to the news and the governmental guidelines since the 1980s, you'd inevitably be a little confused. Guidelines have gone back and forth on whether sugar or fat is the problem. If it is fat, which fat and how much should we remove? Is cholesterol the problem? It is no wonder most people have either never heard of the government's Eatwell plate or at least completely ignored it because they no longer trusted the changing evidence. Also, diets seem to take on a religious-like view, so for some people, once they have made up their mind on what is best, they will stick to their opinion even in the face of evidence to the contrary.

In the 1970-80s, we had the war on fat. One of the names synonymous with this is that of Ancel Keys who helped contribute to the widespread belief that fat was the major contributor to heart disease and obesity. In the famous seven countries study, he displayed a clear association between eating greater amounts of saturated fats and deaths due to heart disease. And thus, the demonising began as it was founded in scientific evidence.

The 1980 dietary guidelines were, as a result: "Avoid too much fat, saturated fat, and cholesterol; eat foods with adequate starch and fibre; avoid too much sugar; avoid too much sodium". I mean, not that hard to understand why this didn't work to help the obesity problem.

We know in hindsight now that Keys had cherry-picked these countries because they supported his hypothesis and, in fact, left out 15 countries that did not reveal any association between saturated fat consumption and heart mortality. Ignoring countries like Denmark and Sweden, which had very few deaths despite their diets high in saturated fat, or Chile, which had high cardiac mortality rates but ate little saturated fats. The problem is, as I said, once we see the headlines, "Saturated fats cause heart attacks", an internal bias has already been formed and the damage has been done.

When foods are incorrectly demonised, it is inevitable that this will have a knock-on effect on the consumer. If you read the headline preaching that saturated fat caused heart attacks, it is possible you will internalise some of this bias and follow suit. You see, our brains don't let go of negative stories easily. They tend to hang out at the forefront of our consciousness, where our mind can easily access them. This causes old information to colour our views and assessments of new situations. So, even if I temporarily believed saturated fat was the problem, it is likely that my brain will store this. Then, in future situations when addressed with the issue of saturated fat, my brain will go in search of previous examples and latch on to those easiest to recall in order to assess the validity of the issue. The bigger the impact the story had on us, or the more compelling it is, the easier it will be to recall, even if it is based on misinformation.

In an age where clickbait articles are the norm and, therefore, misinformation is rife, it has skewed many people's perceptions of nutrition. The articles that flooded the media from Ancel Keys' study permeated the media and government policy and found its way into many people's minds and eventual biases. Even though, around the same time, work by John Yudkin and others implicated excess sugar in coronary disease and cancer. Ultimately, the emphasis on fat won and governmental policy and people's biases recorded this.

Unsurprisingly, prospective cohorts and dietary intervention trials showed that a focus on total fat produced little measurable health benefit, and actually, the results of people eating things like eggs and red meats usually showed it conferred health benefits. For weight loss and glycaemic control, it appeared that the focus on low fat diets was not the answer as studies came out showing that foods rich in healthy fats produced benefits, while foods rich in sugar caused harm. You see, we were yo-yo-ing back and forth from sugar to fat as the problem, while more and more misinformation and religious-like dieting cults developed. We created the sphere for fad diets to be born, and with fad diets came yo-yo dieting culture.

I always think of it like sharks vs. mosquitoes. If you think about which one kills more every year, the numbers aren't even close—mosquitoes wipe the floor with the sharks, but you don't read of every mosquito-related death, and that's no real surprise, it would get boring given the numbers, and let's be honest, it's not quite as dramatic as being killed by a shark (imagine if Jaws was based on mosquitoes instead... not exactly a plot for a Hollywood blockbuster now). When some tourist goes swimming in the wrong area and ends up being shark chow... well, this is more often than not front page, worldwide news.

We end up fearing the wrong things. You probably fear being eaten by a shark a lot more than being bitten by a mosquito. In our diet, we end up beginning to fear what the media wants to focus on (or the douchebag influencers)... we fear chemicals, preservatives, seed oils, dairy, artificial sweeteners, while forgetting the simple things like eating more fruit and vegetables, increasing lean protein sources, oh, and being in a calorie deficit if we need to lose weight... IT'S not the SEED OILS or DAIRY that's causing your obesity, even if you want to throw words like inflammation in the mix. Unsurprisingly, it's the continued overconsumption of calories... we can't escape this.

These next few chapters are all on how our mistakes trying to tackle the problem have only worked to further the obesity problem. Well, that coupled with the diet industry and social media trying to get you to part with more of your money in the process.

CHAPTER 16: FAD DIETS

I love this quote from the book *Why Smart People Make Bad Food Choices* by Jack A. Bobo. He writes: *"It seems that the more weight we gain, the more diets there are to choose from"*.

In fact, in 2022, according to the International Food Information Council (IFIC), 52% of Food and Health Survey participants reported following a specific diet or eating pattern, a sharp uptick from 39% in 2021. A quick Google of dietary practices and up pops lists of literally thousands of dietary methods. I can't say I'm surprised... I think part of the allure of fad diets is that they take responsibility off of us in a way that implies that obesity is caused by a dietary mistake rather than just an overconsumption of calories. If sugar or high fructose corn syrup is to blame for obesity, then it's not our fault. It is the devilish macronutrient's fault and the big food companies that get us addicted to their products (completely ignoring calorie consumption and the fact that we have studies disproving this). I'm not saying you or we are completely to blame for this obesity epidemic, as you have already probably learnt that there are many reasons for our overconsumption, but it still boils down to it being an overconsumption problem.

It seems the failure of doctors and governmental guide-lines to provide an appropriate working solution for the obesity epidemic led to the creation of different dietary guidelines by self-help gurus, social media influencers, and weight loss experts alike. Dieting was big business, and this was the Wild Wild West. If you could develop a diet, package it up to provide people with simple and fast results, you were not only creating a cash cow but, in essence, creating almost a religious entity in the process.

I found this definition on PubMed: "A fad diet is a broad term used to describe dieting methods that rec-ommend altering the intake of macronutrients to specific proportions or instruct people to intake or avoid par-ticular foods, often with the goal of rapid weight loss".[59] The diets that came out around this time reflected vary-ing levels of scientific rigour and forethought. From the Atkins, Ketogenic, Palaeolithic, Mediterranean diet to the Vegan, Carnivore and Intermittent Fasting diets, you name it, someone came up with it. If some of these aren't bad enough, this is literally the tip of a very strange diet-ing iceberg. Most of us are probably trying to forget some of the more embarrassing ones that we may have tried in the past. Like the cabbage soup diet, the blood type diet, the alkaline diet, the grapefruit juice diet... I even found someone writing about the tapeworm diet (yep, people got desperate and... well, desperation doesn't lend itself to smart decision-making).

The problem with these fad diets is that while many provided you with quick weight loss as promised, it was unsustainable and, therefore, resulted in failure in the long term. It did, however, provide people with nice before and after photos and temporary results to which they could then swear that the diet was a success and sell it to someone else before reverting back to their old eating practices and putting all the weight back on. We have already gone over why the only diet that will work will be the one that you can stick to for the long run. But let's just hammer that point in again, if you go back to eating what you ate before your weight loss, you will not only return to your prior weight but it is likely you will return even heavier than before #crashdietlife.

With this new era of fad diets taking hold, so too was born the yo-yo dieting culture, and along with it, dissemination of confusion and misinformation into our world. I personally think this is one of the biggest reasons behind the continuing obesity epidemic. Obviously, it is not the cause as we had already developed obesity at this point, but what I mean is that, since people aren't sure who to trust and what diet to follow, they are caught in a cycle of weight loss and weight gain, only exacerbating the problem, so the number of people remaining a healthy weight is slowly becoming the exception to the rule and not the norm.

Dieting became a huge business with supplements coming out promising to burn fat, the food industry inevitably got involved pumping out fat-free foods, or reduced sugar versions of common foods to appeal to the more health-conscious. Diets gained followers and funded research to help back up their theories, but the world became more confused in the process.

Let's take the Atkins diet, for example. Created in the 1970s by cardiologist Dr. Robert Atkins, this was a low-carbohydrate, high-protein regimen. Atkins believed that metabolic imbalance resulting from carbohydrate consumption is the major cause of obesity. His solution involved an extreme reduction of carbohydrates, i.e., less than 5% of total calorie intake, ad libitum intake of proteins and fats, adequate fluid intake with vitamin and mineral supplementation, and regular exercise. Doesn't sound too ridiculous, but again, will this work for everyone? Absolutely not. There are many studies to confirm that low-carbohydrate diets are unlikely to produce significant long-term weight loss and may lead to health complications as a result. I am not shitting on low-carb diets, but we have to think long-term—as I said, if you can't see yourself on that diet in six months or six years from now, then the results it produces will be short-lived.

And the Atkins diet is one of the more reasonable ones… what about one of the ridiculous ones like the blood type diet? Created by Peter D'Adamo, a naturopathic physician, is a diet based on the theory that your blood type determines the foods you should consume (and the exercise you should do) to achieve optimal health. D'Adamo claimed that the foods you eat react chemically with your blood type. If you follow a diet designed for your blood type, your body will digest food more efficiently. You'll lose weight, have more energy, and help prevent disease. Sounds great except for one thing… oh, that's right, there is no scientific evidence that this diet works. You might as well read your horoscope at the same time and then use that to help you pick the winning lottery numbers while you are at it.

It really became a free-for-all. What I do think this should highlight is that nutrition should be personal. The word diet actually means "the kinds of food that a person, animal, or community habitually eats". You see, we are all on a diet, it is not just something to follow in times of weight loss. We can improve anyone's dietary practices, but the idea of cutting out whole food groups to achieve weight loss just will not work for most people as it is too restrictive and can result in nutritional deficiencies. Most of these fad diets seem to look to create a deficit by removing whole food groups without taking into account any of your personal preferences, habits or lifestyle. If all diets work by creating an energy deficit (and they do, despite you saying the word *autophagy* over and over again), why we tackled a simple problem with differing levels of complexity and misinformation will forever be embedded in the problem we now face.

Yes, eating a Paleo diet to be like an early man who never suffered obesity sounds great, should we also get rid of all our possessions in the process, stop using technology and walk barefoot everywhere because that's what he did? Taking what worked hundreds and hundreds of years ago in a completely different environment, differing food availability and differing lifestyles and assuming that makes it healthy is a bit nonsensical. Yes, we can learn from studying these populations and maybe extract beneficial qualities from it, like walking more or eating meat and berries, and avoiding ultra-processed food. But to then go, "Well, they didn't eat yoghurt or oats so those are unhealthy", immediately makes the diet restrictive, at risk of increasing nutritional deficiencies and, therefore, defeats the point. Remember, diet should be personalised to the individual. Just because the inhabitants of Okinawa, Japan—a well-known Blue Zone—have a longer life expectancy (Blue Zones are regions of the world where people regularly live longer than average) doesn't mean that if I adopted their diet, I would live longer. We have different genetics (shock), we handle stress differently, we have different lifestyles. Trying to break down obesity into one macronutrient, one dietary practice or food into good or bad completely ignores what health actually is and that is the accumulation of all your habits, from diet to exercise to sleep, stress and more.

The internet and the ability for everyone's voices to be heard led to rapid exposure and increases in fad diets. These fad diets not only didn't solve the problem (shock horror), but they introduced a new problem, and this came in the form of demonising specific foods and food groups. Have you ever heard of a food referred to as good or bad? I'm guessing you probably have, but why is this? Food hasn't got an agenda—no food is inherently bad for you. Fat is not bad for you, carbohydrates are not bad for you nor is protein, even a small dose of alcohol has some reported health benefits (although, not really, but if it makes you feel better about that glass of wine, then let's just go with it). So, why are some foods labelled as good or bad? The fact that foods are classified in this manner reveals a fundamental problem of fad diets. We focus on the individual health benefits of a food, and we forget to consider the context, yet it is the context that determines how that food may contribute to an individual's health.

If I were to eat half a bag of Haribo sweets (Tangfastics obviously... or maybe the giant strawberries) once a week while otherwise consuming a diet predominantly of whole foods, fruits, vegetables, and lean protein sources, do you think that my consumption of some Haribo would undo all the health benefits from my otherwise 'good' diet? On the contrary, do you think if I ate a diet predominantly of fast food and highly processed foods that one serving of that 'good' broccoli I ate, even if it was every day, would offset all the negative effects of my otherwise 'bad' diet?

Individual eating episodes are pretty insignificant in the context of your overall health. We are the sum of habits. Enjoying pudding once every month when you're out for dinner isn't going to negatively impact your life or your waistline (as long as it doesn't become a habit and you start doing it every night). If anything, it's good for your mental health and is associated with greater adherence to a diet.

Let's go back to the scenario where I eat a diet of whole foods, vegetables, fruit, and lean protein sources all week, but I like to enjoy half a bag of Haribo Tangfastics on a Sunday. I want to lose weight, but instead of just reducing total calories from all foods, I decide I'm no longer going to have my Haribo because it's 'bad' for me. After two weeks, I see a little drop in weight, but I start to feel very restricted in my diet. Eventually, my so-called willpower gives out and I end up eating a whole bag of Haribo. But that's not where it stops… the guilt that accompanies this leads me to overeat on Haribo and I end up feeling depressed and ashamed afterward.

You see what happened there… if I told you not to think of a giant pink unicorn, what did you just do? That's right, you thought of a giant pink unicorn. The more I focused on not having Haribo, the more I thought of my Haribo. When restriction goes up against my willpower, there will always be one outcome. If I had instead continued to enjoy my Haribo while reducing overall calories in order to lose weight, I would not have felt so restricted by my diet, therefore, avoiding the eventual binge. Ultra-restriction has been proven to lead to increased episodes of binge eating. Food psychologists have referred to this as an unanticipated consequence of self-imposed food restrictions. If we look back at the Minnesota Starvation Experiment and the effect (albeit extreme) restriction has on individuals, they found that participants became more and more preoccupied with food.

Allowing yourself that piece of chocolate or Haribo, or whatever your guilty pleasure is, does not undo the health benefits of the nutritious foods you eat, nor does it ruin your goals. If your goal is weight loss, if you are still in a deficit at the end of the day, then there is no reason to stress or feel guilty. You need to look at your diet as a whole and not just individual moments.

You see, the aftermath of the creation of this dieting culture is one that many people will sadly never escape from, even unknowingly, since the effects are still playing a massive role in the psychology of weight loss. While the mantra to just eat less and move more, works to an extent, it ignores areas that many people are unaware of, and this comes in the form of confirmation bias, health halos and social influence, which we will touch on and then we can see how these have found a way back into marketing manipulation.

CHAPTER 17:
IT'S ALL IN YOUR HEAD

O ur brains are an amazing culmination of hundreds and thousands of years of evolution. The growth of our brains directly led us to climbing to the top of the food chain. Yet deep down at our core, some of our thought processes don't seem to be as evolved as we first thought. Our stress response is still triggered to respond like we are being chased by a tiger, yet most of the time, it is being set off by a barrage of stupid work emails, not enough people liking our recent Instagram post, or missing the bus on your morning commute to work. Having just finished reading the book, "Sapiens" (definitely worth reading), I think it's safe to say we have culturally and socially evolved quicker than we could biologically.

Why do I say this? Well, it seems that there are a few psychological reasons that might be standing in the way of you and your weight loss.

Let's start with the basis for most of these psychological traps, which are termed heuristics. In psychology, they refer to a mental shortcut that helps us make decisions and judgments quickly without having to spend a lot of time researching and analysing information. Heuristics are essentially rules of thumb to help us solve complex problems quickly, however, they can leave us susceptible to influence we aren't aware of and into making consistently incorrect decisions based on our goals. Remember, our senses are bombarded in today's environment. If we read everything carefully and fully deliberated on every decision we ever made, we would get fuck all done.

We have already touched on one of these heuristics (decision fatigue) when talking about how our brains cope when shopping in our giant supermarkets and how this can negatively impact our decision-making abilities. I also touched on another called availability bias when talking about the demonising of fat, once Ancel Keys reports on the dangers of fat had come out, many people internalised this bias against fat without even realising it. Essentially, consumers assess the probability of an event with the ease by which occurrences can be brought to mind. Because the demonising of fat was well publicised, it was easy to access this memory in people's minds and, therefore, strengthening the internal bias.

The other two that I think are super important when we look at our diets are confirmation bias and the health halo effect. Let's start with confirmation bias:

Confirmation bias is the tendency for us to favour information that confirms our beliefs or ideas and discount that which does not. So, when we are confronted with new information, we tend to do one of two things. If this information confirms what we already believe, then great, our natural instinct is to accept it as true and accurate. We accept it and are happy to have seen it. Even if it has some problems, we ignore those and incorporate this new information into our beliefs quickly. We are, therefore, also more likely able to recall this information later to help reinforce our views during an argument. On the other hand, if someone provides us with information that contradicts what we already believe, we have a completely different response. We become highly critical of the evidence and defensive immediately, nit-picking any possible flaw in the information, even though the same flaw would be ignored if the information confirmed our beliefs. Because we don't accept the information presented, it also fades quickly from our mind so that, in the future, we cannot even recall being exposed to it (probably why carnivore diet preachers never seem to remember the thousands of studies done showing the benefits of fibre on health).[60]

Confirmation bias plays an important role in our diets, whether we like and trust a certain brand, our perceptions of whether something is healthy or not, really all our food choices are affected by some form of confirmation bias. Confirmation bias is what allowed fad diets to survive for so long without slowing down. Let's take the keto diet for example—you have a friend who lost a lot of weight following the keto diet, you are then approached by a trainer who calls himself 'Keto Ken'. He gives you a big spiel about how carbohydrates are what causes weight gain because they spike insulin, which is the fat-storage hormone... he says it with enough conviction, and it sounds like it makes sense.

You are thinking about it. He then shows you a few testimonials from his clients, telling you how they, like you, had struggled with weight loss until following his plan, and with some sexy before and after pictures, just like that, you are sold (without realising you have just agreed to give up all carbohydrates). You start the diet, and with every pound you lose, you credit the diet. "This is amazing, why did I not try this sooner?" you think to yourself (without realising most of this initial weight loss is water weight). Three weeks go by, and you are beginning to crave those good carbohydrates you have always enjoyed. You also want to go out drinking with your friends, but your coach has told you this will take you out of ketosis. That weekend, you slip up and enjoy a few glasses of wine and a croissant the next morning as part of your hangover cure. You feel guilty but it was inevitable. You go to step on the scales the next day and, unsurprisingly, you have gained back 1kg. "Well, that was my fault, I cheated on my diet", you tell yourself. You end up blaming your lack of willpower and not the ridiculous rigid nature of this unsustainable diet. You see we make excuses for things we believe in and only question the successes of those we don't like (sound familiar?). If you ever speak to someone who actually demonises carbohydrates, we have hundreds of human studies showing that diets rich in carbohydrates and sugar can still work for weight loss. If you try to present them with this, watch them squirm and then go off on some mental gymnastics segway into how sugar causes cancer or something equally moronic.

Now, this works for every fad diet or eating habit... I don't want to just shit on keto people although it's an easy target. The same can be said for vegans or carnivores. There is evidence for and against both diets, and while a rational person might be able to see that combining the best practices from both diets would result in the best results, unfortunately, this would mean at some point you would have to admit you were wrong and, well, we don't like doing that as a species.

We are more likely to go in search of information or follow people on social media that already support our views. For example, someone who doesn't really like fruit or vegetables is more likely to follow some health guru who proposes that the carnivore diet is the best for our health. When they watch a video of said health guru demonising something like spinach because it contains oxalates that apparently cause kidney stones or take minerals from your body, they don't bother to fact-check the information and, instead, take it for truth because fuck it, they hate spinach and now they have the evidence they need. If they were to fact-check, they would type into Google a phrase like, "Spinach causes kidney stones", and be supplied with a list of equally questionable results supporting their theory. You see, you can pretty much find anything these days to support your opinion (and, apparently, opinion is worth more than fact these days). Not that surprising I guess that they don't use a more neutral phrase when looking for information like, "Does spinach intake cause kidney stones?" Or, "Are there health risks to eating spinach?" as this will inevitably turn up research that argues against the opinion they already hold... and we wouldn't want that. On the other hand, if I wanted everyone to eat spinach, I would be googling, "Why spinach is a superfood?" Or, "The health benefits of spinach". You see, we look for information to back up our beliefs.

I might as well clear this point up... yes, spinach does contain an antinutrient called oxalate (oxalic acid). Your body can produce oxalate on its own or obtain it from food. Once consumed, oxalate can bind to minerals to form compounds, including calcium oxalate and iron oxalate. So, yes, it can reduce the amount of iron or calcium that we get from eating spinach, however, this doesn't mean it removes all the health benefits of eating spinach or that you have a net loss of these minerals. The formation of these compounds mostly occurs in the colon but can also take place in the kidneys and other parts of the urinary tract. So, there can be a risk of kidney stones. However, for most of us, these compounds are normally eliminated in the urine or our stool with no problem. Urologists now prescribe a strict low oxalate diet (less than 100 milligrams per day) only for patients who have high levels of oxalate in their urine. For the most part, oxalate restriction is no longer recommended for every person with kidney stones. This is because half of the oxalate found in urine is produced by the body rather than absorbed from food. Most foods high in oxalates contain many antioxidants and fibre, so it is not something worth demonising... but the truth rarely gets you likes on Instagram or sells carnivore cookbooks.

One bias that definitely plays into our diets can be illustrated simply by the word "natural". What immediately comes to mind when you hear this world? Probably ideas like healthy or chemical free popped into your brain, right? If you immediately associate positives with this word, doesn't it make sense that you will be more likely drawn to a product if it has a label on the front saying "natural".

According to research, the food industry in 2014 sold almost $41 billion worth of food each year labelled with the word 'natural'. Another survey released by Consumer Reports in 2016 shows that the majority of consumers (73%) seek out foods labelled as 'natural' when they make food-purchasing decisions. Seems like natural is quite a pull factor (maybe this is why women lie about having work done or men lie about taking steroids… just a thought). Isn't it amazing that such a simple word can have such a powerful influence on our purchasing decisions. The IFIC found that 70% of consumers who were surveyed perceived the products labelled 'natural' were highly likely to be healthier, even when compared to identical products without the label.

But what does natural actually mean when it is on a food? Well, if you go directly to the US Food and Drug Administration (FDA) website, it turns out it is not really defined, this is exactly what the website says: *"Although the FDA has not engaged in rulemaking to establish a formal definition for the term "natural", we do have a longstanding policy concerning the use of "natural" in human food labelling. The FDA has considered the term "natural" to mean that nothing artificial or synthetic (including all colour additives regardless of source) has been included in, or has been added to, a food that would not normally be expected to be in that food. However, this policy was not intended to address food production methods, such as the use of pesticides, nor did it explicitly address food processing or manufacturing methods, such as thermal technologies, pasteurisation, or irradiation. The FDA also did not consider whether the term "natural" should describe any nutritional or other health benefit".*

So, there are no strict criteria for labelling your product 'natural' really. Okay, it might not have artificial ingredients, but it could contain pesticides from the food processing method as this is not included in the policy. When it comes to the UK or EU, it also appears that there is no legal definition of the term 'natural' in law, therefore, regulations covering its use in relation to food are open to legal dispute. The Food Standards Agency (FSA) issued this guidance in 2008: *"Natural" means essentially that the product is comprised of natural ingredients, e.g., ingredients produced by nature, not the work of man or interfered with by man. It is misleading to use the term to describe foods or ingredients that employ chemicals to change their composition or comprise the products of new technologies, including additives and flavourings that are the product of the chemical industry or extracted by chemical processes".* You see, we sort of understand what "natural" means, but it's not straightforward and companies can try and get around this by implying natural without saying it. Think of all the adverts you see in beautiful natural settings, and they talk about nature or how mother nature made it better… yes, they risk a potential lawsuit, but there must be so many adverts that tread the line and get through without any problem.

So, "natural" is a big driver of bias because of the positive connotations we attach to this word, but with this bias, we seem to completely forget that we still work within the realms of energy balance. People assume natural means lower calories… but we shouldn't make this assumption. I mean, Brazil nuts are natural (about the only thing in Brazil that is), but in just three nuts, there are an impressive 99 calories. As I've said before, you can still get fat shopping at Whole Foods or Planet Organic and eating only "natural" foods. We have also spoken about how people can reward their good decisions with potentially bad ones, so maybe you grabbed a "healthy natural" lunch only to chow down on some cheesecake and wine for dinner because you were "healthier" earlier in the day. The truth is, the natural label doesn't tell us whether the food is good or bad. Just because something isn't natural doesn't mean it's bad (the same goes for tits, I think).

This natural bias actually plays into a bigger bias that is coined the health halo effect. When we consider a particular food to be healthy in some respect, we quite often disregard any negatives that might be attached to it or ignore the fact that one "healthy" item doesn't suddenly make our diet "healthy". It would make sense to assume that as obesity rates go up, people clearly just care less about their health. The opposite is true though—more people are on diets than ever before, the weight loss and diet industry are growing every year, people google and go in search of the latest so-called healthy foods more now than ever before. This has created a food landscape of health claims, health labelling, and as a result, health halos and even more confusion.

Let's take something like veganism and fake meats as an example. After the Netflix documentary, "The Game Changers", came out, how many people do you know decided that they would give up animal products because of the alleged health benefits of going vegan and the apparent risks associated with an animal-based diet? This documentary was an example of someone cherry-picking studies, using straw man arguments, logical fallacies and false dichotomies to help argue their point. They also used celebrity and athlete endorsement while misrepresenting the data... oh, and also completely ignoring the conflict of interest given that all the experts they called are those that make money off vegan books or products, including the producer, James Cameron, who owns a pea protein company... shock. I won't go into everything wrong with the documentary as that is outside the scope of this book, and I also want to say I'm not against vegan diets (although I do advise caution as you can become deficient in a number of essential vitamins and minerals if you are not well educated in the nutrition sphere). I only bring this up because this documentary helped create a health halo effect around plant-based foods. I'm also not saying this was purely down to the documentary, however, it definitely helped create more buzz around plant-based diets.

The global vegan food market is projected to grow from \$26.16 billion in 2021 to \$61.35 billion in 2028. Sales for meatless burgers and sausages soared 18% in 2019, and 45% in 2020. In 2019, Beyond Meat had the most successful stock market debut of any company since the 2008 financial crisis. It seems that the meat-free section was the new gold rush, but why? Is a meatless burger actually healthier for you or is it just playing off of the health halo created by the media buzz around vegan diets? Honestly, if you actually read the packet of some of these fake meat products, it is a hard argument to make that it is actually healthier for you. While I am, again, not going down the rabbit hole of which is better for you, the label "meat-free" suddenly became a selling point much like the "natural" label. You see, the health halo is a type of error in perception that distorts how we see products. People would see "meat-free" or "vegan" labels and attach positive impressions to the product, assuming that it is healthier, without hesitation. It's a bit like if I show you a picture of a well-dressed man in a suit, clean haircut, and no facial hair, you might assume that he's smart or successful, maybe works in an office. This is the assumption we make. If you saw me, on the other hand, as a bearded, bald-headed man with a facial tattoo, you are likely to think drug dealer, criminal, hostile… and you would be wrong (on at least two of these assumptions). You would have to talk to me or the suited man to actually know who we are and see if your assumptions are correct—a bit like having to actually look at the nutritional info, ingredients and cooking process of the burger or meat-free burger to understand better if it is a good introduction to your diet or not. But this requires more work. You see, our brain wants things to be nice and simple, so it likes to classify things as good and bad, beneficial or harmful. Someone who watched the Game Changers and believed it was then able to create this clear distinction in their mind: Meat = Bad and Vegan = Good. Unless we push to find out more, our mental autopilot will overlook the complexities of the decisions and instead favour a simple assumption/bias.

I think the vegan angle is interesting because the statistics show that the majority of actual long-term vegans are vegan for ethical reasons (animal welfare), whereas health is only the second reason for choosing a vegan diet. Why is this interesting? Well, in an interview, Beyond Meat CEO and founder, Ethan Brown, said that "meat reducers" are Beyond Meat's target market, rather than vegans. The brand's own research shows that 70% of the Beyond Burger's buyers are meat-eaters. And according to recent research by The NPD Group, 86% of consumers who purchase vegan products are omnivores.[61] The fact that the vast majority of people purchasing Beyond Burgers aren't vegan, I think, shows the impact that a health halo can have on our purchasing decisions, given they are quite often more expensive than their actual meat counterparts.

I think along with "natural", we can put the phrase "organic" up there as this also seems to carry weight with consumers, although it usually prices most of us out of being able to afford the product. You see, these health halos are everywhere—take, for example, protein. Everyone, myself included, started preaching about the benefits of a high-protein diet. Well, companies are not stupid, they latched onto this, and we started seeing the appearance of "added protein" or "high protein" labels being attached to all products. Even Mars and Weetabix got in on the trend. The thing is, just because a product is higher in protein doesn't make it healthier. Also, most of the time, what the company really means is that they have added the smallest amount of protein to the product and added the label to get you to pay more for pretty much the same product. If we quickly look at Weetabix vs. Weetabix protein, while per serving, yes, Weetabix protein does, in fact, contain more protein, this amounts to just 3 grams more. That's not even half an egg more of protein! So, if we look at the label, we can see it's just a marketing ploy. I guarantee it works as protein has formed its own health halo. People will see the label and immediately assume health or attach positive associations with the product.

I don't blame companies for it either. As I said, I am constantly preaching for people to increase their protein intake, so while someone with nutritional knowledge will realise when we say to eat a high protein breakfast we are referring to something like an omelette, scrambled eggs or maybe a protein shake with porridge, for Cheryl, a 30-year-old office manager who hates cooking, she sees the high protein labelled Weetabix and thinks, "Great, everyone's always telling me I need to eat more protein to lose weight, that will do". And just like that, Cheryl thinks she's being healthier without realising that she's actually now just consuming more calories as all she used to do was have a slice of toast before leaving for work. (And we often reward ourselves for what we deem good behaviour, so maybe Cheryl has an extra glass of wine in the evening to pat herself on the back for making smarter food choices... wow, actually, the more I think of it, the less surprised I am that we are slowly becoming a fat species). Interestingly, for something to be labelled as "high protein", it needs to have 20g of protein per 100g, so Weetabix can only label itself "Protein" rather than high as it only has 19g per 100g. Many of the foods labelled protein or high protein may have more sugar or fat than the original version, and as a result, more calories, so in some cases, you are actually worse off reaching for the so-called "protein" option. Research has shown that the word "protein" positively influences consumer perception of how healthy a product is, but more interestingly, people made assumptions because of the "protein" label on other health markers off the product. For example, research found that protein bars with protein on the label led consumers to assume greater levels of both iron and fibre content in the bar! Which are two completely unrelated dietary concerns.[62]

Health halos also alter our perception of restaurants or takeaway restaurants. I do a calorie quiz on my Instagram where I get people to guess which meal or food item is the lowest in calories. The idea was to help people understand that their intuitive brains are useless when it comes to guessing calories, so while people think their basic understanding of nutrition means they can tell which is the best option, it is not normally the one you actually think. I bring this up because it immediately shows the health halos of some restaurant chains compared to others. Take McDonald's as an example, this is the poster child of unhealthy fast food (although I feel that is unfair), so therefore, must be calorie-dense and always lose. Well, let's take their signature burger, the Big Mac coming in at a reasonable 508 calories... if we add a medium fries at 337 calories and a Diet Coke (1 calorie), then our Big Mac meal comes to an impressive 846 calories. Now, let's compare it with two chains in the UK that have a healthier image. Nando's, for example, is just grilled chicken and everyone knows chicken is a lean protein source, so healthy. I ordered a simple half chicken (588 calories), regular chips (465 calories), and some macho peas (141 calories). Well, my "healthier" meal comes in at 1,194 calories. Let's try the same but with Wagamama, which is an Asian chain inspired by the flavours of Japan, I believe. I ordered the Vegatsu (the vegan Katsu curry). It's vegan, so obviously healthier, right? The meal comes in at 1,191 calories...

If my goal was fat loss, then judging by the three meal options I have laid out, McDonald's is your best option given its lower calorie content, but we just assume McDonald's is the worst option because of the negative health connotations we have attached to it, and the positive ones we have attached elsewhere. Just because a chicken breast is a lean protein source doesn't mean any chicken dish will be healthy. It might be breaded, fried, or marinated, remember restaurants want you to have a taste sensation so you keep coming back. It is, therefore, highly unlikely to be just a bland grilled chicken breast. Health halos not only impact your decisions at home but also when you are on the go, when you go to restaurants, and in most of your choices. These mental shortcuts help our brains to keep up with the millions of decisions we make every day. Unfortunately, our autopilots are prone to oversimplification and buzzwords. You might think that a salad box from the supermarket is your diet friend, but once you add the thick dressing, put the croutons on it, and add the little bits of bacon, you may have been better off reaching for that dirty burger.

CHAPTER 18: FOOD LABELS

N ow, there is a lot to unpack in terms of food labels as they play a role in a lot of the different fad diets, demonising trends, and health halos that have occurred over the years. But for the purposes of introducing food labels, let's just start with the basic principle of nutritional labelling. This makes me think of that quote, "Knowledge is power", often attributed to Francis Bacon from his *Meditationes Sacrae* (1597). This quote is used to transmit the idea that having and sharing knowledge is the cornerstone of reputation and influence, and therefore, power. Today, knowledge is shared through publications that not only inform but have the capacity to influence decision-making.[63] If we blame—as we should—an increase in consumption of calories on why we are putting on weight, then surely it makes sense that if we added calorie labels to food products, people would start to make more conscious decisions surrounding what they eat, and this would lead to a reduction in the obesity problem. On the surface that makes sense, right?

In the 1960s, obesity rates were quite low, yet people's knowledge of nutrition was rudimental or poor at best.

So, how is it that now we know more, we appear to be worse off?

In 1990, the Nutrition Labelling and Education Act was signed into law, and there were two primary objectives. Firstly, to provide information on food labels to help consumers make better food choices, and secondly, to encourage food companies to improve their food products. I mean, surely, since we know that too many calories cause us to gain weight then people would stop buying high-calorie food products and companies will have to change their ingredients to improve the nutritional profile of their food products? Again, it makes sense.

Information regarding serving size, total calories, number of grams of sugar, fat, protein, fibre, milligrams of cholesterol, and sodium will surely help people make better food decisions. Just quickly ask yourself how often you check food labels. And then how often this influences your decision-making process. Do you check it on products you've always been eating? The Food and Drug Administration in the States points to surveys that report 77% of consumers claim they use the nutrition labels "always/most of the time/or sometimes" when buying food products. I mean, that doesn't sound wrong, although if that is the case, why are we not making better food choices?

If we look at consumer psychology, we begin to understand that actually giving people more information isn't necessarily a good thing. Remember, an increase in product variety already causes decision fatigue, leading to impaired decision-making... and that was before we were asking people to try and read the small print on every packet on the supermarket shelves. Nowadays, there is even more information on some of the packets you buy. Don't you think most people are going to run out of their already limited decision-making capacities even quicker if we ask them to read all the calorie contents and compare products? I feel a box of cereal now provides more information to appear on the shelf than I have to do to fly overseas. While I love reading the labels on food packets, I am probably the exception to the rule and definitely not the norm. I mean, as a single man, I have the luxury of shopping for myself with no real time constraints... imagine being a single mum trying to get her two kids around the shop and behaving while trying to suss out which of the 100 options of pasta sauce has the least sugar or is the least processed, and fits your budget, and this is before mentioning any allergies or intolerances that suddenly everyone seems to suffer from. To be honest, sometimes I even get lost reading all the small print on some packets. Seriously, sometimes trying to figure out servings per container or calories per serving can be confusing. Packets sometimes include calories when adding milk, but I haven't added milk and maybe my milk is a different calorie level, and maybe I like to add more milk... anyway, I digress.

When we actually look at it from the context of the average consumer, it is no wonder it doesn't have the dramatic effect that we first thought it might. Most of us are creatures of habit and are probably reaching for the same old products we always have—if we haven't fallen for some marketing ploy already of "50% off this" or the use of some new shiny packaging. There is also something termed 'moral licensing', 'self-licensing', or 'licensing effect', in psychology or "balancing" (okay, I found a few different names for this psychological effect). Essentially, this is the subconscious phenomenon whereby past good deeds 'liberate individuals to engage in behaviours that are immoral, unethical, or otherwise problematic, behaviours that they would otherwise avoid for fear of feeling or appearing immoral.'[64] If we think of checking a food label, we are making a decision (hopefully) to make a better/healthier food choice. Imagine, for example, you pick up a bag of crisps and check the calorie and fat content. Due to its high level, you decide to avoid purchasing them today and instead add some extra apples to your basket. We internalise this as a good behaviour and subconsciously pat ourselves on the back. But what do most of us do when we make a good decision? Let's be honest, we feel that good decisions should be rewarded (yes, we are that simple). But wait... we are still in the supermarket, so I may have put back the packet of crisps (score 1 for being healthy), but by doing so, I have given myself permission to make a slightly unhealthy decision next. Well, I don't have crisps but because my dinner is going to be healthy, I might just buy that Magnum ice cream I've been eyeing up for the last few weeks.

Because we feel virtuous of our first decision, we feel we can afford to treat ourselves with something else. It is hardwired into our psychology, and just because we have slapped a large calorie label on a product isn't going to overpower this. Think about how many times you have come back from a good workout only to reach for that pizza because... well, you earned it. Honestly, how many of you reading this fall into that trap? You don't like exercise, so you view exercise as a punishment. Therefore, by doing it, you should be rewarded, and you do this by enjoying those ultra-processed treats that helped you gain weight in the first place. When you don't see the progress you think you should have earned (despite you constantly rewarding yourself along the way), you tell yourself exercise clearly doesn't work, so you stop. Having stopped your exercise and not changed any of your eating habits, you only continue to gain weight. The system is against you... or at least that's what you tell yourself.

I think this also just says something about the state of the human race and how exercise is viewed. I'm not saying you need to fall in love with CrossFit or try and become the next Mr Olympia, but if I were to list all the health benefits of exercise and tell you that a pill could give you this, I guarantee you would be willing to pay hundreds and thousands of pounds/dollars/euros or whatever currency you use to get your hands on that pill. Now, when I tell you it's free and just involves a few squats and moving your body a little... oh no, how dare you try and trick me into using my body into doing what it was designed for. Sorry, I got side-tracked on a little rant there, but you get my point.

If we think about what will actually improve our health or shopping habits, it is not the changes in single items in our shopping basket but whether the basket as a whole is becoming better over time. If we are simply switching one bad thing for another, we are essentially taking one step forward to take one step backwards.

Okay, so we added calorie labels to our supermarket foods. *"But, Chris, you said we are now eating out more than ever before".* Yes, this is true, but do you think adding calorie labels to restaurant and fast food menus will change people's decisions? On September 26th, 2006, the New York City Department of Health proposed the nation's first menu labelling law (regulation 81.50). Its provision applied to all restaurants that voluntarily disclosed the nutrition information of their food and was designed to primarily impact large chain restaurants. The idea was aimed to help reduce obesity by giving consumers more information about their food at the point of purchase. After some initial opposition from the restaurants, the law was changed to apply to any restaurant that had more than 15 locations operating under the same name, and this was then upheld by both federal and district courts and was eventually approved. It went into effect in 2008. The presumption was that consumers would hopefully be better educated and hopefully adjust their usual choices, opting for lower calorie versions. This was based on the assumption that we are all rational creatures who want to potentially reduce our weight. It did not take into account that people at fast food restaurants are often more motivated by convenience, budget and taste rather than calories and health. Consumers who already care about health probably don't shop in fast food stores regularly, and those who do likely already know enough to know which choices to make.

Also, when we factor economics into the equation, people with smaller budgets may actually look at getting more calories for less money as a bonus and, therefore, only change their decisions in the wrong direction if we are looking at it from a health perspective. Following the implementation of New York City's menu labelling law, there were studies conducted to examine the results. Interestingly, the initial results showed that consumers reported seeing and using the nutrition information to decrease the number of calories consumed when eating out. Unfortunately, this doesn't necessarily translate to an overall daily reduction of calories as they may later reward themselves with extra snacks since they were healthier at their previous meal. Also, these changes are likely limited to only certain populations. Unsurprisingly, the effects of these changes in food choices didn't last and later studies found that it had no overall impact on calories purchased. In the long run, had you been going to McDonald's three times a week before the menu labelling law, it appears that, after a year, you were probably still going to McDonald's the same three times a week and ordering exactly the same number of calories.

People now have the information available to them, but we are creatures of habit and convenience, and these appear to be stronger drivers than the need for change.

While discussing food labels, we have to bring our attention back to our health halos since these two work together. How often do you see something labelled "fat-free" or "gluten-free" and place a more positive health assumption on the product? Remember, the food industry is consumer-driven—we want people buying more. Since we were able to produce more calories per person from a food production point of view, the need for people to purchase more has increased. When we started demonising fat as the reason behind people gaining weight, it made sense for companies to change their products and reduce the fat content to make them more consumer-friendly. The example that always comes to mind is yoghurt. A naturally high in fat product, we suddenly saw a massive growth in "low fat" or "fat-free" versions hitting our shelves. And unsurprisingly, we ate these up, with the "fat-free" label disguising the fact that companies had to replace the fat with basically double the sugar content of the original product in order to improve the palatability. The calories hadn't gone down, and instead, otherwise fairly natural whole-fat versions of food had been replaced with high-sugar, chemical concoctions. I'm not saying all fat-free products are unhealthy or high in sugar, I am a big fan of Total Fage 0% yoghurt myself, however, this is more the exception than the rule, so be careful when reaching for anything labelled "fat-free". One article I found noted that "nutrition claims, which are used at the discretion of food manufacturers to highlight particular attributes of the food, can mislead consumers since they are used to highlight positive characteristics of the food, but do not warn consumers about the content of nutrients of public health concern".[65] Not sure that most fat-free yoghurts would sell very well if there was another label underneath the "fat-free" one that read "high-sugar content".

Other labels that may draw your attention can be "no added sugar", "no artificial colours or preservatives", or "free-from". It seems the more a product is "free from" things, the more expensive it becomes and the more health benefits we attach to it. Gluten—a type of storage protein that, for anyone other than people with celiac disease or a wheat allergy should not worry about it being in their diet—suddenly became the poster child for all gut issues, brain fog and belly fat. I can't say where this demonising started, but you can probably guarantee it was some naturopathic doctor or chiropractor online who started shitting on it (as these are the ones who I always see have the biggest problem with gluten... although no idea why). Anyway, suddenly, our shelves were inundated with "gluten-free" products that usually just translates to less tasty, crumbles more and is higher in calories and more expensive. Yet people were sold—gluten-free diets became the rage and self-diagnosis of gluten intolerance exploded.

As someone who specialises in gut health, I am continually bombarded with people self-diagnosing food intolerances, and with things like gluten and dairy demonised by so many online, is it any surprise that more and more people are removing these foods from their diets? You read an article talking about the negatives of gluten or the prevalence of gluten sensitivity and think to yourself, "What if I have gluten sensitivity?" "Should I remove gluten?" And judging from the broad symptom list they provide, it's not hard for you to tick off some of them in your mind. "Yes, I do get tired, and I get bloated after eating breakfast... I must have it!" Without addressing potentially the lack of sleep making you tired, the nutritional deficiencies adding to your fatigue, or the quantity of food that made you bloated, the frequency of bloating you experience, the fact that you chugged a large coffee before eating breakfast… you see, it is easier for people to self-diagnose an intolerance and blame that for their health symptoms rather than actually addressing the larger picture of their lifestyle choices. Gluten is not a lifestyle choice, it is a protein, and unless you have an actual intolerance, there is nothing wrong with it.

The demonising of foods can affect us mentally—I think I've demonstrated this—but can this also affect us physically? The answer is yes. Hopefully, you have all heard of the placebo effect, the phenomenon where people report real improvement after taking a fake or non-existent treatment. Because the placebo isn't a real treatment, any beneficial effects reported are due to a person's belief or expectation that their condition is being treated. It is basically the positive power of perception. Well, there is a reverse to this called the nocebo effect. Essentially, have you ever read the potential side effects of a medicine only to then develop them? Had you not read those side effects, would you have developed them? There is evidence that negative words (or suggestions of harm) are also affecting us. These influences tend to be mainly subconscious. But our fear of a substance can be enough to trigger a symptomatic response to it. With the continued attack on gluten on social media and in the news, do you think this is impacting our ability to digest it?

Jessica Biesiekierski and colleagues from Monash University conducted a study to discover whether patients who described themselves as gluten sensitive/intolerant were either physically sensitive to gluten OR if it was psychological.[66] This was done as a double-blind, placebo-controlled, randomised cross-over trial (which is a method used to remove the scientists' biases and their likelihood of finding what they suspect they'd find). Participants couldn't be celiac as this is a serious auto-immune condition, and gluten for people with celiac is incredibly harmful.

Each participant was assigned to a gluten group or to a gluten-free group (they were not aware which group they were in). All meals were provided to both groups for several days, where they also minimised other potential food irritants. What the scientists found was odd. During the experiment, both the gluten and the gluten-free group experienced symptoms that are characteristic of a gluten sensitivity! After the first experiment, the participants swapped groups (without being told). This crossover allowed the scientists to compare gluten and gluten-free diets in the same individuals. There was also a washout period in between the two phases to avoid any carryover effects.

The second time around, the results were even more puzzling. The sensitivity symptoms showed up again in both gluten and gluten-free diets. How could that be? The scientists concluded that the cause was likely psychological and explained by the nocebo effect. The participants expected the diets to make them sick, so they did, even when gluten was removed. "A strong anticipatory sympto-matic (i.e., Nocebo) response was present independently of the nature of the challenge protein (gluten)".

So, believing something is bad for you might be enough to cause a reaction... is this just in gluten though? Well, in another study done by a team of Italian gastroenter-ologists,[67] they asked people with and without diagnosed lactose intolerance to take lactose for an experiment on its effects on bowel symptoms. In reality, the participants didn't receive the promised lactose. Instead, without knowing it, they received low-dose glucose (which does not harm your gut).

Shockingly, 44% of people with known lactose intoler-ance and 26% of those without lactose intolerance com-plained of gastrointestinal symptoms typical of lactose intolerance! Again, it appears that the expectation that they would receive lactose created a negative physical reaction. Their minds and bodies emulated the damage.

The misinformation about health risks and negative expectations that permeate the internet, our magazines and news outlets, can prompt nocebo effects in individ-uals. When someone says there is a rise in gluten sen-sitivity, do we think that's because suddenly epigenetic changes are coming to the front and more people are now unable to digest gluten, or is it that we have created this health epidemic through misinformation alone? I'm not saying the media is entirely to blame, but it is an interesting point. Also, I'm not blaming the nocebo effect for people suddenly gaining weight, but if it is altering people's eating habits, then it is having an influence and obviously not a positive one. In 2015, Fiona Crichton and Keith Petrie (University of Auckland), in their paper titled "Accentuate the Positive: Counteracting Psychogenic Responses To Media Health Messages In the Age of the Internet", noted, "The Internet has expanded the scope for creating health scares and increased the risk of nocebo responding in individuals exposed to misinformation about threats to personal health posed by aspects of modern life".[68]

It is worth noting there are no actual food intolerance tests (except for a Hydrogen breath test used to diagnose lactose intolerance), so if you have paid a company to stab you or analyse your hair, then well done... you basically pissed away your money. It is also worth noting that for many people who get symptoms after eating too much dairy, it is more down to the quantity of the lactose, and if you just reduced the portion size, you should be okay. Research suggests that even those who are lactose-intolerant can usually tolerate up to 12g of lactose at once (about 250ml of milk) and up to 24g of lactose spread out across the day (about 500ml of milk). I'm not saying these intolerances don't exist, but we must be careful when just removing large food groups from our diet based on misinformation and fear.

It seems that the food labelling and nutrition labelling that now covers our food packages hasn't helped at all. It has only fed into our mental shortcuts and health halos. Knowing the calories doesn't deter people from a product, and labels like "gluten-free" or "fat-free" only work to confuse people more about what they should or shouldn't buy. Again, we have created confusion while providing more information. Knowing more than ever before, we end up actually saying less and people seem to know less as a result. Confusion breeds chaos and distrust, and that is the world we live in now.

CHAPTER 19:
THE SOCIAL MEDIA DIET

Where to start...

What if I asked you, "What do social media and guns have in common?" Strange question, I know, but when you think about it, I guess both could be used for either good or bad. You could shoot and kill an innocent bystander (bad, obviously), or you could be using it to protect your family from a home invader (good...). Well, social media can be used for the same, I guess, and while your first reaction might be that it's a bit extreme... there are many cases where cyberbullying can result in people taking their own lives. And while many people (like myself... shameless plug) may be trying to put out educational content or motivational content, there is also a lot of toxic information and misinformation. I am not going into my opinion on gun laws... I am just trying to come up with an analogy... not my best... but not my worst.

I posed this question on my Instagram story recently and was intrigued by the results. The question was, 'Do you think as a whole social media is good or bad/useful or dangerous?' Posing the question on social media is obviously biassing people who actually use social media, so I'm not suggesting that this is a good sample size. But despite expecting the vast majority of my followers to think it was a positive tool (given they are using it), a large number of them actually believed that it was bad/dangerous. (Strange, although I guess people drink every weekend despite knowing the health risks concerned with alcohol intake…)

I think the overall opinion (from my poll) was that people are indifferent, it is a bit of both as it were. For me, I think social media is what you make of it—obviously, it is important to follow people you believe are either delivering positivity or good education. The problem is knowing what good education is and what is toxic, a fad, or potentially harmful. One of my clients and good friends constantly deletes and then reinstalls social media as she claims it can be detrimental to her mental health seeing all these half-naked women with bodies that she aspires to. When I suggest she doesn't follow these pages, she replies that she doesn't have the self-control not to look at this content. I guess even if you are trying to use it for good, it is hard to filter out the negatives, and while social media allows me to reach a larger audience and help promote my education, it's also a reason why I end up seeing many clients who have suffered as a result of the misinformation they learned through social media and media in general. So, I can see the good and bad of it.

Do I think it is having a positive impact on our overall diets and lifestyle? The answer is probably not. Despite knowing more about our health and nutrition than ever before, we are still faced with a growing obesity epidemic and an increasing rate of disordered eating patterns. While influencers may think they are helping, and I think many of the intentions behind posts are positive, posts like: 'A day in the life of…' or 'Here's what I eat in a day,' are only helping to compound disordered eating rather than educating or inspiring (which I'm sure was the rationale behind the post).

You see, social media is a powerful tool. Food nutrition myths have only been exacerbated by social media. This, again, is the Wild Wild West of information where you can say something, and if you say it with enough conviction, people will believe you. Apparently, providing evidence to support your advice is an unnecessary prerequisite rather than a necessity. Take, for example, the famous case of Jordan Younger, a "Wellness" blogger, who, in 2014, had amassed an impressive 70,000 followers on Instagram. What were her credentials to give nutritional advice? Oh, wait… she had none. What did she promote? A "gluten-free, sugar-free, oil-free, grain-free, plant based, raw vegan diet". Essentially, the poster girl for so-called "clean eating". Surely, anyone with two brain cells to rub together should have realised this was a dumb diet to follow, however, when you say something with enough conviction and sex it up into #foodporn pics and #fitspiration quotes, you can really convince people your diet is better than theirs. What had begun as an attempt to be healthier and promote this to her followers quickly developed into extreme low-calorie diets, juice cleanses and detoxes resulting in her hair falling out and her developing the eating disorder, orthorexia (refers to an unhealthy obsession with eating "pure" food).

Before I move on, let's pick apart this "clean" eating trend. What is clean eating? What is clean food? Is there any evidence that so-called clean eating works for weight loss and health? According to a 2019 survey of over 1,000 US adults, 38% of them had followed a diet over the past year, of which "clean" eating was the most commonly cited diet, so its popularity is clear, but is the definition of what clean is?

It appears that the definition of what is "clean" depends on who you ask since there are no clear definitions or oversight from regulatory authorities. This means that there are differing levels to the lengths people go to in order to eat clean. Obviously, Jordan Younger is an example of someone who went to more of the extremes. I think the main definition of "clean" emphasises the consumption of whole, unprocessed foods—not exactly a bad pursuit, however, others involve eliminating entire food groups such as dairy, refined sugar, wheat, and so-called acidic foods. The further you go clean, it appears the more disordered your eating becomes... not exactly healthy.

Clean has essentially become an umbrella term for you to demonise what you want to and promote that which fits your narrative. How many of you have seen people on Instagram promoting so-called "clean recipes" like, 'Here is my healthy clean brownie recipe,' only to watch that person fill a tray full of peanut butter, butter, cacao, avocado, almond flour, and agave syrup (okay, don't quote me on that… I try and ignore these people so my memory is fuzzy, but it is usually something like this) under the illusion that these natural ingredients are clean and, therefore, the brownie will be "healthy". Fuck me sideways… most of these concoctions are more calorie-dense than the store-bought versions, and while they may not contain any "artificial" ingredients or "preservatives", it will definitely be working against you in your pursuit of weight loss or health. Also, if you are slapping "clean" and "healthy" labels onto your home-cooked brownies, it's even more likely that you will overindulge on them guilt-free. At least when people buy the store-bought "dirty" ones, they know exactly what they are doing and don't try to pretend like it's a healthy choice.

A look at the Clean Eating Magazine website and they are trying to pretend their brownie recipes are good for you because they are "gut-friendly and free of additives and preservatives". Although, and I quote the title of the article, "I Can't Stop Eating Dalci's Decadent, Clean and Gut-Healthy Brownies"… doesn't sound very useful if your goal is weight loss no matter how good for your gut it supposedly is (and judging by the ingredients list, I really don't see how good for your gut it will actually be. They are trying to claim that unrefined natural coconut sugar, avocado oil and some pectin from apples is enough to label something "gut healthy"… I call bullshit).

Clean eating is a major consumer trend, with 40% of young people aged 18-30 years in the UK reporting dietary practices consistent with clean eating. In the USA, the consumer demand for clean eating is even driving changes

in the food supply. For example, manufacturers are refor-
mulating food products to modify or remove certain ingredients and additives in response to consumer demand for
"cleaner" processed foods.[69] No wonder companies are
bowing to this since it appears people are willing to pay a
higher retail price for a food product made with ingredients they recognise and trust. I always use the example of
an RX bar. These are marketed as clean protein bars with
the ingredients list in bold on the front of the packet, since
it only contains four ingredients. It is genius marketing,
and the ingredients are all "natural" and "clean". Three egg
whites, six almonds, four cashews and two dates (and No
B.S.). I mean, brilliant, what genius marketing, and they
actually taste quite nice, and yes, if you fear chemicals, then
this is a bar for you. Also, it calls itself a protein bar so
has the halo of being a protein bar and a clean one at that.
Considering though, for a protein bar, it only has 12g of
protein yet 210 calories… is it really the best option? With
9g of fat and 13g of sugar, I'm confused—aren't we against
sugar? Insert the, "Well, it's natural sugar" argument (like
that makes a difference to how our body uses it), and it's
almost like you can't argue with these people. If I were to
look at, say, PhD Diet Whey Bars, while I may find a longer
ingredient list, I would also find a bar that has fewer calories (199 calories) but 20g of protein and only 2.7g of
sugar. So, is your clean diet really leading you to make the
best choices? Doesn't seem like a forgone conclusion from
where I'm sitting.

Where does labelling something clean stop? Now
people are demonising ingredient lists because they can't

pronounce some of the ingredients! And demonizing something because it's a chemical... despite the fact that everything is a fucking chemical. Water is dihydrogen monoxide, so shall we remove that from our lives since that's a chemical? There is this fear that big food companies are trying to poison you to either get you addicted to their foods or to profit off of your illness because they also own big pharma companies... or some sort of conspiracy narrative like that. I can't begin to express how dumb this is. Many of the ingredients in our foods serve a beneficial purpose and are there for a reason—your ability to pronounce or recognise that ingredient doesn't determine its health or benefits. Beyond flavour, many ingredients are there to prevent spoilage and extend the shelf life. So, they are improving food safety and reducing food waste, but just because you can't pronounce it, it must be bad for us, so let's get rid of it. How self-righteous and self-involved have we become? Also, bear in mind this is definitely a privileged standpoint. I don't think lower economical countries are throwing their hands up because they can't pronounce the ingredients or because their food is lasting longer. Yes, some woman making thousands of pounds or dollars every month from being a twat on Instagram can afford to pay extra for so-called "clean" products and to live that so-called "clean" lifestyle, but you think people living in the third world benefit from your moronic clean narrative.

Creating fear around foods and ingredients does not help anyone (apart from the social media gurus getting followers from it). If you see an ingredient list that has the ingredients cobalamin or pyridoxine on it, do you recognise those? No... well then, don't eat it—those are chemicals. Except, cobalamin is the name for Vitamin B12 and pyridoxine is the name of Vitamin B6. You see how stupid this narrative is? The British Dietetic Association identified "clean eating" as their number 1 "worst celebrity diets to avoid in 2017". Research even suggests that positive attitudes toward "clean" diets are linked with disordered eating attitudes and behaviours and that those who followed advice from "clean" eating websites exhibited higher dietary restraint—a risk factor for disordered eating.

As Dr Max Pemperton wrote in one article, "At best, clean eating is nonsense dressed up as health advice. At worst, it is embraced by those with underlying psychological difficulties and used to justify an increasingly restrictive diet — with potentially life-threatening results".[70] Look, I believe everyone is entitled to follow whatever eating patterns they choose, but when this is being promoted out to large audiences of potentially young and impressionable people, this is a real problem. More recently, a vegan raw food influencer named Zhanna Samsonova with the Instagram name 'Raw Vegan Food Chef', with 33k followers died of health complications. Now, while I can't say for sure it was 100% due to her diet, even though most reports I could find say she died from starvation and exhaustion, I think it is safe to say that a raw vegan diet is not a healthy diet to promote either. It seems almost ridiculous that social media sites are more concerned about potentially blocking any videos or pictures that might show a woman's nipples because, heaven forbid, a young person sees those... however, they don't do anything about people spouting incorrect and actually dangerous misinformation, which can quite literally kill people.

More than 3.6 billion people are connected worldwide, and this number is projected to increase to 4.41 billion by 2025. I was lucky enough to grow up without social media until I was about 14, and even then, most of it was about just poking your mates or trying to change someone's status to read something highly non-PC (ah, the good old days of Facebook), and this all had to be done while connected to very slow internet (that you were attached to with a cable... I know, it's hard to imagine), so by the time Instagram and YouTube were big entities, I was at least old enough to not be quite so impressionable. Nowadays though, kids are getting smartphones and social media accounts around the time they have only just learned to take a shit for themselves (okay, don't quote me on this as I don't have a kid, but I see kids who have to be younger than five playing with iPhones). At this age, we are so impressionable, it can't really be of any surprise that the introduction of social media—a world of cyber bullies, unrealistic body images, violence, wealth and diverse culture all rammed down the throat of someone who is not old enough to drink, drive, vote or work (not in that order)—is probably not going to lead to good outcomes!

Social media use is directly linked to increases in disordered eating patterns and body dysmorphia (in both men and women, although women suffer more). In fact, according to the National Association of Anorexia Nervosa and Associated Disorders, approximately 24 million people in the United States suffer from an eating disorder, and this is probably underreported and only increasing. Not only that, but The Eating Disorders Coalition reports that every 62 minutes, at least one person loses their life as a direct result of an eating disorder. Out of the population with disordered eating attitudes, 16% of them present with overeating. Moreover, recent data has discussed the increase of the minimum age of the people with disorders is around 12 and decreasing still. Now, again, I'm not suggesting social media is entirely to blame, but the association between the two is clear.

Why do I mention this? Well, disordered eating spans the spectrum of over-controlled eating, resulting in anorexia nervosa, to a variety of forms of under-controlled eating such as bulimia nervosa and binge-eating disorder, or night-eating syndrome. Both binge-eating disorder and night-eating syndromes are often present with those who are overweight and obese.[71] Those with binge-eating disorder are, in fact, an estimated three to six times more likely to be obese than those without an eating disorder. So, increased social media use can lead to an increased risk of disordered eating patterns and negative body image, which is not a recipe to be a healthy weight. And while it can lead to being both underweight or overweight, it is definitely not helping the obesity problem.

It is no real surprise that social media, while being a useful tool for education, has actually become more of a problem than a benefit in the obesity puzzle. With thousands of followers behind some of these social media influencers, consumers place more weight on what that person says. They assume they know more and assume that because of how many followers they have, they must be telling the truth. Consumers also want to fit in, in a world that is becoming more and more governed by online communities. People get rewards for being part of a group and fitting in, even if that means giving up meat, or preservatives or common sense. Gabor Maté M.D. writes in his book, *When the Body Says No*: *The Cost of Hidden Stress*, "We attempt to understand the body in isolation from the mind. We want to describe human beings- healthy or otherwise- as though they function in isolation from the environment in which they develop, live, work, play, love and die…" The reality is, our bodies and minds are one. Things that impact our mental and emotional state inevitably have an impact on our physical selves. Now, while he writes about the impact of trauma on auto-immune conditions and disease, it probably isn't a stretch to say that the negative impacts of social media use on our mental health will also be impacting our phys-ical health. Whether this is through an increase in disor-dered eating or stress leading to patterns of binge eating or comfort eating, the result is an increase in weight gain in certain individuals.

On one side of social media, we have health gurus and nutritionists seemingly cherry-picking studies and mechanistic data to blame small components of other-wise healthy foods to demonise them, like demonising oats because they have phytic acid, while ignoring that most of the phytic acid will be lost when you cook or soak the oats and that we have lots of studies in humans showing that oats can actually make up part of a very nutritious and balanced diet. Using words like inflammation or cancer to scare their followers, all while probably selling cookbooks, diet plans or other nonsensical products. On the other hand, you have fitness influencers who are probably on more performance-enhancing drugs than most of the Russian Olympic gymnast team or who have hidden their eating disorders to then promote so-called cheat meals, or how they can eat mountainous amounts of food and still maintain their ridiculous lean physiques year-round. How is the average impressionable user meant to navigate up this stream of bullshit without developing some irrational eating patterns? I, myself, with a wide knowledge in nutrition can be left scratching my head when I see some doctor on Instagram giving nutrition advice that seems to go completely against another doctor's advice. How can two doctors have completely different views? Aren't these the people who are meant to know how to heal the body? It seems that medical practice is also more focused on treating symptoms rather than tackling their root causes. We are predominantly lazy as a species and would rather take a pill that tackles symptom X, than doing work on ourselves to correct the habits that caused X in the first place. The demand for weight loss drugs sort of highlights this.

Celebrities will reveal their diets, only to have people try and replicate these unhealthy protocols because they want to emulate them, even though, actually, most of these routines are unsustainable and were only followed in order to get that actor very lean for a small period of time (not to mention the undisclosed drugs they were using alongside this). Other celebrities promote expensive health trends that aren't always founded in actual science. Take Gwyneth Paltrow for example—her company, Goop, at one point was promoting Yoni vaginal eggs made of Rose Quartz or Jade that, when inserted inside a woman's vagina, could help balance hormones, regulate menstrual cycles and increase bladder control. Unsurprisingly, these didn't work, and gynaecologists even warned the materials could cause infections or toxic shock syndrome. Goop had to pay $145,000 in civil penalties to resolve allegations that it made unsubstantiated claims about its products. Realistically, if we also think of celebrities, they are, in general, a terrible example. Does the average person have the time and resources that an actor does? You hear how some of these actors get ready for such roles like Batman or Superman, where they are training for two to three hours every day with a trainer, they have a chef prepare all of their meals and a massage therapist, and all manner of recovery aids. I think most people would be able to improve their physique with this setup.

Most of the Fitfluencers you see on Instagram or health experts, if we ignore drug use, eating disorders and genetics, just look at their day… it is quite literally their job to be in shape. You can almost smell the irony in some of these people promoting "clean" diets or eating "natural" foods when they don't come clean about their drug use and are about as natural as the cast of The Only Way is Essex. You have about as much chance of achieving their physique by following their plan as I would have of being the next poster model for L'Oréal (bald joke). That is not to say there aren't any good influencers because there are, but they seem to be the exception to the rule rather than the norm and, unfortunately, usually drowned out by the majority.

There is a quote from Jordan Peterson's viral interview with Cathy Newman that I feel sums up social media use for me. He said, "In order to be able to think, you have to risk being offensive". And I think we could paraphrase this to read something like, "In order to use social media, you have to risk being triggered". There will always be good and bad elements of social media, I think a bit like what I teach people when trying to lose weight to control their environments, the same could be said for your social media use. Maybe you only follow certain accounts that empower/educate you... maybe you can set a daily allowance for how long you can use it. However you choose to use it, be a voice for good. If you find yourself complaining about what someone is posting, simply unfollow or mute them.

CHAPTER 20: STRESS

Stress—that six letter word we can't seem to escape. It only seems right that we have a chapter in this book regarding stress, and it probably makes the most sense to have it immediately after one on social media. You see, as I mentioned before, we shouldn't look at the body and mind as separate entities, we know from looking at things like gut health that the brain and the stomach communicate together, and what affects one can have an impact on the other. It is no real surprise that we have studies showing that those with IBS symptoms or even conditions like IBD tend to have higher levels of anxiety and depression, although a bit like the chicken or the egg conundrum... it's not so easy to say which came first. Did the stress and anxiety cause the IBS symptoms or did the IBS symptoms cause the stress and anxiety. Speaking as someone with IBD, I can attest that stress is the worst thing for my stomach. It is, unfortunately, the one area that is hardest to control.

Anyway, in order to understand and discuss the link between stress and obesity, we first have to understand what stress is. Hans Selye, an endocrinologist who coined the word stress in the 1930s, joked that, "Everyone knows what stress is, but nobody knows what it is". He later defined it as "Nonspecific response of the body to any demand". While there are different definitions depending on who you ask (an engineer, for example, would describe it as an "External force which produces physical strain in the materials exposed to it".), let's stick with Hans's given the man is basically the father of stress research.

Stress affects and involves virtually every tissue in the body. As Seyle noted in his work, The *Stress of Life*: "A general outline of the stress response will not only have to include brain and nerves, pituitary, adrenal, kidney, blood vessels, connective tissue, thyroid, liver, and white blood cells, but will also have to indicate the manifold interrelations between them". While we predominantly think of stress as negative emotions, anxiety, defiance, worry, panic, anger, defensiveness, depression and tension, there is a lot more that happens on a physiological level when we are stressed. Stress is not a matter of subjective feeling, it is a measurable set of objective physiological events in the body, involving the brain, hormonal apparatus, the immune system and many other organs.[72]

The stress response we experience happens due to a stimulus (loud noise, lion, angry email), which causes our body to react in some way (increased heart rate, rapid breathing, sweaty palms...). This is because we have perceived the stimulus as a threat by the part of the brain called the amygdala (if you specialise in stress and are reading this, please don't crucify me, I'm just trying to make it slightly more bitesize). If the amygdala perceives the situation as threatening, it relays the threat signal to the hypothalamus. The hypothalamus is essentially the command centre here, and with the information it receives, it then carries out several actions like activating the autonomic nervous system, stimulating the secretion of corticotropin (hormone involved in the stress response), and producing vasopressin (another hormone that decreases urine output and thirst).

The autonomic nervous system maintains normal organ function, it is the branch of the nervous system that operates without conscious thought, regulating digestion, respiration and temperature. There are two branches of this system: the sympathetic (SNS) and the parasympathetic (PSNS) nervous system. The SNS is the main branch involved in the 'fight or flight' response. The PSNS can be thought of more as the rest and digest system. The two systems work together to maintain balance in the body. When the SNS is activated, the sympathetic-adrenal-medullary (SAM) axis, the hypothalamus-pituitary-adrenal (HPA) axis and the gut-brain-axis (GBA) all play a role in regulating stress. In times of immediate acute stress where a fast reaction/response is needed, the SNS releases acetylcholine (neurotransmitter), activating the adrenal medulla. This results in the release of catecholamines (epinephrine and norepinephrine) into the bloodstream. Epinephrine, or adrenaline as you probably know it, is the fight or flight hormone, and is responsible for rapid reactions, heightened focus, and increased heart rate. Norepinephrine is essentially its backup.

When anxiety or fear is present for an extended period, two important hormones are secreted—corticotropin-releasing hormone (CRH) and vasopressin. The combination of these two being released activates the HPA axis. CRH is transported to the pituitary gland where it stimulates the secretion of corticotropin, also called adrenocorticotropic hormone (ACTH). The pituitary gland sends a signal to the adrenal gland, which produces more messenger hormones to be directed around the body... still with me? One of these messengers is called cortisol. You have no doubt heard of this one. Cortisol, also sometimes referred to as the "stress hormone", plays an important role in regulating metabolism, the immune system response, memories and sleep-wake cycle. Cortisol is not released immediately after a stressor stimuli, it lags behind epinephrine and norepinephrine. You see, cortisol takes longer to have an effect, but it also stays longer.

Cortisol levels normally fluctuate over the 24-hour cycle. As I mentioned, it plays a role in the sleep-wake cycle, so the body regulates the release of this hormone. Although it fluctuates on a day-to-day basis, an excess of cortisol in the body can indicate the activation of the stress response system, this might be due to a bad day at work or sitting in traffic. Now, normally, once the stressor has passed, the body has a negative feedback signalling system to shut off the stress response. This is important to remember when someone demonises cortisol because many things can raise cortisol levels in the body, which doesn't mean they are immediately bad... remember, cortisol naturally goes up and down. Following a hard workout, for example, cortisol levels are raised... this doesn't mean working out makes you fat. It's important to understand this, as charlatans on Instagram always like to use cortisol as a buzzword to make you fear things.

Okay, science lesson over, but it's important to understand the basis of the stress response (trust me, this was the abridged version). What is important to note is that there is a stimulus that is deemed as a stressor by the body, which activates the stress response. All stressors start as a stimulus but not all stimuli are necessary stressors. The process of deciding whether a stimulus is considered a stressor or not is called appraisal. Essentially, stressors fall into two main categories—physiological (chronic illness, physical pain, extreme temperatures, poor sleep, injury) or psychological (giving a talk at work, problems in a relationship, threat to your self-esteem, verbal abuse). Interestingly, the body does not seem to care much about whether the stressor is physical or psychological; in either case, it triggers the stress response.

Our bodies are constantly working to adjust to any changes, both internal and external, to maintain homeostasis. This process is referred to as "allostasis", which is a normal process and is happening all the time. When the body gets overwhelmed and can no longer keep up with the onslaught of pressure and stress, this is called allostatic overload. In the case of allostatic overload, the hormones that have a beneficial effect on the body will now become excessively released, disrupting homeostasis and leading to both psychological and physiological problems. Now, it is no real surprise that since the body doesn't really differentiate between a stressor like a lion chasing us (which helped us survive back in the days of early man) and having received a bad review at work that our bodies are probably now under a lot more stress. According to the Mental Health Foundations study in 2018, which surveyed 4,619 people in the UK, 74% of participants reported having felt so stressed that they had been overwhelmed or unable to cope in the last year.

So, is stress or an increase in stress impacting our waistlines? The simple answer is yes, however, remember that we are still working within the realms of energy balance.

When we talk about stress leading to obesity, we are referring to chronic stress. Chronic stress is usually a strain that has been present consistently for at least 6 to 12 months. So, don't worry if you stub your toe, this type of acute stress usually isn't what we are worried about. Remember, we are talking about allostatic overload—if our bodies experienced this after every little stressor, we would be fucked. There is an increasing amount of evidence that stress, and particularly, an increase of the glucocorticoid stress hormone, cortisol, plays a role in the development of obesity. You see, chronic stress, for instance, is a predictor of elevated body mass index (BMI) and waist circumference in men and women.[73] It has also been demonstrated that high levels of stress are a predictor for significant weight gain in female university students.[74] There is also evidence that stress-increased cortisol secretion can lead to an increase in abdominal adiposity.

Now, it is important to note that fat doesn't just materialise out of thin air. The reason behind the link is that stress may influence obesity behaviourally through increased "stress-related eating". Cortisol can also increase your appetite and usually results in a craving of hyperpalatable ultra-processed foods. Dr. Charlie Seltzer, a weight loss physician, also notes that excess calories consumed in the setting of high cortisol appear to be preferentially deposited around the middle. There is also a knock-on effect with other systems, for instance, if elevated cortisol levels can negatively impact sleep, then this, in turn, can negatively affect food-eating patterns and behaviour. Stressed people also tend to exercise less and drink more alcohol, all of which can contribute to excess weight. But, you see, we are still operating within the realms of energy balance—it is just that stress can negatively impact both the *energy in* and *energy out* parts of the equation. One study I found even showed that stress and depression can alter metabolic responses to high-fat meals in ways that promote obesity. "The cumulative 6-hour difference between one prior day stressor and no stressors translates into 104 kcal, a difference that could add almost 11 pounds/year".[75]

So, yes, when discussing the obesity epidemic, it seems that increases in rates of chronic stress go hand in hand with our growing waistlines. I mean, to be honest, the increases in rates of chronic stress also seem to go hand in hand with an increase in autoimmune conditions and most cancers... so, while I will now give you some more information on stress and weight gain, I advise you to read Gabor Maté's books (*When the Body Says No*, and *The Myth of Normal*), which really help you understand how trauma and stress impact our bodies and health. Let's first tackle stress eating or emotional eating.

Emotional eating can be described as using food to provide comfort in response to mood and feelings rather than hunger. Now, it is important to note that some people can undereat when stressed or when confronted with emotion, however, when we are talking about emotional eating or stress-related eating, we are usually referring to increased total caloric intake, as well as the overconsumption of food items high in fat and sugar. One study looking at the emotional eating habits of 8,580 men and 27,061 female college students found that higher emotional eating scores were correlated with being overweight or obese. Interestingly, it also found that emotional eating scores were higher in those who said they were currently dieting (restrained eating), so not only being more stressed but also being on a restricted eating regime showed an increased association with more emotional eating and weight gain.[76] This also clearly illustrates why our simple *eat less, move more* mantra is short-sighted if we haven't first addressed potential psychological aspects of the individual. Interestingly, dieting itself is considered a risk factor for an enhanced tendency towards emotional eating.

Stress eating or emotional eating is essentially a coping mechanism to control and decrease negative emotions, such as depressed mood, anxiety, and stress. The prevalence of emotional eating, based on a survey performed by the American Psychological Association, found that 38% of adults stated that they have been implicated in emotional eating during the past month, with 49% of them engaging in it weekly.[77] That is quite a shocking statistic. Is an increasing amount of the population self-medicating with food? As I have mentioned, emotional eating has a positive relationship with increases in weight gain over time and difficulty in losing weight. One of the main reasons for this is the fact that emotional eaters are more prone to greater consumption of sugary and high-fat foods, in response to stressors, and tend to snack more frequently compared to non-emotional eaters. So, quite simply put, it is leading people to choose more calorie-dense foods. Unfortunately and unsurprisingly, this rarely bodes well for our waistlines. One of the reasons food is used to cope with stress is that hedonic food can help release dopamine in the body, and this neurotransmitter is what helps you feel good. It is strongly associated with pleasure and reward. Craving for this food can be a way of trying to balance your emotions—increasing your appetite at a time when you actually don't need more calories from a homeostatic standpoint. It seems that while acute stress usually results in a loss of appetite, chronic stress can override the brain's natural response to satiety, leading to non-stop reward signals that promote eating more highly palatable food.

Imagine I have sat you in front of two bowls. One contains red seedless grapes, the other contains M&MS (which kind, Chris? Whichever kind you fucking love… and if you don't love M&Ms, choose a sweet you do)… I tell you that you're allowed to pick at either bowl during our session. Do you think your choice will depend on how you are feeling in the session? Do you think your decision might change due to stress? A study published in 2006 performed this exact experiment on college students.[78] It turned out unstressed participants were likely to pick at the grapes, however, when stressed (by being given unsolvable anagrams... I know, boring. I was hoping it was some form of electric shock or something), the students tended to reach for the M&Ms more. This study helps illustrate the immediate impact a simple stressor can have on our immediate food choices.

Professor Herzog, the senior author of a study looking at how chronic stress amplifies the brain's rewards system, noted, "Our findings reveal stress can override a natural brain response that diminishes the pleasure gained from eating—meaning the brain is continuously rewarded to eat... We showed that chronic stress, combined with a high-calorie diet, can drive more and more food intake as well as a preference for sweet, highly palatable food, thereby promoting weight gain and obesity".

How does increased cortisol come into this equation? So, I explained that when the stress response is activated, cortisol levels increase as part of this process. If this is acute stress, cortisol levels will fall after the stressor has passed and homeostasis will be maintained. When we are chronically stressed, cortisol levels are elevated and can remain elevated. Why is this a problem for our waist? Well, simply put:

Step 1: Cortisol stimulates your fat and carbohydrate metabolism to give your body a rush of energy as it prepares to fight off a threat (the stressor). So, your appetite naturally increases to signal that your body needs more fuel to keep up with the energy demand. As cortisol levels remain elevated, so does your appetite and your desire for more calorie-dense foods.

Step 2: Elevated levels of cortisol also appear to interfere with insulin action on several different levels, leading to an increased risk of insulin resistance.

So, increased cortisol levels work to not only increase our appetites but also steer them towards more calorie-dense foods, and at the same time, reduce our insulin sensitivity. Quite a good combination for weight gain if you ask me.

Why the increased abdominal adiposity though? Well, this is a complicated issue, however, one paper I found stated that "although the molecular mechanisms remain to be fully elucidated, there is increasing evidence that glucocorticoids (like cortisol) have multiple, depot-dependent effects on adipocyte gene expression and metabolism that promote central fat deposition".[79] Which essentially translates to… we aren't sure but it is our understanding that the hormonal milieu caused by stress in conjunction with a calorie surplus promotes central fat storage. Okay, I may have used a bit of artistic licence with that conclusion, but I'm trying to keep this simple for you. The evidence suggests it increases abdominal fat storage (in 87 obese women, 24h urine cortisol excretion correlated significantly with abdominal diameter and abdominal obesity), although the mechanisms aren't entirely understood. One paper I read suggested it was due to the increase in the neurotransmitter, neuropeptide Y (NPY), directly into the adipose tissue. The studies were done in vitro, so I don't like to assume this as FACT, and actually, who cares? Just know that chronic stress does lead the body to favour central or visceral fat storage. It is important to also note that an increase in visceral fat significantly increases your risk of many serious health complications. It is also a diagnostic marker for what is called metabolic syndrome (a group of conditions that, together, raise your risk of coronary heart disease, diabetes, stroke, and other serious health problems).

Hopefully, I have demonstrated that stress is not good for our waistlines, however, this again still operates within the realms of energy balance… you may be bored of me saying that, and trust me, I don't love repeating myself, but it is worth it to make sure this point is hammered home before we get onto the next part of the book, which is where people try to explain obesity beyond the confines of this equation.

PART 5: ARE YOU SURE IT ISN'T?

Okay, okay… having discussed what I believe to be the major players in terms of the weight loss equation and how they all impact our energy balance, I think we should address some of the angles that the online snake oils salesman like to ram down our throats in order to sell diet books, recipe guides, podcasts… you name it, they will set it to you. Let's start with the carbohydrate-insulin model of obesity so that we can dispel what I deem the herpes of weight loss myths (since it never seems to go even in the face of undeniable evidence).

CHAPTER 21:
THE CARBOHYDRATE-INSULIN
MODEL OF OBESITY:

Ah, insulin and carbohydrates (sugar)... two of the most fractious terms when it comes to discussing your religious-like dietary beliefs. This topic essentially ties up most of the low-carbohydrate and keto zealots out there who hate the argument of calories in vs. calories out. The need/desire to remove or blame an entire food group on the obesity epidemic seems to make about as much sense as it does that women can now have penises, but apparently, we live in a society that likes to confuse and keep us on our toes.

Firstly, we should probably address what insulin is for those of you who are unaware so that we can understand the rationale behind this model of obesity. Simply put, insulin is a hormone (chemical messenger) produced in the pancreas that allows cells to absorb glucose—a sugar— from the blood. The higher the level of glucose, the more insulin goes into production to balance sugar levels in the blood. The carbohydrate-insulin model puts the blame for rising levels of obesity on the processed, fast digesting carbohydrates that have flooded our diets during the low-fat diet craze. Diets are now heavily ladened with white bread, white rice, breakfast cereals, sugary drinks, sugary snacks, etc. It posits that the consumption of these carbohydrates raises insulin levels too high, and this produces hormonal changes that promote calorie deposition in adipose tissue, exacerbate hunger, and lower energy expenditure.[80]

There are even those who argue that you can gain fat while in a calorie deficit if you are eating carbohydrates because insulin drives obesity—it is not about calories but where they come from. The rationale is that insulin (the hormone that shuttles glucose into cells) drives fat gain and obesity because of its inhibition of lipolysis and fat oxidation. If this hypothesis were true, we would see this represented in any human studies done looking at sugar or carbohydrate consumption. Unfortunately for these low-carb zealots, the opposite is true.

They will usually say higher fat diets burn more fat, but that is because they are consuming more fat, so of course you will be burning more fat as it is more available, but this doesn't mean you will lose more fat. You see, they ignore one side of what is essentially the body fat equation. Our body fat is governed by fat storage minus fat oxidation (burning). Because a diet that consumes more fat will burn more fat, it will also have more fat to store as well. A higher carb diet will burn less fat but will also have less fat to store (interestingly, when actually studied using metabolic tracer studies of the fat that winds up in adipose tissue, over 98% of it comes from dietary fat, and less than 2% comes from dietary carbohydrates[81]).

The body is always simultaneously burning and storing fat, and the rates of both of these determine the net gain or loss. What makes the difference is total calories. What do we see when calories are equal in diets? A meta-analysis by Kevin Hall of 32 controlled feeding studies where calories and protein were identical but fat and carbohydrates quantities varied showed that there were virtually no differences in fat loss between diets that were high in carbohydrates vs. those low in carbohydrates when calories and protein were identical.[82] In fact, one study— where participants were either fed a high carbohydrate baseline diet or a ketogenic diet (calories and protein matched)—found that following the high carbohydrate diet was more effective at inducing body fat loss than the reduced carbohydrate diet, which flies directly in the face of the carbohydrate-insulin model of obesity.[83]

There are even studies that vary the sugar content. One study I found wanted to compare the effects of high vs. low-sucrose, low-fat, hypo-energetic diets on a variety of metabolic and behavioural indexes in a six-week weight-loss program.[84] Both the high and low sucrose diets contained the same number of calories with 11% of energy as fat, 19% as protein, and 71% as carbohydrate. The high-sucrose diet contained 43% of the total daily energy intake as sucrose, and the low-sucrose diet contained 4% of the total daily energy intake as sucrose. If sugar and spiking insulin drove obesity, you would expect to see greater weight loss in the low sucrose group, right? However, the results did not show this, and they concluded: "that a high sucrose content in a hypo energetic, low-fat diet did not adversely affect weight loss, metabolism, plasma lipids, or emotional affect". This roughly translates for everyone who doesn't read PubMed articles every day, that when calories are the same and you are in an energy deficit, the level of sugar did not negatively impact the participants' ability to lose weight.

Have you heard of a man called Walter Kempner MD? This man is the creator of what is called the Rice diet. Kempner's Rice Diet began at Duke University in North Carolina in 1939. The treatment was a simple therapy of white rice, fruit, fruit juice, and sugar. The rationale was that by altering a person's diet and lifestyle, they could reduce the work the kidneys needed to do and could save the lives of those with malignant hypertension and renal failure. Why is this relevant? Well, not many diets are as high in carbohydrates or sugar as this. What is interesting is that in a study of 106 massively obese patients, by following the rice/reduction diet, in combination with exercise and motivational enhancement and under daily supervision, they were able to lose at least 45 kg. The average weight loss was a massive 63.9 kg.[85] Now, I'm not recommending this diet, but considering it's very high in sugar, if calories didn't matter and only insulin, then why were participants able to lose so much weight?

Hopefully, we are beginning to see the flaws in this argument. What's interesting is that even in overfeeding studies, it appears that, for the most part, there is no meaningful difference between overfeeding on a high-carbohydrate or high-fat diet.[86]

If we are blaming sugar, we would assume that sugar intake would have increased hand in hand with obesity rates, sounds fair. And yes, sugar intake has increased over the last hundred years. However, a very interesting study called the Australian Paradox[87] found the existence of an inverse relationship between trends in the prevalence of obesity in adults and children, where it experienced a three-fold increase in obesity rates yet the consumption of refined sugar over the same time frame declined by 16%. The findings directly challenge the assumption that increasing sugar consumption is to blame. If insulin was to blame, then surely as we decreased refined sugar intake, we should see a decrease in obesity rates, not the numbers tripling.

I would suggest the final nail in the carbohydrate-insulin model of obesity is that of Semaglutide. You may have heard of this, hailed as the most effective pharmaceutical obesity treatment on the market. Why is this the final nail in the coffin? Well, Semaglutide binds to and activates the GLP-1 (glucagon-like peptide-1) receptor to INCREASE insulin secretion, suppress glucagon secretion, and slow gastric emptying. You see, if the insulin model was correct, how would a drug that increases insulin secretion lead to weight loss when they blame increased insulin on obesity? This is another direct contradiction. Semaglutide use improves insulin sensitivity in the long run, and that is because it helps patients lose weight.[88]

Some arguments can be made that insulin can increase appetite. This is a weak claim, however, I would agree that high-sugar, heavily processed foods like Haribo sweets, for example, are usually very unsatiating, so you can overeat them. However, it is usually the case that heavily processed foods are high in both sugar and fats, so it is quite rare that someone who is eating a diet high in heavily processed foods is eating only a lot of carbohydrates but low-fat levels. And so, this claim that insulin is making you overeat is actually incorrect. When we look at studies in controlled settings, if insulin did indeed increase hunger, we'd expect to see people eat more on higher carb diets than lower carb diets, but the exact opposite was observed in recent studies, comparing ad libitum food intake in high carb diets vs. low-carb diets.[89] The researchers concluded that *"Exposure to the low-fat diet resulted in significantly lower ad libitum energy intake compared to the low-carb diet, potentially due to its lower energy density and greater fibre content".*

Insulin increasing appetite also, from a mechanistic standpoint, doesn't really make sense since insulin secretion usually increases leptin secretion, which is the satiety hormone. Furthermore, some studies show that when insulin was administered, it actually decreased energy intake in humans (and rats, but we want to focus on the human studies... a concept lost on most insulin/keto zealots).[90],[91]

Okay, I said the final nail, but I just thought of another. If insulin was the cause of obesity, what if I told you that protein is quite insulinogenic? In fact, a very famous study showed that protein-rich foods induced as much insulin secretion as did some carbohydrate-rich foods, e.g., beef was equal to brown rice and fish was equal to grain bread.[92] So, if protein increases insulin secretion, then according to the insulin zealots, we would expect that high-protein diets would cause you to gain weight. BUT... drum roll, please (not sure that works when it is written, but hey, I tried), there is no evidence to suggest that high-protein diets cause you to gain weight when calories are equal. In fact, due to protein-rich foods usually increasing satiety, having a higher thermic effect, preserving muscle mass, and actually improving glycaemic control, they are usually associated with improvements in body composition.[93],[94]

While people can lose weight without tracking calories using low-carb/ketogenic diets, the simple act of not tracking calories does NOT mean those people aren't restricting calories. It does not mean energy balance no longer matters or calories don't matter. It is a form of restriction, that is all, it is not some magical formula. It still works the same way a higher-carb diet would work if used for weight loss, and that is by creating a calorie deficit. Insulin and carbohydrates aren't the devil. It is IMPOSSIBLE to gain weight in a calorie deficit. If you gained weight, then by definition, you are not in a deficit or have calculated your deficit wrong (which also means you are not in a deficit). If, for example, you have low thyroid hormones (hypothyroidism), this can indeed make it more difficult to lose weight due to it reducing your BMR, but that does not mean you won't lose weight in an energy deficit, it just means your deficit will be lower than predicted. You see, still within the realms of energy balance.

The people who follow low-carb/ketogenic diets often report amazing and fast results. This is simply due to the initial reduction in water weight caused when you cut your carbohydrates. For every 1g of carbohydrates stored as glycogen, around 3g of water is stored. When our glycogen stores become depleted (when we reduce our carbohydrate intake), we will immediately see a loss in scale weight due to a loss in water weight—this is not body fat though. Body fat is only lost by being in an energy deficit or, as we have established, a calorie deficit since it means the same fucking thing.

CHAPTER 22:
IS OMEGA-6 TO BLAME? SEED OILS ARE THE DEVIL

I n a similar vein of demonising carbohydrates and blaming sugar for the obesity problem, there is another camp of people who like to demonise seed oils or essentially omega-6 as the underlying cause for obesity. While I take offence to anyone telling me not to drink oat milk in my coffee because of a little canola oil, I feel like it is worth trying to understand their argument, even if it will more than likely uncover that these "experts" are just spouting more shit.

Ideally, and throughout our history, the ratio of omega-3 to omega-6 within our bodies would have been between 1:1 to 1:4 (that's four times more omega-6 to omega-3). However, since the creation of the Western diet, where we moved away from fresh whole foods (shock) towards processed, longer-lasting foods filled with differing nut/seed/ vegetable oils, we have seen this ratio transition to between 1:20 to 1:50 in some Westernised cities. This change in the composition of fatty acids parallels a significant increase in the prevalence of obesity. So, I guess not a massive stretch to suggest that X (increase in omega-6 in our diets) is causing Y (increase in obesity). I mean, again, somehow this argument completely neglects *energy in vs. energy out*, but who knows… maybe this is what we have been getting wrong all this time.

Before concluding this though, it is always worth seeing what the evidence says rather than just assuming correlation proves causation. What I think is worth doing is first explaining what omega-6 fatty acids are, where they are found and what the research says before shitting on another food group. Bit boring, I know doing your due diligence, but if you wanted to read a book that butchers what the evidence says, just look for the word biohacker, or fasting expert on Instagram, and I have no doubt you will find a book more your speed.

Omega-6 fatty acids belong to a group of unsaturated fats known as polyunsaturated fatty acids (PUFAs). Omega-6 fatty acids are also essential, so you need to obtain them from your diet. Linoleic acid is one of the most common forms, while arachidonic acid and gamma-linolenic acid are also omega-6s. Some good food sources of these PUFAs are walnuts, pine nuts, almonds, cashews, sunflower seeds, peanut butter, and tofu. Most of the omega-6s that appear in our diet are usually from oils like sunflower oil, grapeseed oil, corn oil, soybean oil, avocado oil, safflower oil and canola oil.

The rapid increase of omega-6s in our diet came from the government's push to reduce saturated fat intake in our diets and instead replace them with vegetable oils that were considered healthier and protective of the heart. Vegetable oil consumption skyrocketed from 15lb/year in 1970 to over 60lb/year in 2009—a rise of 300%. It is important to note that this also led to a rise in the total amount of fat consumed as a whole (63% rise from 1970-2005).

Now, despite the correlation between increased consumption and a rise in obesity, I can't for the life of me find any strong evidence suggesting that we can blame obesity on an increase in omega-6s alone. I was even googling and actively searching for evidence shitting on omega-6s (especially canola consumption), and honestly, other than some misguided nutrition experts trying to twist the data to fit their narrative, the evidence is weak at best.

The argument I seem to keep stumbling across is that getting too much omega-6 increases the risk of chronic inflammation, which can lead to obesity (their logic, not mine). While linoleic acid isn't inflammatory, the body converts it to arachidonic acid, a building block for inflammatory compounds. This theory was reinforced by studies, predominantly in lab animals[95] (shock horror). With increased inflammation in the body, this increases TNF-alpha (inflammatory molecule), which acts to block the action of leptin (the hormone that tells us to stop eating), leading to leptin resistance, which is linked with obesity.

Firstly, only a small amount of the linoleic acid we eat (about 0.2%) turns into arachidonic acid, and not all of the compounds it produces cause inflammation. If linoleic acid or omega-6s did increase inflammation in the body, we would expect human studies to support this, right? However, this is just not the case. In one meta-analysis I found, it was concluded that increasing dietary linoleic acid intake does not have a significant effect on the blood concentrations of inflammatory markers.[96] And another paper stated, 'Studies in healthy human adults have found that increased intake of arachidonic acid or linoleic acid does not increase the concentrations of any inflammatory markers'.[97] Finally, in an analysis of 30 prospective studies, scientists found that higher levels of LA were significantly associated with lower risks of total cardiovascular disease, cardiovascular mortality, and ischemic stroke, while arachidonic acid levels were not associated with higher risk of cardiovascular outcomes; in a comparison of extreme quintiles, higher levels were actually associated with lower risk of total cardiovascular disease.[98]

Not exactly evidence to support this claim that omega-6s increase inflammation. You know what does increase inflammation though? Oh, yes, that's right... being overweight does as adipose tissue actually increases inflammation in the body. (*Obesity is currently presented as a pro-inflammatory state with an expansion in the outflow of inflammatory cytokines, such as interleukin-6 (IL-6) and tumour necrosis factor-alpha (TNF-⍺).*[99]) They seem to have mixed up the cause-and-effect parts of their argument. If someone is in a state of energy balance and remains that way (healthy weight), then omega-6s will not increase inflammation.

The next argument is that omega-6s can decrease the sensitivity of the cell wall to insulin in muscles and leptin in the brain. Higher insulin and leptin levels again increase your risk for obesity. Again, if we are to dive into the research, we would expect to see increased omega-6 intake would, therefore, be linked to type 2 diabetes, however, again, this just isn't the case.[100], [101] In fact, in one meta-analysis where they summarised findings of 102 randomised controlled trials, including a total of 4,660 participants, which provided meals varying in the types and levels of fat and carbohydrate to study participants and evaluated how such variations affected various measures of blood glucose control, insulin sensitivity, and ability to produce insulin. *The findings suggest exchanging dietary carbohydrate with saturated fat does not appreciably influence markers of blood glucose control. On the other hand, substituting carbohydrate and saturated fat with a diet rich in unsaturated fat, particularly polyunsaturated fat, was beneficial for the regulation of blood sugar.* [102]

A direct retort to the claims then that omega-6 increases insulin resistance, leading to obesity. It baffles me that people either try to misinterpret what the actual data says or make claims without actually assessing what the evidence first says. This goes back to the religious element of nutrition where people choose what to believe and ignore facts or the underlying fact that it is huge business, and actually telling people to eat a balanced diet doesn't really grab headlines or drive sales, so making bold statements like, "Why your oat milk is making you fat", (yes, I won't let that go… still angers me now that these tits are able to put out content like this on Instagram and TikTok, which can reach millions of people and impact their dietary practices... anyway, more about this later).

The final argument they make is that omega-6 fatty acids act as a precursor to endocannabinoids, which are signalling molecules that stimulate the cannabinoid receptors located in the brain. The effect of stimulating the cannabinoid receptor when you smoke weed is an elevated mood, and if the dose is high enough, you may experience feelings of euphoria as well (I can honestly say that I am not writing this from personal experience but instead taking it from a book as my own experience with the two times I have tried weed have not been pleasant at all... but I digress). Most people then go on to experience a sudden increase in appetite. When food has eventually been eaten, the feeling of pleasure from the food is usually enhanced.

So, when our omega-6 ratios are massively elevated, this produces an excess of endocannabinoid messengers and the system becomes chronically over-stimulated. This is not to say people eating processed food will walk around cheerful and stoned (trust me, the people sat in the McDonald's by my house are rarely in a good mood, although judging by their mental faculties, they might be stoned, or at least I hope so), but, as the same system is being continuously stimulated over time, the more our appetite and the weight-regulating system will be switched towards a system of weight gain.[103]

While I am not going to argue with this, I think that this is focusing on the wrong part of the argument. Foods like walnuts, pine nuts, almonds, cashews and tofu are high in omega-6, yet most people who have a diet rich in these are unlikely to then be overstimulating this endocannabinoid system as a result. The ones we do see an increase in appetite are the ones overconsuming heavily processed foods that combine sugar, fat and salt. Demonising omega-6 because it is found in heavily processed foods is like demonising me because I'm a white man, therefore, I must be privileged, racist and misogynistic. You can't make this assumption (or at least you shouldn't). The evidence clearly shows that omega-6s are healthy as part of a balanced diet. Obviously, if you are taking in too much omega-6 because you are eating too much fried, ultra-processed foods, you are likely to be unhealthy/overweight because your diet is very micronutrient-poor and will contain too many calories. But it is a calorie/energy problem, not an omega-6 issue.

I am always advising my clients to increase their intake of omega-3s in their diet to help improve many health markers that omega-3s provide, it will also help improve our ratio of 6 to 3 in the body, which will be a better approach than demonising omega-6s. Having said that, we can remove most of the unnecessary omega-6s from our diet just by decreasing the amount of heavily processed foods we eat. A message that seems to hold true for most of the health topics I write about... and is obviously key when it comes to a topic like weight loss.

In the interest of providing information and looking at improving health, I would add this (although, again, this is mostly concerned with ultra-processed fast foods, and as we have established, we should reduce those as much as we can), the bigger concern with seed oils or oils, in general, is when you heat them up time and time again. When you bring unsaturated fats repeatedly to high temperatures, you'll get a build-up of free radicals, increasing oxidative stress in the body. The main problem is restaurant and factory deep-fryers are changed infrequently, making these foods significantly more toxic for the body. This does not mean cooking with seed oils at home is an issue as we are not reusing the oil (a note these zealots fail to mention).

CHAPTER 23: IT'S NOT ME, IT'S MY METABOLISM

Does how we perceive others or how we perceive ourselves influence who we become? Johann Wolfgang von Goethe once said, "If you treat an individual as he is, he will remain how he is. But if you treat him as if he were what he ought to be and could be, he will become what he ought to be and could be".

It might make sense then when people blame their genetics or other factors on their inability to lose weight that, actually, they are making it immediately harder just by having this mindset. Let's take this example as I'm sure we have all either said this or heard someone say it before: "I used to be able to eat what I wanted to when I was younger, but now that I'm getting older, my metabolism has slowed down. I just put on weight". We can hear from this statement that their mindset is one that says, *"It's not my fault, it's because I'm getting older".* They are either trying to excuse themselves for having put on weight or at least trying to convince themselves that this is why they haven't been able to lose the weight they want, so why bother trying. They have accepted this new reality.

We need to look at changing this paradigm. Contrary to the popular belief that metabolism slows in middle age, research suggests that energy expenditure does not change until close to the age of 60, when it starts to slow down. In fact, the research concluded that adult expenditures (20-60), adjusted for body size and composition, are remarkably stable, even during pregnancy and postpartum. After 60, there was a progressive decline in total daily energy expenditure/BMR, even when corrected for losses of fat-free mass and fat mass, but this decline was relatively slow at approximately 0.7% per year up to the age of 90. Those 90+ years of age adjusted total expenditure was ~26% below that of middle-aged adults.[104]

What this roughly translates to is... sorry, that old excuse actually doesn't track when we look at what the evidence actually says.

So, why do so many of us find that we are putting on weight as we age?

Well, simply put, for most people, they simply move less. If we look at the normal office worker who is sat at a desk from 9 to 5, it is likely he/she/they (yes, we are inclusive in this book) is walking less, playing less sports and generally moving a lot less than they were doing in maybe their teenage years or early 20s (one reason we advise many clients to start actively paying attention to their step count and making a conscious effort to increase it). This reduction in activity level plays one role. Research has actually demonstrated that elderly people stand and walk significantly less than young people, leading to significant reductions in calories expended via non-exercise activity thermogenesis (NEAT), and exercise activity.[105]

If we also remember that muscle is more metabolically active, we can start to understand that if we are able to maintain muscle as we age (through resistance training and a high-protein diet), we can prevent or at least slow down the gradual decline of muscle mass and prevent sarcopenia (the loss of muscle mass specifically related to ageing), which can help prevent this gradual decline in metabolic rate.

So, from a reduction in general activity level to a reduction in muscle mass, we can see why our metabolism may slow down if the right lifestyle choices aren't put in place. The other point is that, for a lot of people, priorities change (work/family), bad dietary habits can start to creep in without realising it. Imagine you now have kids and are having to cook something quick for them and at the end of the day, instead of making yourself a nice roasted veg dish, its quicker and easier to keep the kids happier by banging a couple of pizzas in the oven, and well, fuck it, you're tired and stressed… let's have a glass of wine to treat ourselves. Very quickly, this becomes a few bottles of wine each week, impacting our sleep, food choices and waistline as a result. This is just one example, but you can see how quickly we can lose those good habits that kept our weight in check before without us realising it.

The point of this is not to shame you for that glass/bottle of wine or for making the easy choices for cooking dinner (as I can't begin to imagine how stressful looking after kids is…) but to explain that wherever you are now, you can make progress. You don't have to admit defeat to middle-aged weight gain. If we know that we can have a positive impact on our metabolism moving forward, we can be empowered to make the right decisions, we can create positive and healthy habits and we can switch the narrative. So, instead of blaming our genetics or our age, we can take back control and move forward with a spring in our step.

Maybe that starts with trying some quick healthy recipes for the family that are high in protein and lower in fat—maybe that's starting to make sure you are fitting in two to three resistance sessions a week to help improve your muscle mass instead of going for after dinner drinks at the pub with the boys most nights, maybe it's increasing your daily step count by walking the final two stops to your office rather than getting on the bus. I'm not suggesting you change your entire life, but change your mindset first and then start adding habits to this change that will lead you towards your goals. "To change ourselves effectively, we first have to change our perceptions".

I also think the biggest flaw in the old slow metabolism argument is that research has demonstrated that both obese and obese with type 2 diabetes have similar or greater metabolic rates compared to lean people.[106],[107] If your metabolism being slow was why you had an obesity problem, you would expect to see the opposite. One study I found titled 'Does basal metabolic rate predict weight gain?' concluded that *"Adults with low BMRs did not gain more weight than did adults with high BMRs, implying that habitual differences in food intake or activity counterbalance variations in BMR as a risk factor for weight gain in a typical Western population".*

So, if we can't blame our metabolism slowing down, what can we look at blaming next?

CHAPTER 24: I'M IN A DEFICIT AND CAN'T LOSE WEIGHT

Before we come to the final part of this book, where I will discuss what to do as it were in order for you to achieve long-lasting weight loss, it is worth just going over this final point one last time. You see, we have all heard that one friend who claims they are in a deficit and can't lose weight, and it is because of this sentence or dilemma that people usually veer off into the blame game… oh, it's my hormones, or I have a slow metabolism. The thing is, this is just again a simple misunderstanding of the problem presented—if you are in a caloric deficit, then by definition, you will lose weight (you have to give this enough time… we aren't suddenly skinnier at the end of one day fasting… although we may weigh less if there is no food now in our system).

If we compare energy balance to a savings account, simply put, if I am spending less money than I am making, my savings account will increase (assuming you put it into a savings account)… it's simple maths (unless I get robbed). Then, if this continues for a month, at the end of the month, I will have a healthier-looking savings account… FACT. The opposite is also true. If I start spending more money than I am making, I will have to go into and withdraw from my savings account… if this continues for a month, my savings account will be depleted as a result (yes, I am assuming you have a savings account… otherwise, okay, I have built up debt… thanks for trying to complicate the analogy). You see, we can't escape this simple fact, you can try and muddy the water by talking about interest rates or taxes, but when we boil it down, it is quite simple: more money coming in than going out equals more money saved.

When we talk about energy in vs. energy out, hopefully, having read up until this point, we now understand that there is a lot more to this equation than just food and exercise as things like hormones, macronutrients and even your gut microbiome can impact the *energy in* or the *energy out* part of the equation. BUT… it is still part of the fucking equation. The fact that this confuses people is more a glaring indictment of the forever-dropping IQ levels of the general population and not because we suddenly evolved to operate outside the laws of thermodynamics. If my hormones cause me to have an increase in appetite, then guess what? I increase the energy I take in… if my gut microbiome causes me to extract more calories from the foods I eat, then guess what? That impacts how much energy I take in. Yes, we have confused the topic of weight loss, but at its core, it is really quite simple. Hopefully, you understand this, although hopefully you also understand that there are personal complexities to everyone's weight loss journey. Hence, I try to steer you away from just blanket prescribing people to eat less and move more.

Now that I've got that rant out the way, I think it is important to explain more clearly the common reasons why someone will make the statement, "But I'm eating in a calorie deficit and can't lose weight".

Let's assume the example of Kate, a 30-year-old from Brighton who is struggling to lose weight. Over the last six years, she has repeatedly gained weight over the colder months, only to find herself unhappy with her body image as it gets to around April each year. In a desperate attempt to get ready for the summer holiday to Ibiza with the girls that they always go on, she goes into an extreme diet one month prior to the holiday in order to shift the 4-5kg she's gained since last year. Every year, this becomes progressively harder as Kate has found that her weight has been creeping up incrementally—five years ago, it was just 1kg she wanted to lose, and now it's four. Kate usually tracks calories only when dieting and uses an online calorie calculator to work out her calorie target. This year, she types in her new weight and is given her deficit calorie level to be 1,600 calories. Kate begins tracking, and to her dismay, after two weeks, she hasn't lost any weight! Why is this?

Reason 1: If you are the product of three or more crash diets or yo-yo dieting culture, then it is more than likely that your metabolism is operating at a lower-than-predicted level. This means the 1,600 calories that the calculator gave to Kate was not, in fact, her calorie deficit.

Remember, when we calculate your calorie targets, it is a guide. Using different equations, we can get a fairly accurate idea, however, it is not an exact science. Because of Kate's history of yo-yo dieting, we could have guessed that her metabolic rate was now more efficient (so as to prevent future weight loss) and, therefore, her deficit calories would need to be lower. So, she is not actually in a deficit. If we were to drop her calories more, having adjusted for this metabolic adaptation, putting her in a deficit, then she would lose weight.

(This is also the reason why health conditions like PCOS or women who are perimenopausal might need to adjust their deficit calories to lower than the predicted level of most calorie calculators. You can still lose weight with these conditions, but your deficit might be lower than predicted due to hormonal and lifestyle factors.)

Reason 2: Okay, so we recalculated Kate's adjusted deficit calories and she's still not losing weight. The most common reason why this is not working is that you aren't tracking your food intake properly. You see, in order to be in a deficit, we do actually need to know how many calories we are eating (shock). Now, I know that tracking calories has inaccuracies, I have written about it, so I'm not saying it is 100% accurate. Remember, we don't want to confuse accuracy with precision. Just because the act of tracking isn't 100% accurate doesn't mean it doesn't work. Once we have worked out our calorie deficit and have started tracking, if we are not losing weight, one of the main reasons I usually find is that people are miscalculating or not tracking their food accurately, or just forgetting to track. How easy is it to grab a handful of almonds as a snack and forget to track? Oh well, it was only about 12 almonds, that won't really matter (100 calories not tracked... assuming they haven't got a gut microbiome that extracts even more calories from the almonds). What about the few teaspoons of olive oil you used for your stir fry and didn't track (120 calories)... or the little splash you had of milk in your four teas and two coffees. These are just little examples... but it is very easy for these to add up quite quickly to take you out of your deficit.

Say Kate isn't losing weight at 1,500 calories but that's because, unknowingly, she is actually taking in 1,800 calories (through miscalculation). She decides to drop her calories a little lower in order to see weight loss. She starts tracking her calories at 1,200 now. Unknowingly, she is still taking in 1,500 calories as she is still miscalculating her food intake, but her miscalculated level now is actually bringing her to her actual deficit calories. And guess what? She loses weight!

There are other examples like the weekend warriors, who are strict through the week only to binge on the weekends, never to make any progress despite being in a deficit five days of the week. Well, if we look at their total calorie intake for the week, we see that they actually ate at maintenance or above, thanks to their weekend indiscretions. So—shock horror—it is again easily explained by the energy balance system.

You see, we can explain why without just going, "Oh well, this means calorie deficits don't work". This is a ridiculous reaction when we think about it. It would be like my car breaking down, and instead of taking it to a mechanic to see what was wrong, just scrapping it because cars don't work. While cars drive past you as you walk to work, you mutter to yourself, "Well, cars don't work for me... it's because of my genetics". You see how ridiculous this is, although it is made more believable because there will inevitably be some cunt on Instagram called @ CAR_CUNT.MD who blames big pharma for getting us addicted to cars, and that you should buy his eBook on "Walking with nature" or some shit like that.

Look, being in an energy or calorie deficit is the only way to lose weight... FACT. If you aren't losing weight then it is because you aren't in a deficit. Either because the calculated deficit is wrong or because you are not accurately tracking the calories consumed. But I'm sorry to say, we can't escape it. Even with all the complexities of weight loss that I have explained throughout this book, whether genetics, gut microbes, stress, macronutrients or hormones, they all still work within this energy balance. Even all the psychological reasons for why you aren't losing weight still operates by impacting your energy balance.

Remember, energy balance doesn't care if your food intake is "healthy", "organic", "natural" or whatever bias you want to dress it up in. Yes, if it is higher in fibre or protein, it will impact the *energy out* part of the equation. Yes, if it has less pesticides in it, it's probably better for your health in the long run... but in terms of weight loss and calories in, it doesn't matter. Ignoring our friend, the energy balance, is like ignoring contraception when having sex... it's your choice, but don't come crying to me when you fuck up your life.

"Oh, I eat intuitively and it's all healthy foods". When a client says a statement like that to me, what I usually do is ask them to run through a typical day of eating so I can get an idea of their food habits and suggest potential changes. What usually follows is... hmm, how to explain this... okay, imagine that wanky Instagram fitness influencer you follow who thinks it's helpful to post a 'full day's eating video', then imagine someone narrating that back to you—that's usually how that conversation goes... followed by the, "I don't understand where I'm going wrong". Without again going into the million reasons why this isn't best serving them and refraining again from calling them an idiot, it is worth mentioning that if we aren't in any way aware of how many calories we are taking in on a daily basis and we are unhappy with how much body fat we have, it probably means we are (drum roll, please) consuming too many fucking calories for our current lifestyle.

Hopefully, this is now beyond a reasonable doubt, although just like some people believe Earth is flat, I have no doubt there will be some who continue to blame artificial sweeteners, seed oils, dairy or sugar for the obesity epidemic. What I have hopefully done is give you the tools/knowledge to either correct them or the good sense to ignore them.

Now, the part of the book where I give you some direction on what to do...

PART 6: WHAT TO DO

The conclusion in a PubMed article titled "Regulation of Food Intake, Energy Balance, and Body Fat Mass: Implications for the Pathogenesis and Treatment of Obesity" perfectly summed up my aim for this part of the book, so I have extracted the exact conclusion verbatim and inserted it below so that you have this yourself. Hopefully, you can understand the recommendations included:

> *"If obesity involves the biological defence of an elevated level of body fat, as current evidence suggests, advice to simply "eat less, move more" cannot be expected to remedy the problem. This is because interventions that reduce body fat stores without a corresponding decrease in the defended level of fat mass elicit compensatory responses that promote the recovery of lost fat and are difficult to consciously override. Because these responses constitute perhaps the single largest obstacle to effective obesity treatment, breakthroughs in understanding the biological defence of elevated body fat mass may be required to enable the development of effective new obesity prevention and treatment strategies".*[108]

When I wrote that the diet that works is the one you can see yourself on forever, I mentioned that this doesn't mean we need to be in a deficit forever. What it means is that we still need to control/limit our increase so that we can help reduce/defend against our bodies' self-defence system. We also need to improve lifestyle factors that can help contribute to defending a higher metabolic rate. In the remaining chapters, I will go through the most important things you can do to help reduce the speed of the body's metabolic adaptation during a diet and help defend against the weight regain after a diet. Having explained this, I will then attempt to give you some actionable tips to use, however, I'm hoping having run through something like why resistance training is so important, I won't have to tell you to then add it—as that much will be obvious, even for the slower people out there. The tips I will provide, however, will be working on how to increase adherence and ways in which you can increase satiety or improve your relationship with food. By the end, hopefully, you can create your own personalised action plan and get started on creating a healthier, happier you.

CHAPTER 25:
RESISTANCE TRAINING

P art of me thinks it is the fear that many women have for resistance training (classic don't want bulky muscles scenario) that causes a disproportionate number of women to struggle more from the classic yo-yo dieting model I described above. Now, before you jump at me like, "Chris, there are so many other reasons like the pressure that the media put on women to be size zero, and social media, culture, femininity, etc". I am not saying it is the only reason, I am saying it is part of the reason. With many women avoiding resistance training, they are likely to have much lower levels of muscle mass and, therefore, their BMR is lower at their given weight.

I think many people also just view exercise as a way to burn calories. This is the first mistake, while exercise does make up a portion of our TDEE, it is usually a very small part. And actually, if we look to increase our energy expenditure by a significant amount by increasing cardio exercise quite often due to the adaptive nature of our metabolism, we will probably see a decrease in our NEAT as a result, and therefore, it doesn't actually increase our weight loss. As mentioned before, our bodies also become more efficient, hence the plateauing of weight loss for the average cardio bunny at the gym. The old saying less is more, or too much of a good thing sort of applies here, I feel. I'm not saying don't do cardio, I am just stressing that resistance exercise is the main tool in our weight loss belt and not cardio.

Viewing exercise as a way to burn calories is doing it a disservice anyway because it has so many other more important benefits, from improving sleep, gut health, bone density, mental health… etc. The reason we preach resistance training to everyone is to increase our muscle mass. Remember, this is more metabolically active tissue, so someone with more muscle will naturally have a higher BMR. While in a deficit we are not likely to be building muscle, what the resistance training will be doing is making sure we maintain what muscle mass we have, therefore, limiting the reduction in our BMR as a result of muscle loss. This point can't be stressed enough. The more muscle we hold onto during our deficit, the longer we are able to diet before metabolic adaptation causes us to plateau.

Systematic review and meta-analysis of 18 studies concluded that resistance training was effective at increasing resting metabolic rate, whereas aerobic exercise and aerobic and resistance combined were not as effective.[109] Resistance training, as we increase our calories, can also help traffic the excess nutrients away from energetically efficient storage mechanisms (our bodies are primed to store fat post-diet) and use them for other energy costly mechanisms, which decreases the likelihood of fat storage.[110]

Maintaining or increasing your exercise after your diet (calorie deficit) has come to an end has been demonstrated to prevent the increase in the number of fat cells we spoke about earlier as part of the body's self-defence system.[111] Exercise also increases your sensitivity to satiety hormones, which can prevent the inevitable increase in appetite during a deficit. Hopefully, you are beginning to see why resistance training is so important. Also, in general, people who regularly exercise typically have more discipline and better overall habits (although this is a generalisation, not a rule, there are quite a few people who come to my local gym that have just got bigger since I've known them, and they have been coming consistently for the last six years, so it is clearly not a fail-safe). Exercise is also important for helping maintain insulin sensitivity or improving insulin sensitivity in overweight people or, say, in women with PCOS who are likely to have some level of insulin resistance.

If we think about longevity (which we should), then resistance training is again a must. Maintaining your skeletal muscle is essential, not just for strength, power, and exercise performance, but for life. A 2022 study of 1,200 women and men aged 40 and older even found that skeletal muscle mass is a better predictor of mortality than BMI or fat mass.[112] I mention this because if resistance exercise is beneficial for our long-term weight management, and if we think about it, our ability to simply move also improves our ability to stay lean (think step count and NEAT), then surely being able to main-tain our muscle and bone density later in life is essential for our ability to move in our later years, which is essential not only for weight control but for quality of life. You will see the difference in older populations of those who have been able to stay active vs. those who haven't. I have seen 80 and 90-year-olds in the gym deadlifting, and who are able to get out of chairs unassisted, go for long walks, and play with their grandkids. Yes, there are a few things at play, but the main correlating factor is that they have stayed active and maintained greater muscle mass into their later years. In comparison, I have seen many people in their late 60s and 70s unable to get out of a chair without assistance, not because of any underlying medical issue—they are simply too weak to now support their own body weight. Having spoken to these people, again, there is a common theme—a lack of physical activity throughout their life.

There is obviously a crossover from the benefits of exercise to other factors that improve weight mainte-nance or weight loss. For example, we know that a lack of sleep can lead to increased fatigue and excessive daytime sleepiness, it can also impair the metabolic, endocrine, and immune systems. While I will talk more later on the benefits of sleep, it is important to note that exercise is associated with improvements in both sleep quality and quantity. One review of all the evidence concluded: "*We found strong evidence that both acute bouts of physical exercise and regular physical exercise improved sleep outcomes. Moderate evidence indicated that longer bouts of Physical exercise (both acute and regular) improved sleep, and that the effects of physical exercise on sleep outcomes were generally preserved across adult age groups and sex. Finally, moderate evidence demonstrated that physical exercise improved sleep-in adults with insomnia symptoms or obstructive sleep apnoea".*[113]

Based on the available studies, Charlene Gamaldo, medical director of Johns Hopkins Centre for Sleep at Howard County General Hospital, stated, "We have solid evidence that exercise does, in fact, help you fall asleep more quickly and improves sleep quality".[114]

Exercise can also help improve stress resilience, which can improve your sleep and reduce your risk for episodes of emotional eating. While evidence is a little all over the place as to why and by how much it helps (probably due to poor study designs), it is safe to say that regular exercise is frequently associated with general well-being and lower rates of mood and anxiety disorders in cross-sectional studies. The mechanisms underlying the benefits of exercise are not clear, but I think the cross-stressor adaptation hypothesis makes the most sense. Since intense physical activity is also considered a stressor since it increases heart rate, raises blood pressure, and increases levels of cortisol, the idea that activation of the stress response through exercise may produce beneficial adaptations so that the body is able to respond more effectively and efficiently to acute stress in the future, hence enhanced resilience to stress.

Anyway, in layman's terms, exercise also increases your production of endorphins—the brain's feel-good neurotransmitters. Sometimes referred to as a runner's high, you get a release of endorphins from any style of exercise really. It can also improve gut motility and, therefore, improve gut health, which can lead to an increase in serotonin production, further helping improve mood. Also, if we think about it from a vanity perspective, if I start training hard and I start to see progress, this is likely to improve my self-confidence, helping me relax and lower symptoms of depression and anxiety.

If you listed all the benefits of exercise, specifically resistance training, and you could bottle it into a pill, you would be richer than Elon Musk or Jeff Bezos easily. It would be the most sought-after drug in the world. The strange thing is, we have the ability to already get all those benefits if we just commit some time each week to making resistance training and exercise part of our lives.

"Oh, Chris, but I just don't have time..." You don't have time not to! I'm not telling you to become Arnold Schwarzenegger and live in the gym, I'm not prescribing three-hour workouts or hundreds of burpees. If you can commit to three resistance sessions a week, say 30 minutes each, that's an hour and a half as a minimum you need to commit. If there are 168 hours in a week, that's not even 1% of your fucking week (assuming I've done the maths right (1.5/168) x100= 0.89%).

"Oh, but I don't know what I'm doing..." Hire a coach? *"I can't afford one..."* Okay, hire an online coach? *"I don't want to do that..."* Well, go on YouTube and just follow a video along... there is more fitness content online than ever before. If anything good came from Covid lockdowns, it was the massive increase in the number of quality train-

ers creating fitness content for you for free to be followed online.

"*Oh, but I have dodgy knees...*" Then go swimming or see a physio and get a plan to rehab your injuries...

There is no reason not to... stop making excuses. Yes, some people will find it easier than others, and yes, some people have more responsibilities and commitments to take care of on top of everything else... but if you aren't taking at least 90 minutes a week to exercise for yourself, then it won't be long until you run into health complications that will make it a hell of a lot harder to continue to fulfil your already full list of commitments and responsibilities. If you have seriously read a weight loss book and expected that you wouldn't be told exercise is important, then you have probably been sniffing or smoking something you shouldn't. "*But Chris Tim Spector said exercise isn't important for weight loss!*" Yes, he did, and while I like the man and understand he was trying to flog his book so what better way to stand out than to say you don't need to exercise... he was, however, wrong. It's like people who say calories don't matter... they obviously do, but that doesn't exactly grab headlines. I know it's hard to see all the wood through the trees at times in this health and fitness space, but if you are concerned about long-term weight loss, weight maintenance and longevity, then some form of resistance exercise is essential no matter what you hear.

CHAPTER 26:
PROTEIN AND FIBRE

Before you open your mouth to eat anything, I always tell my clients, "Think protein and fibre". We need to get into the habit of structuring our meals around good protein sources, but this doesn't mean ignoring carbohydrates or fats. Hopefully, you realise by now I am against demonising macronutrients, but our focus should first be on where our protein is coming from, and then what fibre can be added to the meal. Let me explain why:

Remember when we were discussing the *energy out* part of the equation, I mentioned something called TEF or the thermic effect of food. This is the effect of actually using energy in order to get the energy out of the food we eat. Why is this important? Well, during a diet or after a diet, we are trying to increase the *energy out* part of our equation in order to improve weight loss or limit weight regain. Different foods require varying amounts of energy to be processed and digested. Generally speaking (and this is why we usually focus on these two when setting up diets), protein and fibre have the highest TEFs. Both of these also usually help to increase satiety, which, as you can imagine, is quite important when we are trying to control our appetites.

Let's start by looking at protein. Protein isn't just for getting jacked, although, yes, it is important, nay essential for the creation of new muscle. Protein is actually involved in nearly every process of the body, from making hormones, enzymes, transporters, improving recovery, and yes, stimulating muscle protein synthesis. Making sure we consume enough protein is essential for the anabolic reactions of our metabolism. You see, we need enough in order to have sufficient building blocks from which to synthesise new tissue. This is essential to remember as we are trying to increase our muscle mass or at least prevent the loss (catabolism) of muscle mass during a deficit. Sparing more muscle mass during a diet has been associated with decreased incidence of weight regain, as well as maintenance of metabolic rate. Winning.

Interestingly, the recommended daily allowance for protein in the States was based on what was needed to prevent protein deficiency. Since we are concerned about improving body composition, we can probably ignore these pitiful guidelines and go to what the research suggests is optimum when it comes to improving muscle mass, preventing catabolism in a diet, or reducing the risk of sarcopenia (muscle loss due to the ageing process). Honestly, without getting too sciencey (that's a word), I usually advise clients to aim for 2g per kg of bodyweight or their goal bodyweight (so, if I weigh 90kg or was 100kg but my goal is to be 90kg then, I would need to aim to consume 180g of protein #Quickmaths) as most people don't know their lean body mass, so getting into more complicated recommendations seems a bit of a moot point. Honestly, some studies I have found online go as far as using 4.4g per kg, which seems a bit extreme for me, and I think for the majority of people out there who are probably consuming closer to 0.8/1g per kg of body weight, this target would be stupid. It is probably better advice to get them to increase their intake slowly, aiming to try and reach 1.6-2.2g per kg over the course of a few months. Trust me, if you went from eating 60g of protein normally to 120g overnight, you are likely to run into some rather unpleasant digestive complications.[115]

High-protein diets have been demonstrated to be superior to low-protein diets with regard to fat loss, even when calorie intake was identical. This is most likely due to the increase in TEF of protein, which is around 30%, whereas carbohydrates are only at 6%-8% and fat at 2%-3%.[116] The higher the TEF, the more energy out we have in our equation. Further, as previously mentioned, high-protein diets have a greater satiating effect than low-protein diets.[117]

Because reductions in fat-free mass (essentially from a loss of muscle) during diet-induced weight loss typically account for about 1.2 of every 6kg of total weight loss, it is no surprise that resting energy expenditure or BMR decreases alongside most dietary practices. However, if you are on a higher protein diet, we should hope to see a smaller reduction in FFM and, therefore, a smaller reduction of resting energy expenditure while dieting. In one meta-analysis, I found that was of 24 randomised controlled trials, it compared high-protein diets (HPD) and standard-protein diet (SPD), both isocaloric energy-restricted diets (so the same calorie deficits for both groups).[118] Interestingly, despite the calories being the same, participants on the HPD diet produced greater reductions in weight, fat mass, and had lesser reduction in FFM and resting energy expenditure. Because diets were energy-matched, the relatively small difference in weight loss observed between diets was not surprising, however, there was still a significant 0.79kg greater weight loss produced with the HP diet. So, quite clearly, we can see that having a diet higher in protein not only favoured fat loss, but also helped reduce the metabolic adaptation that takes place alongside dieting. Remember, holding onto that muscle or increasing it is key to helping our long-term weight management goals.

To further illustrate the benefits of a higher protein diet, researchers have tested the theory that increasing the protein content while maintaining the carbohydrate content of the diet lowers body weight by decreasing appetite and spontaneous caloric intake. By comparing ad libitum calorie intake (meaning eating as much or as often as necessary or desired) with higher protein diets, researchers concluded that "An increase in dietary protein from 15% to 30% of energy at a constant carbohydrate intake produces a sustained decrease in ad libitum caloric intake that may be mediated by increased central nervous system leptin sensitivity and results in significant weight loss".[119] Essentially demonstrating that higher protein diets improve your satiety, so even when we aren't counting calories, a higher protein diet helped to increase participants' satiety, therefore, helping to reduce their overall calorie intake. I have already spoken about how diets full of ultra-processed foods have shown ad libitum increase in calories by up to 500 per day. It seems the reverse is true for increasing your protein intake in your diet. Great news for all you, *"I don't want to track my calories, it's triggering"*, people out there. Just focus on increasing your protein intake and this should help decrease your overall calorie intake (I mean, it should... don't challenge this because I guarantee there will still be people out there eating high-protein diets who are still overweight).

The researchers of one study noted, "Additional protein consumption results in a significantly lower body weight regain after weight loss, due to body composition, satiety, thermogenesis, and energy inefficiency, while the metabolic profile improves".[120] Do I really need to say more?

I would also suggest that women are made even more aware of the importance of protein in their diet as not only are women usually worse when it comes to protein intake (generalisation again, so don't bite my head off, but from what I tend to find in my work, women are usually the worst offenders when it comes to protein intake), but women's hormonal profile can make protein requirements that much more important. Let me explain... after ovulation and during the luteal phase (second half of your cycle), progesterone rises. This is important to note because progesterone breaks down protein (as well as carbohydrates and fats) to provide amino acids as the building blocks for the uterine lining. Therefore, you may want to increase your protein intake in times of elevated progesterone to mitigate those effects and maintain your muscle mass. Also, when women go through menopause and their oestrogen levels drop, they lose the anabolic stimulus that oestrogen helps provide. So, again, you may need more protein to pick up the slack as it were. Research also shows that, with age, you also need more protein to help offset the increased risk of catabolism that causes sarcopenia.

Finally, for all you *"Well, high-protein diets are bad for your kidneys or your bones"* idiots, let's just double-check what the literature says.

Now, since the kidneys are involved in nitrogen excretion, it has been theorised by some that a high nitrogen intake (protein) may cause stress to the kidneys (seems logical, I guess). Additionally, since low-protein diets are typically recommended to people who suffer from renal disorders, it makes sense to jump to the conclusion that high-protein diets can stress the kidneys… but just because something sounds good doesn't suddenly mean the science backs it up. I mean, the theory of fasted cardio sounds convincing, yet when we actually research it (in humans), we see that theory doesn't mean FACT. So, what happens when we test renal function of those on high-protein diets? Well, one study using both bodybuilders and well-trained athletes on diets up to 2.8g of protein per kg of bodyweight (well above the recommended amount) concluded, "It appears that protein intake under 2. 8 g.kg does not impair renal function in well-trained athletes as indicated by the measures of renal function".[121] In fact, a review looking at the effects of Protein Intake on Renal Function and on the Development of Renal Disease, concluded that, "Concerns about an adverse effect of high protein intake on renal function, and in particular on its decline with age, appear to be ill advised... there is no reason to restrict protein intake in healthy individuals in order to protect the kidney".[122] It is also probably worth noting that very low protein diets don't appear to be that beneficial when it comes to stopping the progression of chronic renal failure. Now, I'm not saying to ignore your doctors, but if protein was that stressful on the kidneys, surely you would see some improvements in chronic renal failure in subjects on very low protein diets. However, "Among patients with more severe renal insufficiency, a very-low-protein diet, as compared with a low-protein diet, did not significantly slow the progression of renal disease", it appears it doesn't... just saying.[123]

What about bone loss then? Well, since high-protein diets can cause an increase in calcium excretion, it again makes sense the theory that high-protein diets could lead to an increase in bone loss and maybe increase your risk of osteoporosis. Again, the theory sounds good but what does the evidence in humans actually tell us? Well, most of the evidence I could find seemed to suggest that higher protein diets were associated with improved bone mineral density scores, not with a decrease, so directly in the face of this stance.[124] While your calcium excretion might increase (although this is not always the case as some evidence suggests[125]), it appears that there is no evidence that this increased calcium loss is from your bones or the overall net calcium balance is affected. So, we can ignore this argument, and any arguments for liver damage, heart disease or diabetes are just moronic, and I won't waste any more of your time discussing it. Just eat your fucking protein!

Okay, let's talk fibre now...

Fibre, while technically a carbohydrate, acts quite differently in the body. You see, it is this portion of the carbohydrate that cannot be completely broken down by digestive enzymes. There are two types of fibre—soluble and insoluble—and it is worth including a mixture of both in your diets (luckily, most plant sources contain a combination of both, so don't stress on this too much). Fibre has many health benefits, from lowering cholesterol, improving blood glucose and insulin sensitivity, and gut motility. When it comes to weight loss, the TEF of fibre is similar to that of protein, so again, increasing the *energy out* part of our weight loss equation. Let's be honest, good sources of fibre (fruit and vegetables) all tend to be low energy dense foods, meaning that they add bulk to your meals without adding lots of calories. This can help with our satiety levels. One of the most effective methods of improving weight loss for my clients, especially those who like to feel full when they eat, is getting them to focus on low energy dense foods. This allows them to eat a larger quantity of food while reducing their overall calorie intake. In numerous studies conducted by Rolls et al., consuming low energy dense foods as a first course reduced the energy intake of the main course and of the entire meal. Serving large portions of chunky veg-etable soup at the start of a meal has been shown to increase satiety and reduce the total amount of calories you eat in your main meal by 20%. Having salad or fruit beforehand also reduced the number of calories in the main meal by 15%. Aim for 30g of fibre per day. More than this can lead to some gastrointestinal distress (con-stipation, bloating).

Fibre is also useful for helping promote bowel regu-larity, can improve the diversity of your gut microbiome (important for overall health), improve blood glucose control (reducing blood sugar spikes), regulate hormones (especially in women as it helps remove excess oestro-gen), reduces your risk for colon cancer… it even actually reduces your risk from all-cause mortality… so, from an overall health perspective, we need to eat more. Accord-ing to research, only 5% of people in the US meet the Institute of Medicine's recommended daily target of 25 grams for women and 38 grams for men. That amounts to a population-wide deficiency… but let's go back to weight loss for a second.

A large bowl of boiled spinach contains just 50 calo-ries, which is about the same as a nibble of cheese. Hope-fully, we can start to see that if we are smart with our food choices and add more fibre and low energy dense foods to our meals, we don't have to eat tiny portions that don't satiate us. You can still feel full on a diet. Let's try and get away from the mindset that dieting or reducing our calories has to mean eating tiny portions and feeling hungry the whole time. Bulking up your meals with more protein and fibre can help to increase the volume/size of the meal and, therefore, improve your satiety. In one study where participants were asked to either eat more low-density foods or to restrict portions, the ones who ate more low-density foods lost 23% more weight. Interestingly, this group also ate 25% more food by weight and reported feeling less hungry and greater satisfaction with their diet than the portion control group.[126]

If you were on a low calorie diet of say 1,500 calories and you only ate lean protein sources, lots of fruit and vegetables and wholefoods/whole grains, this is actually a lot of food. This could be a large portion of oats and a large mixed omelette of two whole eggs and four egg whites, a large chicken salad, a protein shake for a snack and a big serving of Bolognese in the evening (assuming you substituted some of the pasta for extra veg or some courgetti). This may even leave you with enough calories for that chocolate bar you've been craving and still be within your calories. If, on the other hand, you were to only eat ultra-processed foods, this might be a vanilla latte from Starbucks (253 kcal) and a small bowl of granola (350 kcal), leaving you feeling hungry, a bag of crisps for a snack (130 kcal), still leaving you hungry, a meal deal from the local supermarket with a rather unsatisfying cheese sandwich (350 kcal), another packet of crisps (130 kcal), and an orange juice for lunch (120 kcal). The subsequent sugar crash from this meal leaves you needing an afternoon pick-me-up, so you reach for some biscuits in the office (three Oreos = 159 kcal... although, let's be honest, you probably swallowed half the pack), and before you know it, you've hit 1,492 calories, so unless you are eating air for dinner, you will be going over your calories and probably still feeling hungry in the evening. So, fuck it... I can't do it—cue the feeling to reach for that sharing bag of Maltesers and inhale it yourself. You see, if you are smart with your food choices and think protein and fibre first, then those 1,500 calories can still go a long way. If you are not smart with your food choices, what might have started off as a good intention to lose weight will probably end you worse off than when you started.

Even if you are someone who doesn't want to track calories, then purely focusing on protein and fibre content of your meals can lead to improvements in body composition and calorie intake. In fact, instead of focusing on restriction and portion control and instead focusing on increasing your protein intake, and your intake of high-fibre, high water, nutrient-rich foods will help promote satiety and automatically help reduce overall calorie intake, meal frequency and cravings. I will be giving you more tips in terms of nutrition at the end of this book, but the focus on your diet should always start with "Think Protein and Fibre".

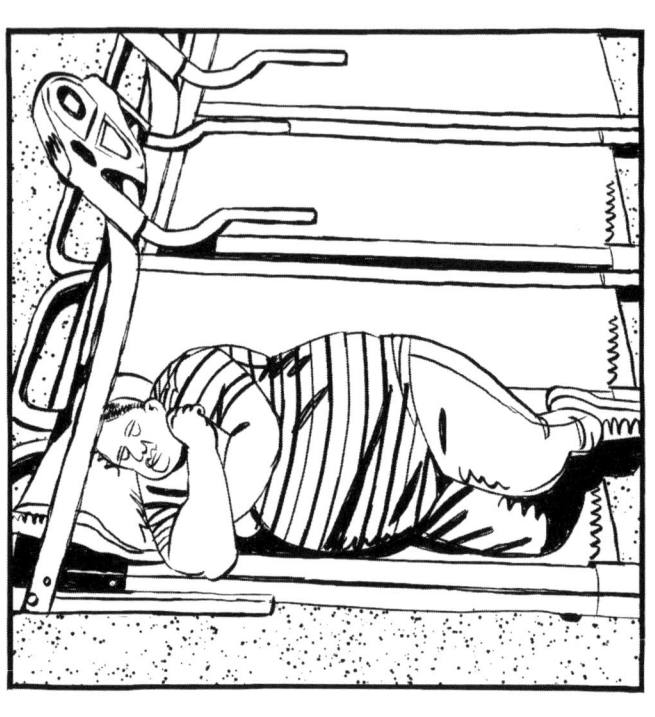

CHAPTER 27: SLEEP

Sleep: A duration of 7-9 hours of sleep a night is considered appropriate to support good health in adults aged 18 to 60 years. Due to the changing demands of work, social pressures and lifestyles, the advent of artificial lighting at the turn of the last century, and with more screens and electronic devices attached to us and spread throughout most rooms in the house, it is no surprise that the average sleep duration reduced from nine hours a night in 1910 to seven and a half hours in 1975, and today, the average—depending on what country you are looking at—is probably closer to six and a half.[127] In fact, in the US, more than one-third of adults sleep less than seven hours a night on average. The modernisation of our world seems to have come at a cost to sleep, and while that might not sound that bad, the health ramifications of this are far-reaching and quite pronounced. I am constantly bombarded by social media content where people are promoting waking up at four in the morning like that is the only way you can get ahead in life… apparently, losers sleep in past four. It seems the early bird doesn't just get the worm—he apparently gets rich as well. Although, unless he went to bed at nine, he's probably reducing his mental faculties, weakening his immune system and increasing his chances of becoming overweight... but that doesn't exactly roll off the tongue or increase your followers on Instagram.

Now, sleep is part of the weight loss puzzle that is often the most ignored. Let's be honest, in today's world, where people are more sedentary than ever, I feel like it almost seems counterintuitive to suggest that you should sleep more to help you lose weight. Also, if we were to believe the theory that we sleep to help conserve energy, it doesn't sound too illogical to suggest we should be moving more and sleeping less... well, maybe not the sleeping less part, but you can see why we don't often factor it into the equation. The focus is on calorie burn. A quick look at any social media platform won't take you long to find some influencer, fitness professional, or expert talking about burning calories and why we need to do x, y, and z in order to maximise your calorie burn. People are even selling tips on hacking your metabolism to burn more calories like we are some kind of computer or machine.

I was watching a podcast recently of the brilliant Mathew Walker, who is essentially Mr Sleep himself (if you haven't read his book, *Why We Sleep*, I suggest you do... and also, why haven't you already? Have you been living under a rock?). He was asked why his focus was on sleep and why he believes it to be so important. I loved the simplicity of his reply, so I will try and capture it here (although, I'm doing this from memory so I might be butchering what he said a little and I tend to waffle).

If you take anyone and remove either food, water, exercise or sleep from them for a 24hr period, which will have the most physical and psychological impact on the body? The answer is sleep, and it isn't even a close call. The immediate impacts of sleep deprivation on the body are quite pronounced, where we can definitely survive without exercise for a day (as so many seem to do by choice). Given the obesity epidemic, I think most people could go a lot more than just one day without food, and while I would never suggest going a day without drinking water, I think the general consensus is the rule of three. As in three minutes without oxygen, three days without water and three weeks without food. Okay, so oxygen is the most important for life, but compared to all the other things we seem to focus on in terms of food, water, exercise and sleep, it is true that the immediate impact from one night without sleep is a lot more pronounced than the others, so why is it often the footnote in conversations about health?

Let's pretend for a second you have no prior knowledge of why we lose or gain weight. Let's also pretend we haven't been conditioned to eat at certain times, but we eat solely when we are hungry, and we stop when we feel full. There are a number of different factors at play when we look at sleep deprivation and weight gain, but the first one I want to discuss is the relation between sleep and the two hormones that control our appetite—leptin and ghrelin. Yes, it's time to play blame-the-hormone game (but this time, men can do it too. See, no sexism here). Normally, leptin signals a sense of feeling full, so when circulating levels of leptin are high, our appetite is blunted. In contrast, ghrelin triggers the sensation of hunger. When ghrelin levels increase, so does your desire to eat.

If we were looking at this for the first time, it would make sense that if we had either low leptin levels or high ghrelin levels, we would be in a position where we would eat more than normal. Becoming super hungry (high ghrelin) or eating more as we wouldn't feel full (low leptin).

Dr. Eve Van Cauter developed an experiment in order to see the link between sleep and appetite. For one part of the experiment, participants were given an eight and a half-hour sleep opportunity each night for five nights, this was recorded with electrodes placed on their head. In the other part of the experiment, participants were only allowed four to five hours of sleep for five nights (again, measured with electrodes). In both parts of the experiment, participants were fed the same amount of food and had the same degree of physical activity. Each day, the sense of hunger and food intake were monitored, as were their circulating levels of leptin and ghrelin.

Dr. Cauter used a group of healthy, lean participants for the experiment, and what she discovered was that participants who were in the four to five-hour sleep group were far more ravenous. Interesting that when the food and the daily activities of a healthy individual hadn't changed but only the sleep length had, the same food that had kept them calm and full when they had gotten eight hours of sleep that night seemed insufficient when they had not... sound familiar? What was also interesting was that this happened rapidly, by just the second day of short sleeping, participants were complaining of being extremely hungry.

The results were two-fold. Inadequate sleep had not only decreased the concentration of leptin, but it had also increased the levels of ghrelin. So, essentially, participants were punished twice for the same offence of insufficient sleep. Okay, so sleeping less mutes the body's chemical messenger that says, "Stop eating", and increases the hormonal voice that shouts, "More food, please". But is feeling hungry and eating more the same? Do we actually eat more when sleeping less?

Again, we can thank Dr. Cauter for answering this question. She devised another study, however, this time, the participants were given free access to food rather than having their calorie intake pre-controlled. When participants were subjected to shorter sleep, they ate, on average, 300 calories more per day than when they were well-rested. While this does not sound like that much, imagine this happened every working night of the week (so, excluding the weekend and maybe a month off for a holiday), this would amount to roughly 69,300 calories extra per year... pretty sure that might add a few inches to your waistline.

What's interesting is that they also noticed that participants in the sleep-deprived group had higher levels of circulating endocannabinoids. Endocannabinoids, you probably guessed, are chemicals produced by the body that are very similar to the drug cannabis. Like marijuana use, these chemicals stimulate appetite and increase your desire to snack—welcome to the munchies, although, this time, it's brought on by a lack of sleep and not that massive joint.

So, a lack of sleep will affect our leptin and ghrelin and release chemicals that make us snack. Starting to understand why we may put on weight from a lack of sleep or at least struggle with our diet?

Another study done in 2012 found that individuals who are sleep deprived consumed on average 549 additional calories per day, and this was only an hour and 20 minutes of less sleep than the controlled non-sleep deprived group... that's a substantial difference—enough to take you from a deficit into a surplus.[128]

"But, Chris, if I'm awake longer, surely I will burn more calories by being awake?" Sadly, this just isn't the case, even in extreme examples where individuals were sleep deprived for a full 24-hour period, they only ended up burning an extra 147 calories compared to those who got a full eight hours of sleep in the same 24-hour period. Sleep is not as metabolically lazy as you might have thought. Remember, despite only making up roughly 2% of our total body weight, our brain actually accounts for 20% of the body's energy use and makes use of sleep in a number of ways, but not sure I need to get into that given the scope of this book.[129]

Also, if you think about any time you have had a really bad night's sleep, haven't you felt more tired? Probably more likely to cancel that gym session? It is quite common for people who have worse sleep to actually become more sedentary during the day. So, while it might seem rational at first glance to assume that if you are awake longer, you will surely move more, in reality, what we tend to find is quite the opposite.

To make matters even worse, sleep loss/deprivation can also change what we eat. Dr. Cauter noticed that cravings in her participants for sweets, carb-rich foods, and salty snacks all increased by 30%-40% when sleep was reduced by a few hours each night. (There have been studies done to show why, but without boring you with too much detail, essentially, when tired, our brain activity shifts from controlled decision-making to a more primal drive, resulting in a desire to consume more high-calorie foods.)

According to research done in 2013, a lack of sleep can directly impact your food purchases. The study analysed whether sleep deprivation could impair or alter your shopping habits. Fourteen men were asked to have one full night of sleep and then one night of no sleep. They were then presented with some food purchasing decisions. With a budget of $50, they were instructed to buy as much as possible from a list of 40 food items, which consisted of 20 high-calorie and 20 low-calorie foods. Before the task, they were all given an identical breakfast to make sure they weren't hungry going into the food purchasing task. The results showed that when participants were sleep deprived, they purchased 18% more food (by weight) and 9% more calories, compared with their purchases after a good night's sleep. It seems tired choices definitely tend to lean towards increased calorie density.[130]

But wait... it gets worse. I even found studies showing that reduced sleep (five and a half hours of sleep instead of eight and half hours of sleep) when in a calorie deficit decreased the amount of weight lost as fat by 55% and increased the loss of fat-free body mass by 60%! That's terrifying. If you remember from our above protein discussion, our ability to hold onto as much fat-free mass as possible is key to long-term weight management. So, even if you are able to stick to your calorie deficit, which will be a lot harder because of your increased hunger levels, you will more than likely lose less body fat and, instead, lose more muscle mass than if you had just got enough sleep. The study concluded, "The amount of human sleep contributes to the maintenance of fat-free body mass at times of decreased energy intake. Lack of sufficient sleep may compromise the efficacy of typical dietary interventions for weight loss and related metabolic risk reduction".[131] Really makes you think that while the government will occasionally bring out guidelines on how to eat healthier and how much exercise to aim for, why the FUCK have they never mentioned the importance of sleep?

Matthew Walker made a point on that podcast I was listening to, that in a capitalist society, sleep is the only time where we aren't producing or consuming anything, so it makes sense that governments and companies don't want to be pushing people to sleep more. While I don't want to hang too much on this idea, it does make you think about the clear lack of information and policy surrounding the importance of sleep. Even doctors—a profession that is designed to help improve the health of human beings (gender neutral term, although now you might label me as a speciesist)—seem to learn very little about sleep during medical school (insert emoji of the woman holding her hand out to the side like "I don't know").

Sleep deprivation also seems to be related to the elevation of cortisol, reflecting impairment of the HPA axis and resulting in glucocorticoid overload, which can lead to large deleterious effects on the body. We have already spoken about stress and the obesity problem, so I won't go back over it, so to save time, let's just say that sleep deprivation is a stressor for the body, working to increase cortisol levels and decreasing insulin sensitivity in the body—both of which are risk factors for obesity and diabetes mellitus, and again, works to increase your appetite for more calorie-dense foods.

So, from altering our hormones to increasing our appetite to changing the foods our brain craves, we can start to see how important sleep is and how it should be a part of any weight loss plan. If anyone remarks, "I will sleep when I'm dead", then just nod politely and walk away, you don't need that type of stupidity in your life.

To stress this point, there is even research showing that when it comes to long-term weight loss, improvements in sleep quality and quantity increase the likelihood of successful weight loss by 33%. In this study, they conducted an identical 24-month weight-loss trial in two groups of women who differed only on their sleep duration, either getting more than seven or less than seven hours of sleep. Both groups followed a multifaceted weight-loss program, including a reduced energy diet prescription, recommendations to increase physical activity, and behavioural counselling, including sleep modifications. A third control group received general weight-loss counselling from a dietetics professional alone. The study concluded that "The results of this study suggest that overweight/ obese women who enter a weight-loss program would have a higher chance of continued weight-loss success (at 6 months as well as later time points) if sleep quality is high and/or sleep duration averages 7 hours or more at the time of study enrolment".[132]

Interestingly, sleep and obesity have a bi-directional relationship. This means that poor sleep can not only help to increase your risk of obesity, but obesity can increase your risk of sleeping poorly. Several studies have indicated that obese individuals have a significantly higher chance of developing insomnia than their non-obese counterparts. And Obstructive Sleep Apnoea (OSA) is also highly correlated with obesity, with 70% of those with OSA being classified as obese. This bi-directional relationship only works to make both issues worse as you end up in a vicious cycle of weight gain, leading to poor sleep and poor sleep leading to more weight gain.

I will put some of my top tips to improve sleep at the end of this book in the Tip section, but hopefully, you now understand the importance of working on improving your sleep quality and quantity when it comes to achieving your goals of long-term weight loss and weight maintenance.

CHAPTER 28: ALCOHOL

Ah, where would a book on weight loss be without me writing a chapter shitting on your love of alcohol (one of the many reasons I feel I am usually uninvited from dinner parties). Well, I think most of you are already aware that alcohol isn't a dieter's best friend, but let me just explain why alcohol gets in the way of your weight loss goals. I want to stress the importance of reducing or removing alcohol from your life... HOWEVER, you can still enjoy a glass or two and reach your goals. I am against rigid and restrictive rules, which will inevitably make you miserable and probably give up your weight loss attempts. What we do need to learn is balance, and, if you are being honest with yourself, if you are looking to lose weight and are currently enjoying more than maybe five or six glasses a week, you could probably afford to work on that balance a little more. Also, stop trying to tell yourself that it's healthy because of articles you read in the Sun or the Mail with headlines like, "How that glass of red wine is keeping you young"... this is clickbait nonsense. The amount of resveratrol in red wine is about as good for you as the level of cyanide in almonds is bad for you.

At the simplest level, alcohol is quite calorie-dense, carbohydrates and protein are only four calories per gram, whereas alcohol is seven calories per gram. And this is just the calories from the alcohol, if you think of the amount of sugar usually contained in cocktails, alco-pops and other drinks, after two to three drinks, you are looking at the same number of calories as a meal. Thanks to a quick Google search, I can report the average pint of Larger, Bitters, Pale Ale contains roughly 180 calories (about the same number of calories in a slice of pizza), and let's be honest, how many of you lads... or ladies drink just the one? An eight-ounce glass of red wine will set you back around 190 calories, and depending on the white wine, it might set you back a little more or less (any wine connoisseurs out there, I'm talking average and not going into detail about the different varieties, so don't shoot me because your chardonnay or what-ever swill you're drinking is only 180 calories per eight ounces).

So, after an evening when you are done polishing off that bottle of red wine, you are looking at close to 620 calories and, come on, ladies, if you stick a romcom on or you go out for dinner with your girlfriends, you can easily polish off a bottle in one evening. Smirnoff Ice—that old reliable alcopop I used to enjoy when I was a fresh teenager—contained 245 calories and that included its 32g of sugar! You can quickly see that our enjoyment of alcohol can quite quickly lead to an increase in *energy in*. (There are complexities to how alcohol is metabolised and there appears to be a large individual variability due to genetics and drinking habits as to how much alcohol energy is available on an individual basis, but without getting into this, it is still safe to say alcohol increases the *energy in* part of our equation regardless of by how much…)

The research on this also suggests that the added increase in energy from alcohol appears to not be sensed by the body, in that consuming alcohol before or during a meal does not influence the amount of food eaten in that meal, despite increasing the energy density of the meal. Thus, individuals do not appear to compensate for the added energy from alcohol in the short-term, and alcohol appears to have little effect on satiety.[133]

It may actually have the opposite effect and stimulate food intake. I mean, we all know that a good session on the booze can work to lower our inhibitions, leading to poor decision-making. For some people, this might mean sleeping with the wrong person, or trying some drugs for the first time… for lots of us though, it might mean staggering into that questionable late-night food establishment that serves a dazzling array of greasy offerings, and despite the fact that you can guarantee they failed their most recent health inspection (despite proudly displaying a rather fake-looking A in the window), you don't care because their garlic mayonnaise is the best and you are going to drown your intoxicated brain in it. Sound familiar? I witnessed first-hand many people in the first year of university suddenly pack on weight as their intake of alcohol and late-night kebabs shot up (myself included). I think this phenomenon has become so common, it even has a name to it... something like the "Freshers Five" referring to the extra 5kg of fat people seem to be carrying at the end of their first year.

If we also go back to basics, how many people move less on days when they have hangovers? Or cancel PT sessions or gym classes? You end up spending the day moving from bed to couch, all while picking at certain foods that you have convinced yourself will improve your hangover. Unsurprisingly, these food choices are rarely high in fibre and protein and, strangely, are either high in sugar or fat or a combination of the two. Drinking water with maybe some added electrolytes in it is probably the quickest way to improve most of the hangover (which is partly due to dehydration), however, you conjure up some mental nutritional gymnastics in order to rationalise why you are now eating chocolate buttons on toast... or ice cream with bacon... *"But, Chris, my body needs sugar and fat-soluble vitamins... it's the perfect combination, this is my family's secret hangover cure..."* Of course it is, you absolute fuck nugget.

Think of how many people also follow a diet and put themselves in a deficit Monday to Friday, only to then go out Saturday night for a few drinks. (I mentioned this example earlier in the book, but it is so common, let's just go over it again to really make sure it sticks.) From a simple number's perspective, say my deficit calories are 2,000, I've been in a 500-calorie deficit during the week, by the end of Friday, I've created a 2,500-calorie deficit. I then eat my normal 500-calorie breakfast on Saturday and my 250-calorie snack followed by another 500 calories for lunch. Still on track, I go out for dinner, and I go for a nice pasta dish because I'm out with friends and this place does the best pasta. Let's assume this is 800 calories (conservative guestimate), I've gone a little over my calories, but fuck it, I've been good all week, and it's only 50 calories, right!? Ah, but wait… I didn't factor in the bottle of wine (620 calories) and the two skinny spicy margaritas (300 calories). It's fine because they are skinny, right? Before you know it, this rather conservative night has almost halved your deficit for the week. This is without any late-night snacks or dessert… which, let's be honest, you always get dessert, and if you don't, you are probably grabbing some late-night kebab or chocolate on your way home. Hopefully, you weekend warriors can start to see why you aren't making progress from a simple number's perspective. You spend the next day on the couch feeling sorry for yourself, so your normal step count of 10k is more than halved to a miserable 3k… oh, and you end up bingeing on hyper-palatable foods and go over your calorie target again by just a little. Come on, it can't be any real surprise that you aren't making the progress you want when that weekend completely wiped out any work you did during the week. If you want to be able to drink, be social, go out to restaurants and still make progress, you need to budget better and learn more about what you are putting into your body. Understanding this actually gives you more dietary freedom, not less.

Now, if we go back to sleep again, interestingly, people often believe because alcohol is a nervous system depressant/sedative that induces relaxation and sleepiness, that a little nightcap can help sleep. Unfortunately, while it may help you fall asleep quicker, it is actually terrible for your sleep and can disrupt the sleep cycle and decrease sleep quality (usually resulting in fragmented and disturbed sleep in the second half of the night). One study looking at the acute effect of alcohol intake on sleep found that having two servings of alcohol per day for men or one serving per day for women decreased sleep quality by 24%, and having more than two servings of alcohol per day for men or more than one serving per day for women decreased sleep quality by 39.2%.[134] Now, I'm not going to dive into this any more as we know how important sleep is for weight loss and our health, and you now know even just one drink can negatively impact your sleep. Hopefully, you are now empowered to at least know the cost of your mistakes. I could always say reduce your intake of alcohol in the evening to help reduce the impact on your sleep, but let's be honest, most drinking is done in the evening, and I don't feel comfortable saying, "Well, if you are going to drink, then do it for breakfast", because that is just daft...

Let's be honest, alcohol is also a type 1 known carcinogen—it damages gut health and can increase your risk for liver damage, depression, and even just one drink per day is linked to a 20% increased risk of mouth and throat cancer, so I'm not being a total killjoy for no reason. Again, having said all this, I don't want to ever tell you to completely remove things as one of the most important factors when it comes to dietary success is enjoyment, so if you need that glass of wine on the weekends because that is what you enjoy, then I say do it… just factor in the calories and make sure to drink a glass of water alongside it. If we gave up everything potentially bad for us, there would be nothing left. Also, remember that life is about balance. If you end up removing all pleasure from your life, then what is really life at that point?

CHAPTER 29:
YOUR NEW MAINTENANCE

N EW MAINTENANCE:
Without a plan after your diet has finished, how does that old saying go? *Failure to plan is planning to fail*! Or something along those lines. I always talk to people about how the dieting culture we have beautifully encapsulates Einstein's definition of insanity, which was, "Doing the same thing over and over and expecting different results". If the changes you make to your habits and lifestyle aren't permanent, then neither will be your results. Do you really think if you stopped eating the way you normally ate (which, bear in mind, caused you to be overweight) in order to lose weight, only to then go back to eating like that again, there would be an outcome other than you being overweight again? SERIOUSLY! And I guess 2+2=7, does it? This is why for any diet to elicit permanent results, it needs to involve improving your lifestyle and habits, hence why this part of the book has been all about the key changes you need to make, whether that is from increasing your protein intake to getting more sleep. There is one final point we

need to address, and this was beautifully captured by obesity researcher, Paul MacLean, when he said, "To ensure success, the regain prevention strategies will likely need to be just as comprehensive, persistent and redundant, as the biological adaptations they are attempting to counter".

You see, when we finish our diet, although I feel I should phrase this differently to read, 'when we finish the deficit stage of our diet', and you have reached your goal weight/look/feel, we need to know what calorie level to switch to. If we were to return to our pre-diet calorie level after we finish our diet, then weight gain and probably body fat overshooting are distinct possibilities, if not a certainty for most. So, what should we do? Well, assuming we are making sure you are continuing the good habits of sleeping for seven to eight hours a night, resistance training and eating a diet high in protein and fibre (and maintaining your new reduced alcohol lifestyle), then the only thing we need to do is recalculate our new maintenance levels, which will have adjusted as a result of metabolic adaptation and, simply put, by being a lower body weight. We do this by using the same method we used to calculate our original maintenance level; just make sure you are inputting your new lower body weight into the equation.

Whatever your goals are at this point, I would start at these new maintenance calories for a week or two so we can see how your body is responding. As I've previously mentioned, the formulas used aren't 100% accurate and, therefore, we want to just give ourselves a little grace period to see how our body handles the change, but assuming your weight is remaining relatively stable (I mean, you will likely add a bit of weight whenever we increase calories purely from either having more food in your system or due to an increase in water weight due to an increase in carbohydrates consumed). We then need to ask ourselves how we feel about these calories. Are you super hungry? Do you feel restricted at this calorie level? If you are not comfortable and able to maintain this calorie level comfortably, then it is worth investing in what is termed a reverse diet.

Layne Norton, who helped popularise the reverse diet, defines it as "A dietary goal to increase calories and energy expenditure while limiting unnecessary fat gain". While different people may have slightly different approaches depending on why they are performing a reverse diet, this definition is the crux of what a reverse diet is and is actually a tool I use with hundreds of women every year who find themselves in that classic post-yo-yo diet dilemma where they are stuck on low calories and not losing weight. While this topic, again, isn't really within the scope of this book, I will quickly give you the premise so that you can understand it better (alternatively, go and buy Layne Norton PhD's book, *The Complete Reverse Dieting Guide*, which is a brilliant read and gives you the tools to set up your reverse diet).

If I were to try and simply explain it, I think the best way is to remember that when we created our deficit, I told you that if you didn't reduce your calories enough, then rather than lose weight, we would just gradually reduce our metabolic rate as our metabolism is more a range rather than a set point. So, if we only removed 100 calories from our maintenance level, we would not lose weight. The same is also true in the reverse. Theoretically, if we increased your calories by 100 calories, we would expect to see a weight gain of about a pound per month, however, more often than not, people do not gain as we increase calories slowly, as the body doesn't sense the energy gap. Instead, the extra calories are favourably dissipated as heat through adaptive thermogenesis and NEAT rather than being stored in adipose tissue. This is, however, person-dependent, and everyone will have different thresholds for weight loss and weight gain, therefore, it still needs to be personalised to the individual. If you are someone who tends to gain weight easily, we will more than likely prescribe a more conservative approach to adding calories back in, like 50 calories every other week, as an example. So, if our new maintenance was 1,500, then after two weeks, we would go to 1,550, then after another two weeks, we would be up to 1,600. Basically, every month slowly increasing our daily calories by 100 (usually from carbohydrates as we should already be eating optimum protein levels at this point) should put us in a position after three to four months where we are at a calorie level we can easily maintain while having limited any fat regain. Make sense? (And this is a very, very conservative approach.) Being able to delay gratification is a great marker for success when it comes to long-term weight loss maintenance.

I actually take many women through reverse diets for many months before attempting a deficit. This helps increase muscle mass and actually get our body used to consuming more calories; we can then lose weight on higher calories. Also, if you think of a woman who is eating 1,200 calories and not losing weight, I could not in good conscience get her to diet without seriously risking her health. And let's be honest, if I put her in a 20% deficit at 1,200, making her new calorie level 960, how long do you think she can maintain that for? How many nutritional deficiencies will probably pop up along the way? How quickly will she lose her menstrual cycle? And how long until she ends up bingeing as a result of over-restriction? Dieting is simple at its core, yet we have gotten it so wrong over the years that the number of people who are now in a worse place due to failed diet attempts is astronomical. Hopefully, having read this book, you now have a better understanding of metabology and why your previous attempts might have failed. You should also hopefully have an idea of the areas you may need to work on in order to improve your lifestyle and create long-lasting habits that help you achieve your goals rather than work against them.

In the final part of this book, I want to discuss how to better control your environment (I know, sounds a bit Mr. Miyagi wax on wax off shit, but really, it is quite simple), which is a very important step when it comes to improving your dietary practices and adherence, and then finally a few mindset shifts I have found useful for me when looking at adjusting my life, improving my relationship with my body, and reducing my overall stress and anxiety. Obviously, stress is an area we want to work on, and while discussing things like CBT and more advanced stress management techniques are a little beyond my expertise, I want to share with you the mindset shifts I have made that may help you. Finally, in the Tips section at the end, there will be some that focus on reducing stress in the body.

CHAPTER 30:
CONTROL YOUR ENVIRONMENT

Our traditional approach to dietary changes is usually based on the idea that consumers respond to knowledge and information and adjust their behaviours accordingly, however, as we can see, this just isn't the case. Despite the vast resources of information on what is healthy and how to improve our diet, it seems that this knowledge on its own isn't enough to guide us. I'm sure even if you go up to any overweight man or woman on the street and ask them what they need to improve, it's likely they would say something along the lines of, "Improving diet or activity levels..." Even those unfortunate people who still believe in star signs probably don't think they put on weight because of bad luck or moon energy. The obesity epidemic has only got worse the more we seem to know about nutrition. Most people are also aware that their eating habits aren't the best and could be improved... if they think otherwise, they are living in denial and essentially sticking their heads in the sand. You see, the problem is more complicated than just a lack of information alone. As we have already explained, our diet is also a reflection of our environment, social influences, peer pressure and consumer influence. These drivers usually work to reduce the quality of our dietary habits and our solution of willpower-based diets just isn't the answer.

If our environment can alter when, where and how much we eat, we need to work on improving our environment in order to improve our lifestyles and steer away from the usual focus on nutritional science and reducing intake of different macros or avoiding certain foods. An approach to long-term weight maintenance that doesn't look at addressing our environment is likely to fail as the powerful biological and psychological drivers of our obesogenic environment will test your willpower, and we all know that unhealthy habits are a lot easier to form in this day and age. The underlying premise is that in order to successfully lose weight, we have to work to help eliminate the frequency with which we are confronted with temptation in our day-to-day lives and improve our underlying habits so that, in times of fatigue or stress, we stick to our healthy habits. Now, let's be honest, we can't completely remove all temptation unless you go back in time and regress to living in caves. Alternatively, we also can't be expected to rely on self-control the whole time. So, what can we do?

Let's think of our home environment first. I already mentioned in the Marketing Manipulation chapter that self-control is an illusion. You see, those who appear to have tremendous self-control aren't all that different from those who are struggling. Instead, "disciplined" people are better at structuring their lives in a way that does not require heroic willpower or self-control. By creating a home environment where you don't have to rely on self-control, then surely your chances of better dietary habits will improve immediately. For example, if you are someone who has no willpower when it comes to sweet treats or snacks like cookies, then simply by not buying them and not having any with you at home, your need to practise self-control at home is reduced. You can't eat it if you don't have it... okay, you can probably go out again and get it, or order it, but when we reduce the immediate convenience of something, we can increase our adherence to our goals.

"But, Chris, my wife always buys it, or we have children that like having sweets in the house". Okay, well, let's start with the first objection, your wife or girl-friend... assuming they like you (which, hopefully, they do), then try talking to them about your goals and how you find having something like sweets in the flat trigger-ing for you. More often than not, your spouse will want to support your goals and will respect your request, or at least you can come to a compromise where they put their sweets in a hidden location or lock them away, or don't bring them home. If they are unwilling to do this, while it's not really my place to say, it is quite obvious they are being a bit of a cunt and they might not be the right one for you. If your excuse is that it's for your children, I mean, we are always trying to improve the diet and health of our kids, right? So, maybe it's worth just not buying them for your kids... OR since we don't want to be too tyrannical, try giving them chores to complete like doing their homework or tidying their room. If they do this, they can earn some spending money, at which point, if they want to go out and buy sweets, then they can buy their own (this may actually also teach them the value of work and not assuming Mum and Dad are just walking wallets. Knowing kids, if they do this, they are highly unlikely to share them with you and, therefore, it's a win-win—they got the sweets they wanted, you don't have the temptation, and their room is cleaner, or the bins have been taken out too... YOU'RE WELCOME.

Our home environment should be the easiest one to have control over. The more we can align our home environment to reflect our goals, the better our chances of minimising the usual dietary pitfalls. Also, usually, from purely just a calorie perspective, research indicates that people who eat out in restaurants, pubs or cafes daily consume between 300-1,000 calories more a day than those who can eat at home or prepare their own food. So, if we can also use that home environment to prepare breakfast and maybe lunch, then we will suddenly be in a much stronger position in our work lives. Irregular meal rhythms and snacking have been shown to increase your risk for weight gain, so by taking control of this and planning ahead, we can establish routines and control more of our environment as a result.

Planning ahead can also involve making a shopping list before heading to the supermarket, or by doing a food shop online (off of a list) in advance. Making sure you have the right foods at home can make sticking to your healthy eating agenda a lot easier and help to avoid the temptation of saying, "Fuck it, let's get a takeaway". When shopping off a list, you are hopefully less likely to go down random aisles, which increases your risk of spontaneous purchases due to decision-making fatigue. If I have a list to stick to, I can make sure I stick to what's on the list and reduce my wandering eye that is drawn to the latest flavour of Ben & Jerry's.

If you are a snack/grazing type of eater, then making sure you bring your own snacks with you to work can help you tailor what you have to your calorie budget rather than relying on the usual selection of biscuits and shit that seems to fill most office communal areas. Again, think protein and fibre when we are organising our snacks to help promote satiety and, hopefully, reduce unnecessary snacking. Single portion snack pots are also a better option than sharing bags, while probably less economical, a little snack pot of cashews can help give you a little hit of calories without testing your willpower not to finish the whole bag, which, let's be honest, is usually the case when you open a normal bag of nuts. If you want to save money, you can always buy the larger bag and then decant it into pre-bought snack pots. I often do this with sweets as, firstly, I have no self-control over sweets, but I like to have a few around my harder training sessions to give me a little hit of glucose, so I bought a pack of mini-Tupperware containers that fit about five to six sweets in them or probably eight to 10 almonds. This means I can divide a big bag up and then just put the snack pot into my jacket pocket or backpack to enjoy around training and I can spread this out easily over two weeks. Remember, it is also important to improve our habits rather than avoid/restrict or deny. By allowing myself to enjoy a few pieces of Haribo around training, I don't ever feel restricted or get insatiable cravings, I get a hit of energy around my training session and my enjoyment and adherence to my diet have never been higher.

We can also keep a large bottle of water on our desks at work, reminding us to sip on it throughout the day. Drinking enough water does help naturally suppress your appetite. Drinking enough water is also the best way of getting rid of excess water retention. Water is also necessary to maximise muscle function and raise your metabolism, so keeping a large bottle on your desk (assuming you actually drink from it) can help reduce your snacking tendencies and actually improve things like cognitive function, bowel regularity, aids digestion and improves energy levels. Remember, our brains want to take the path of least resistance, so by making healthier choices more available to us, we are more likely to be able to make these our default settings.

I also spoke about the benefit of low energy density eating in the protein and fibre section, however, there are many people out there who actually just don't like the types of food that are low in calories (all green vegetables basically), as the average Western diet is predominantly a shade of beige. So, the advice of not reducing portion sizes but rather adjusting the constituents of what is on your plate can fall on deaf ears. So, what advice can we give to these people other than learning to like green vegetables? Because that is like me telling someone to stop being so stressed... it's not exactly constructive advice. We know we tend to eat the food that is put in front of us, so reducing the portion size without reducing the plate or bowl that it has been served on is the quickest way to fail. Our brain will see a partially empty plate and assume we will be hungry at the end of the meal, so it is no wonder we will probably either return for seconds or be left unsatisfied and end up reaching for snacks soon after the meal. If you are looking to reduce portions, make sure to reduce the size of your plate or bowl so that you are still presented with a full plate, giving the illusion of a larger amount of food and helping convince our brains that this will be enough to satiate us (yes, we are that simple).

Let's be honest, we can't really alter every part of our environment. No matter how regimented you are, it is impossible to avoid all advertising. I don't know anyone who isn't caught short on occasions when it comes to having foods prepared in advance, or who never gets stressed or tired. Unless you live in the middle of a forest miles away from civilization, then it is safe to say you now live in an obesogenic environment, slowly twisting your consumption of information and food. But this doesn't mean our fates are sealed—it just means we need the right strategies in place in order to help make healthier choices easier, and unhealthy choices appear harder.

Research shows that many of our daily behaviours are performed mindlessly, and this is particularly true of eating. Even when we act consciously, we often fail to consider all options, so how can we get people to improve their decision-making processes? Let me introduce you to the Four Ps of Behaviour Change, created by Zoe Chance & Margarita Gorlin & Ravi Dhar (Researchers at Yale university). Integrating research findings from behavioural economics, psychology, and marketing, they worked on creating a system to help "nudge" people gently toward making healthier choices by changing what choices are offered, how choices are made and how the choices are communicated and how intentions are reinforced.[135]

1. Possibilities – What choices are offered.
2. Process – How choices are made.
3. Persuasion – How choices are communicated.
4. Person – How intentions are reinforced.

"Possibilities" refers to what choices are offered. To change behaviour, we need to improve how attractive the healthier option appears.

The quantity and variety of offers can impact our decision-making process. As I mentioned before, reducing plate and bowl size at home can work to reduce overall calories consumed. Researchers found that when people were serving themselves ice cream, they gave themselves 31% more when given a larger bowl to use and 57% more when given both a larger bowl and larger spoon to use. This even works with the glasses you use. Apparently, a tall thin glass gives you the illusion of more, so you pour less, while a short wide glass you will fill up with more as a result, while that might be great for water, it is not so favourable for alcoholic or sugary drinks like Coca-Cola or orange juice. Although, let's be honest, most Americans aren't using proper glassware when drinking Coke, so that might not be so relevant.

We have already discussed how variety can increase consumption (remember the 85+ varieties of Oreo cookies); it, therefore, makes sense that reducing variety can also lead to a reduction in food consumption. Research shows that people satiate faster the less variety within a meal, so while I'm not telling you to eat single-ingredient dinners as this will likely lead to nutritional deficiencies, we can limit the variety of food choices in the house and reduce the variety of calorie rich foods in each meal. For example, if I make some porridge for breakfast and add nothing to it, it is going to get a bit boring pretty quick and actually my normal-sized bowl is probably enough to satiate me. But this is a bit boring, and I may not keep doing that every day because I don't enjoy it. If I add some berries on top, that is enough to give me some variety and different textures without increasing the total calories that much and, actually, it adds some vitamins, minerals, antioxidants and increases my enjoyment (and still, my usual bowl size was enough to satiate me). If, however, I start adding some honey, maybe some nuts and seeds, to the bowl, I will be increasing the calories of the bowl massively. I can try and reduce the calories by reducing the amount of porridge in the bowl, but now I am left with a tiny portion that will definitely not satiate me. So, I end up eating 200-400 calories more and am left not feeling any more satiated than the original bowl despite the increase in energy consumption.

If you are serious about making changes that last, you need to make sure you create the path of least friction when it comes to healthy habits. Failure to do so and we know that the unconscious decision-making that led you to become overweight in the first place will kick in, and you won't win. We can help nudge people to make healthier decisions if we bundle decisions together. For someone who normally consumes chips every day and wants to lose weight, rather than saying don't eat chips anymore, instead, bundle chip eating with eating more salad by saying halve the number of fries and replace them with some salad concoction, we can improve fibre consumption, reduce their calorie consumption and hopefully encourage better eating practices in the future.

"Process" refers to the accessibility and order of our choices.

Obviously, the more available something is has a strong impact on consumption. How many times have you reached for those biscuits in the office kitchen because they are just there, not because you have some unavoidable craving for them? I tend to eat more fruit when I go and visit my parents because my mum always keeps a fruit bowl on the table, not because I have some underlying reason to be healthier when I go to see her. As I mentioned before, if we are looking to lose weight, we can remove the potential triggers from our home environment and replace them with healthier options that better fit our goals. Accessibility exerts a gentle yet powerful influence on our choices. How many of us have ended up buying sweets while waiting in the supermarket queue because they are there staring us in the face? In one study where people visited a cafeteria, when the junk food was made less accessible (requiring waiting in a separate line), it reduced the amount of junk food purchased.[136] While it may be difficult to change the environment of the shops and the establishments we vacate, we can make sure our home environment is one that reflects our goals, and again, if you are someone who finds themselves buying those sweets at the checkout counter, maybe you can switch your grocery shop to an doing an online shop, or go at a time where there is no queue so you don't get our limited willpower tested.

Research shows that environmental cues are extremely powerful in shaping our habits. Think about going to the movies... how many times have you then gone to purchase popcorn, not because you are hungry but because you associate the movies with enjoying popcorn? Behaviour can, therefore, be modified when we change environmental cues. Getting rid of bad habits is not easy, let's be honest, but if we can alter the environment that helps shape these habits, we have a better chance of change.

Order also influences your outcomes—we pay more attention to certain items depending on where they appear. For example, children at a school cafeteria ate more vegetables when the vegetables were placed at the front of the line. Where items appear on the menu also impacts our choices. When restaurants place more healthy options on the first page, they are ordered more, or when the waiters list the restaurant specials, we tend to remember and choose the ones at the start or at the end. Knowing this, while we can't alter how a restaurant operates or where food is placed in a buffet line, we can alter how we shop in a cafeteria or what food we put on our plate first, and we can try and alter potentially how we go about increasing the consumption of more fruit and vegetables in our kids' diets (assuming you have a kid, that is, otherwise, probably best not to offer random kids pieces of fruit... even with the right intentions, I'm not sure parents would look kindly on this).

"Persuasion" refers to how your choices are communicated. What information is presented, how it is communicated and who delivers the message? To be honest, this is a hard one to really control as we are subject to marketing manipulation and misinformation everywhere, making it more likely that we are actually steered towards choices that don't support our goals. That being said, we can nudge people towards making better decisions through different visual cues. For example, if you live or work somewhere where there is the choice of stairs or an elevator, research has shown putting up signs by the elevator prompting people to take the stairs instead with a message like, "Burn calories, not electricity", increased stair use by as much as 40% even nine months later.[137] We could always find ways to alter our home or office environments with choice reminders to get up and move more or drink more water, or whatever healthier habit you have decided to adopt. Placing cues in our environments that help persuade us to increase the healthier path is a simple yet effective method of improving overall lifestyle. Even with things like your phone and different apps, we can now set them to remind us of hitting certain goals or targets. I bought an Oura ring to track my sleep a few years ago, but I actually found the nudge it automatically gives me when I've been sitting down for a certain amount of time super useful to help me just be more active on a daily basis... although, not very helpful when it sends me that message and I'm stuck on the loo (where's the empathy setting, Oura?).

"Person" refers to how intentions are reinforced. You see, most attempts to change people's behaviour are done by purely offering advice or providing information. We know that intentions and actions aren't always consistent with our behaviour as we are subject to fatigue, bias and... well, willpower that can't exactly be relied on. There are a few simple ways to support healthy intentions.

Effective goal setting can work to increase your adherence to making healthier choices. When setting goals, we must remember to make those goals SMARTER. Research shows that those who write down their goals in a meaningful way increase their chances of accomplishing them by 30%. What's more, it has been shown that if you keep track and measure the progress towards your goals, your success ratio increases by 60%. SMARTER stands for Specific, Measurable, Achievable, Relevant, Timed, Exciting and Recordable.

For example, the goal to lose weight is a bit too general and vague. Having a goal of losing 10 pounds in five months makes the goal more specific. Maybe to this goal, you can add hit calorie target X and complete three resistance sessions per week, making it more specific, measurable and including some actionable steps. In addition, breaking this into smaller steps can help make it more manageable and effective and increase adherence, and you can also celebrate small wins along the way. Experts suggest that it is best to work on just three goals at a time and build from there, starting with the easiest one. Maybe this is something like hitting a step count or even starting to prep your breakfast or purchasing healthier snacks to take to work with you.

Setting goals and tracking progress can appeal to our intrinsic motivation. We can also incentivise healthy behaviour, promoting extrinsic motivation, for example, paying participants to regularly go to the gym boosted gym attendance even after the monetary incentive was then removed.[138] Incentives help to shift the balance in favour of the healthier habit, increasing motivation as you increase the associated benefits of the action. There are several health insurance companies that offer you incentives to exercise. I also know many offices and companies that will offer to cover the cost of gym memberships or provide yoga classes every week in order to improve their staff's mental and physical health. Incentives can be super powerful when it comes to changing our behaviour. We can even create these incentives ourselves. For example, if I want to lose weight and I also love the latest Lululemon legging collection, I could either incentivise myself that before I purchase the new leggings, I need to drop a size in leggings or hit a goal weight. Alternatively, I could always put £20 aside every week I managed to hit my pre-determined workouts, and then after four to five weeks (assuming price), I can take that money and go and treat myself. If this sounds complicated, you can always just bundle things together, so instead of thinking, "I have to exercise", you can book a class with your friends and then you get to socialise and get a sweat on at the same time, but the focus is on the part you enjoy.

We can further reduce our reliance on willpower by getting people to commit to a future course of action. For example, in a school field trip, children who pre-ordered their lunch entrée were almost twice as likely to choose the healthier option.[139] I have always found with my clients that pre-booking PT sessions (and obviously getting them to pre-pay) increased adherence massively as the act of pre-committing increased the cost (emotional and financial) of not following through on the commitment. I find that if I ever book an exercise class that, even when my level of motivation and enthusiasm/energy is reduced beforehand, I will still attend the class regardless, as not doing so actually becomes the course of most resistance.

Interventions like these that focus on the person building healthy patterns of behaviour over time can lead to the formation of better default habits, increasing the chance for long-term success. You see, the majority of our actions are automatic, which means turning healthy behaviours into habits is the easiest way to sustain them, even in the obesogenic environment. Most people want to lose weight or be healthier/eat healthier, yet their actions and habits consistently fail to support these goals. The most powerful driver underlying the obesity problem is not genetics, or seed oils, but rather our failure to develop the right habits to support our goals. While it can take an average of 66 days for a new behaviour to become automatic, starting small and working to alter our environments to support our goals is key in long-term weight management.

CHAPTER 31: MINDSET

For this chapter, I am going to take you through a few different stories that I found have helped me and my clients when it comes to changing our mindset when addressing the topic of weight loss and health.

For the first story, I want to take you back to over a year ago when I had just arrived back to London from one of my trips to Thailand—my home away from home where I get a lot of my writing or studying done. Unfortunately, at the end of this trip, my Crohn's decided to rear its ugly head, and instead of going back to work, I ended up having to make a trip to my local A&E. Sitting in the waiting room of the hospital feeling rather sorry for myself having only just arrived back, this was not exactly the homecoming I had hoped for. Having been waiting for 30 minutes to no avail, I went back up to reception to make sure they knew I was waiting. Given I was losing blood at a rather alarming level, I was worried about being left alone for too long. The rather large and intimidating woman behind reception informed me that the average waiting time was three hours and that I should try and make myself comfortable (she did kindly offer to get me water, which I accepted gratefully). *Could be worse,* I thought to myself, it was warm in the waiting room and I remembered to bring my new book with me. Given it was nice and quiet, this was actually not a bad setting to keep up with my new reading habit. You see, in day-to-day life, I'm aware that it is harder to find quiet places to sit and read, whereas it is so easy when I'm in Thailand on my own. I think this is one of the reasons why my past attempts to read more have not always been effective—London life is busy and there are so many more distractions, but having just read "Atomic Habits", I felt equipped to implement a new reading habit into my life, making sure I take every opportunity I find to read, where before, I probably would have sat procrastinating on my phone (the ever-present dangers of social media).

I realised in myself that as a result of my Crohn's, I have become a man of habit as I find eating similar things at similar times of the day really helps control it—this also goes into making sure I take my probiotic every day and different supplements aimed at bettering my health, so adding the habit of reading an extra 10 pages onto my current habits like after my evening shower, it actually seems to have worked really well. As I looked up from my book as another name was called, I started to look at the different people surrounding me in the waiting room… it's hard not to be a little nosey in these situations. What was wrong with these people? Why were they here? It was quite a diverse mix of people, although I do feel the average age was unsurprisingly quite high, as was the average waistline (although that is the general population these days). It got me thinking how easy it is to take our health for granted. Until you are sitting in the waiting room of a hospital surrounded by examples of poor health, all while struggling with your own health complications, it is hard to ignore the glaring reality. We are nothing without our health. Why am I writing this? Well, I want to share a lesson from the book I was reading (*The 7 Habits of Highly Effective People*) that I think is a key mindset shift.

Do you remember Aesop's fable of the goose that lays golden eggs? The story is of a poor farmer who one day discovers in the nest of his pet goose a glittering golden egg. At first, he thinks it must be some kind of trick. But before he throws the egg aside, he has a second thought and takes it in to be appraised instead. He learns the egg is pure gold! He can't believe his luck. He becomes even more incredulous the following day when the experience is repeated (that's right, he finds another golden egg). Day after day this happens and he is becoming incredibly wealthy. But with this increasing wealth comes greed and impatience. Unable to wait each day for just one more egg, the farmer decides he will kill the goose and get them all at once (he makes the very stupid assumption all the eggs are hidden inside the goose). But when he opens up the goose, he finds it empty. There are no golden eggs and now he has destroyed their means of production.

The author of the book goes on to explain this fable is the perfect analogy for the basic definition of effectiveness. True effectiveness is a function of two things—what is produced (the golden eggs) and the producing asset or capacity to produce (the goose). If you adopt a pattern of life that focuses on golden eggs and neglects the goose, you will soon be without the asset that produces the golden eggs. You see, effectiveness lies in the balance between production (P) of desired results (golden eggs) and production capacity (PC), the ability or assets that produce the desired results.

How true is this of our health? How many people do you know who work hard or train hard purely focused on one goal (the P) and forget to look after their basic needs (their PC)? What happens when you focus so hard on your work that you forget to make time for your mental health, your sleep or your nutrition? You see, we are so focused on goals that, quite often, we neglect the one thing that matters more than anything... our health. (You can't exactly smash those goals while sitting in the waiting room of a hospital waiting to be admitted.) Without our health, what can we really do? The best businessmen/women, the best athletes all need their health to be optimum in order to excel. Lionel Messi is arguably the best footballer in the world, but if he neglects his physical health (his PC) as he is so focused on staying the best (his P), how long do you think it will be before he can't play because of illness or injury? It is not by chance that most of the most successful people are the ones who have also prioritised their health throughout their careers. Look at Cristiano Ronaldo, he is known to have paid for a private chef to stay with him and to have built a home gym complete with different recovery rooms in order to help him recover quicker so that he could then train harder.

This is actually a great example of someone focusing on creating the perfect balance between P and PC.

Effectiveness lies in the balance, excessive focus on P can lead to ruined health, however, too much focus on the PC is a bit like a person who runs for three to four hours a day, bragging about the extra 10 years of life it creates, unaware that he's spending those extra 10 years running. I see so many of these nutritionists or health gurus on social media who demonise everything that isn't organic or a fucking plant, without realising they are taking all the fun out of food and, essentially, life. You can't lead a toxin-free life, and by trying to do so, you'd be creating a life not worth living. You need to find a balance. I always tell my clients to avoid processed foods where possible, but what I mean when I say this is heavily processed foods. For example, a boiled egg in Tesco has been cooked and put in a packet, it has been processed... but it is just a boiled egg, and its ingredients list reads: Egg. Yes, probably healthier for you to cook it yourself, but in the grand scheme of things, there is nothing wrong with buying a boiled egg from Tesco, especially if you are in a rush and looking for a little snack. This, compared to grabbing a packet of Monster Munch (packet of crisps... although elite choice, I must admit) is quite a considerable difference in the level of processing and nutritional value. You see, there is a balance. When clients start with me, I look at their current eating patterns and lifestyle and make suggestions for ways to improve/optimise it.

We aren't looking for perfection, we are looking to create that balance between improving their health and making it a life they want to live. If they want to lose weight and are currently guzzling down one litre of Coke each day, don't you think it's quite an easy switch to go to a sugar-free version? This is probably a switch they can make and stick to. Yes, switching to water would be better for them, but given that Diet Coke is safe for human consumption (as shown in the human randomised control trials) and will work to help them lose weight by reducing current calorie intake (which is what will help improve their health markers), don't you think this suggestion finds a good balance? This is something the health zealots on social media don't seem to understand. Switching to water may not be appealing enough or realistic for this person, and if that was my only suggestion, they would quickly fail and go back to their litre of Coke every day and we would be no closer to their goal of losing weight.

I could just write a list of strict rules and give this to everyone, however, nutrition and lifestyle changes need to be personalised if they are going to work in the long run—anyone could lose weight if I shoved them on a diet of 500 calories or told them to fast for 22 hours every day, but this, for most people, would be torturous and detrimental to both their mental and physical health.

The P/PC balance is the very essence of effectiveness. While I contemplated this in the waiting room full of people, I most certainly could tell who had not found that balance... I then had to look at myself. How had I ended up in this position where my PC needed some help? If I'm honest, a recent lack of sleep and some added stress through dietary changes had probably pushed enough of my Crohn's triggers to tip me over the edge, and I was suffering the result of this imbalance. Granted, some health complications can arise regardless of how you are looking after yourself. I'm not blaming you for any medical/health complication you may have had, but I think this was a chance to step back and remember that while I'm so focused right now on my goals (my golden eggs), I must never take my PC (my body) for granted, especially as having something like Crohn's usually requires me to have to be even more vigilant than the average person.

I saw a reel on Instagram recently that summed up this paradigm shift perfectly (yes, there is sometimes some good content on social media). The quote from the video went like this, "If you think lifting weights is dangerous… try being weak… if you think eating healthy is expensive… try being ill… if you think fitness is time-consuming… try waiting in a doctor's office… short-term costs pay long-term dividends".

I hope you read this and it makes you take note that we are nothing without our health. Don't take it for granted, continue to work on yours because no matter your goals, you won't be able to achieve them if you don't work on your own health too.

I think the next mindset shift is the illusion of motivation but also the important skill of practising delayed gratification. There are many things we do daily to improve our life, yet we don't ask what motivates us to do these things. Are you motivated to brush your teeth every day? You probably don't think of it as motivation fuelling you…

but you do it anyway (or at least I hope you fucking do... otherwise, sort that out first). You see, we know that if we don't brush our teeth, then our oral hygiene will go to shit, our teeth will look bad, our breath will smell, and we will end up with painful and probably expensive complications down the line. So, most of us remember to brush our teeth (twice a day), but we can go weeks or months without exercising. Maybe it's because we brush our teeth and we get that immediate feedback of that fresh minty taste, whereas when we exercise, although we get a little endorphin rush, the results aren't usually immediate. It might be worth it if you are someone who struggles with this lack of quick feedback to try putting up a large calendar and marking off the days you hit your step count or go to the gym. You will be getting some immediate feedback/gratification by simply checking days off on the calendar when you achieve this habit.

Maybe it is because we were taught from a young age to brush our teeth every day that this is so ingrained in us (parents side note... this is why it is important to instil the importance of exercise/sport/activity in your kids at a young age... oh, and eating vegetables. I was lucky enough to have parents who ingrained the importance of exercise and a mother who forced vegetables into every meal when I was a kid, so maybe that's why I have always found it easier than most to do some form of exercise daily and an enjoyment of eating veg... although not mushrooms, I will never like them... eugh).

But it is never too late to shift our way of thinking, even if you weren't lucky enough to have these habits ingrained in you from a young age. As humans, our tendency is to play the victim. We start blaming outside forces for where we are—it's our parent's fault, our genetics, our work environment, our family responsibilities... in reality, we are the creative forces of our lives, and we are free to choose. You are free to reorganise your time to prioritise your exercise and you are free to choose what you eat for breakfast.

I am not expecting you to necessarily enjoy it at first. If you are new to exercising or eating a more balanced diet, you may even start by hating it. Do it anyway. You are not dealing with a quick fix—you are dealing with a portion of your life that will far outweigh the cost of not doing these things. Ask anyone who has started a new exercise regime or a new diet, little by little, the exercises become less foreign and actually the feeling from doing it starts to become more enjoyable. Maybe the less junk food they eat, the less they find they are craving it. (Often, when my online clients report they decided they wanted a takeaway treat on the weekend, they are surprised to find the takeaway was not as pleasurable as they remembered it to be and actually left them feeling gross with stomach discomfort, water retention and a feeling of lethargy). Instead, when we begin to improve our lifestyle choices, we see improvements in energy levels—you are more productive at work, and suddenly, you are finding benefits in areas that weren't even the original intention behind getting started in the first place.

Motivation and willpower, at their core, are finite resources and are not enough to rely on alone. It turns

out that usually people who we think seem to have motivation to spare actually don't have any more measurable
motivation than those who seemingly lack it. It is just
their underlying habits are set up so that even when they
are tired or stressed, their default setting is geared towards
health. This is why the development of better habits is
essential, so that even in times of stress or fatigue, you
fall back on your subconscious habits and don't have to
rely on motivation. Trust me, I love exercise, but I am
certainly not always in the mood to train, however, it is
part of my default setting.

Now that we understand the importance of habits
instead of relying on something like motivation, it is
equally important to understand how we make habits
stick. Changes that we make need to be convenient but
still effective—a simple switch like from using olive oil
when cooking to using a one-calorie spray is an easy
change to make but can save you a lot of calories. Joining
a gym closer to home or work can help reduce the effort
needed in order to get yourself to the gym. If I have to
travel an hour to get to the gym, it will take a lot less to
convince me to miss the session than if I can fall out of
my office or home into the gym. Think about the changes
you can make that require little effort but make a big difference in the long run.

Next, avoid changes that require unrealistic self-control, for example, banning chocolate altogether. Rather
than banning it, either budget for that particular food or
set a goal to enjoy it once a week. Again, this is where
we can begin to practise delayed gratification. You see,

changes that are most likely to be maintained imply a promise of reward. Motivation is the push that prompts us to act and do something differently, but if we can repeat this action enough times, at some point, it will become automatic and effortless, and will no longer require "motivation" or "willpower". Repetition is key here—we are teaching ourselves a pattern and that pattern becomes unconscious over time. It is important to note that changes based on values and enjoyment rather than restriction are a lot more likely to feel natural and last. Think about it, finding recipes you enjoy and tailoring them to your calorie goals sounds a lot healthier and something you can stick to rather than just going, "I'm never eating bread again..."

The good news should be that anyone can do this—it doesn't take some underlying genetic factor or level of intellect. In order to create a new rewarding habit, you just need to repeat the same action in the same situation to create that unconscious link between the situation and action. If I start having a glass of water first thing in the morning before brushing my teeth and I repeat this (maybe setting a reminder on my alarm clock to do so), then quite soon, this will become a habit (this is also called habit stacking where I attach a current habit—brushing my teeth—with my new habit—drinking a glass of water). Scientists estimate that up to 95% of our daily food decisions happen as a result of habit, so realistically, the obesity epidemic can be explained a lot more easily as a result of the ease at which we can form poor diet and lifestyle habits in this obesogenic environment, rather than trying to twist the science to blame it on our genes or a particular food.

Hopefully, through this understanding of how habits form, you can see why the usual diet model doesn't work. By creating restrictive protocols to follow, this type of eating ends up exclusively relying on willpower and self-control, which, as mentioned, we only have a limited amount of. The development of what is referred to as delayed gratification is believed to be one of the most important characteristics for success in health, work, and life. So, unsurprisingly, the inability to delay gratification is related to obesity, as well as other maladaptive behaviours such as substance abuse, problem drinking, smoking, and pathological gambling. To understand the principle of delayed gratification, let me tell you about the marshmallow experiment. "The Stanford marshmallow experiment", first done in 1960, was used to examine delayed gratification. A child was put in a room alone and given a choice between having a small reward now (one marshmallow), or to wait and then be given two rewards later (two marshmallows).

After the child was given the option, they were then left alone in the room for 15 minutes. When the researcher returned, if they had not consumed the marshmallow, they were given another to consume. For a child, delaying the consumption of a sweet treat is pretty stressful, some kids jumped up and ate the first marshmallow as soon as the researcher closed the door. Others shifted uncomfortably and fidgeted in their chairs as they tried to restrain themselves, but eventually, gave in to temptation a few minutes later. And finally, a few of the children did manage to wait the entire time. Remember, if you suffer from anxiety and have less ability to regulate your emotions, the perception of time may feel longer, therefore, that 15-minute wait for the additional reward may feel longer to certain people. What would you do? It's a bit like the situation of receiving a small amount of money now or a larger sum sometime in the future. Which do you pick?

The really interesting part of this study was when they looked at the kids' lives again 10 years later. They found that those who had the self-control to wait for the larger reward (the two marshmallows) were more socially and academically competent, attentive, and able to tolerate frustration and stress. You see, these kids, even at a young age, were already building skills that were essential for later life. The ability to delay gratification is important for success in all areas of life. Think about it, this can be applied to so many different situations. If you delay the gratification of watching television and get your homework done now, then you'll more likely do better at school, achieving better grades and developing more, intellectually speaking. What about if you delay the gratification of finishing your workout early and put in a few more reps, then you'll more likely get stronger quicker, and potentially reach your goals. Dieting culture and actually most of our culture has almost always focused on quite the opposite—anything that promises fast results and instant gratification is immediately more desirable even when it comes at the cost of future success.

Researchers at the University of Rochester wanted to dig deeper into the question, "What is delayed gratification?" A second study was done replicating the marshmallow experiment with one key difference. This time, children were split into two different groups. Before the marshmallow part of the experiment, the first group was exposed to a series of unreliable experiences (researchers promised to bring them something and then never did), meanwhile, the second group had very reliable experiences (researchers delivered on their promises). Do you think this impacted the children's ability to delay gratification? Of course, it did... if the children didn't trust the researcher due to unreliable past experiences, they, therefore, had no reason to trust that the researchers would bring a second marshmallow, and thus, they didn't wait very long to eat the first one. Because the second group of children had learned they could trust the researcher as he had delivered on his promises earlier, they trusted that if they delayed their gratification, they would get more as a result, therefore, they waited longer. So, interestingly, the child's ability to delay gratification and display self-control was not predetermined, but rather was impacted by the experiences and environment that surrounded them. In fact, the environment appeared to have an almost instantaneous impact as only a few minutes of reliable or unreliable experiences were enough to alter the actions of each child in either direction.[140]

What we can learn from this second experiment is that even if you don't feel like you're good at delaying gratification now, you can train yourself to become better.

The children who were subject to reliable conditions learnt that it was in their best interest to delay gratification, so the environment and their experiences almost immediately helped them to develop this. What does this mean for you looking to lose weight? Well, if you start by promising yourself small and delivering on it, and then repeating this, your brain will learn that, yes, it is worth the wait, and yes, I can do this.

From what I have learned, there are a few valuable techniques to help improve your ability to delay gratification (there are probably others I have forgotten or am unaware of, but these work well for me).

1. Identify your goals: Defining your goals clearly provides you with a vision of what you want to accomplish and why it is important to you and what works against your goals. This clarity helps you stay focused, avoiding distractions and temptations that do not align with your goals. (Keep a picture of your goal on your phone—you can even set it as your wallpaper—to remind yourself what you're working toward. It will make delayed gratification that much easier.) Imagine I am trying to save money to buy a house... I put a picture of the house I want to buy on my phone, this reminds me daily of why I am saving money and helps me avoid making unnecessary purchases like a new expensive pair of gym shoes I don't need, considering I already have five pairs.

2. Try your best to eliminate temptation: Temptations and distractions always cause impulsive behaviour

and can make sticking to your new habits a lot harder. By proactively eliminating or reducing your exposure to these triggers, you will be better able to resist impulsive urges and make deliberate decisions that align with your long-term goals. Controlling your environment, as we discussed in the previous chapter, for example, not keeping any chocolate at home if this is usually a trigger food for you. The best way to stay away from temptations is to make them unavailable most of the time. After all, if you didn't buy that bag of chocolate, you won't be able to pick at it later.

3. What is the real cost?: Ask yourself this question. What's the real cost of the thing or the action you're about to take? If I'm about to have a pint of beer or an indulgent dessert, I ask myself what this is potentially costing my health, and if it's a huge spike in blood sugar and likely to make me feel guilty or potentially cause me to overeat or give me a hangover, this can help to deter me from doing it. You can always create prices yourself for those actions (they don't have to be monetary prices), you can write down the temptations that you usually face and then, next to it, the cost of this temptation. For example, I love donuts, so I assign the cost of enjoying a donut to having to vacuum the entire house and clean the shower. When I next feel like a donut, I have to weigh whether it is worth the cost of having to clean my flat. By doing this, I'm more likely to say fuck that donut, and if not,

at least my flat gets cleaner, and I become more active in the process (this should not be confused with having to earn calories by exercising more). We are just trying to create more friction in the act of succumbing to your temptation; however, we aren't saying you can't ever have it either.

4. Break down challenges and tasks into doable actions. Rather than trying to become the model of health overnight, pick one thing you want to focus on, for example, increasing your step count, by focusing on one thing and making it easily repeatable. We can quickly implement this and stick to it. Then, remember to focus on celebrating the small wins. Hitting your step goal for every day of that week, while sounding trivial, is a great start to increasing general activity levels—celebrate this as it will help reinforce this behaviour, helping to make it become more unconscious. Then we can look at increasing it, or we can then choose our next behaviour to work on once this has become ingrained. We want to avoid the mentality of throwing everything except the kitchen sink at our goals.

5. Using budgets or lists: When you are buying something, the cost of it comes into play, right? Or it should unless you are rolling in it. The same comes to our diets and making sure we have the calories available for our food choices. I always talk about budgeting when people are going out for dinner or a night out. Rather than avoiding

having a social life, you just need to factor in the increase in calorie consumption as a result of the occasion and factor this in for your budget for the week. By reducing your calorie consumption on other days, you can increase your budget for that evening.

Lists can also be a useful way of improving self-control. For instance, if you go to the grocery store with a list in your hand, you might be less likely to veer into the wrong aisle and avoid temptations that are not on your list. A list of daily tasks to complete can help you accomplish things you may not want to do by giving you not only the reminder in front of you, but also by being able to tick it off your list once you've done it, you get some feedback and gratification from doing so.

By developing our ability to delay gratification, we can help improve many aspects of our life, not just our health or our weight loss goals. I think it's time for another story to help illustrate this mindset, and what better than another of Aesop's fables (who would have guessed that these stories written back in ancient Greece would be so profound for life today?). The story of the Ant and the Grasshopper, you may remember this from your childhood, but just in case you don't, let me jog your memory. The story goes… in a field, one summer's day, a grasshopper was hopping about, chirping and singing to its heart's content. An ant passed by, bearing along with great toil an ear of corn he was taking to the nest. "Why not come and chat with me", said the grasshopper, "instead of toiling and moiling in that way?" "I am helping to lay up food for the winter", said the ant, "and recommend you do the same". "Why bother about winter?" said the grasshopper. "We have got plenty of food at present". But the ant went on its way and continued its toil. When the winter came, the grasshopper had no food and found itself dying of hunger, while it saw the ants distributing corn and grain from the stores they had collected in the summer.[141]

This fable perfectly illustrates the virtues of hard work and planning for the future. Yo-yo dieting, on the other hand, is perfectly encapsulated by the short-term thinking of the grasshopper. If your only focus is on the speed of weight loss and wanting results now, then you will forever find yourself battling your body's desire to maintain its body fat set point and will only work to increase it as you yo-yo up and down... not exactly planning for the future... unless you want to be overweight in the future. The next time you are given the option of immediate gratification in any walk of life, think about what cost this will have on your future self. I'm all for living in the moment and enjoying the present (I even just finished reading the book *The Power of Now*, although, if I'm honest, I found it a bit preachy and not exactly my cup of tea), but living in the present at the expense of your future seems like a rather bad investment.

If we go back to the scenario of a woman who has gone through a few years of yo-yo dieting and is now eating 1,200 calories and not losing weight, she has two choices. Firstly, she can continue to look for quick fixes, increasing her activity levels more and further reducing her calories. She could even try the new weight loss drug (assuming she qualifies for it). In this scenario, she is not planning for the future, but rather focusing on results now, and we know where that will lead her (more failure... remember the definition of insanity...). In the second scenario, she understands that right now, she is not actually in a position to try to lose weight and will need to ignore the short-term goal of weight loss and focus on improving diet quality (increasing protein targets), focus on a small calorie surplus alongside resistance training to increase her muscle mass, and then work on improving lifestyle factors like sleep and stress. While you can see this is a lot harder sell since she wants weight loss now and you are actually telling her that, in order to achieve her goals, she may first have to put on weight and that her results are predicated on over a year of hard work and consistency... it's quite easy to see why this may fall on deaf ears. However, if she is able to stick to this and invest in her future, in a year's time, she might be a few kgs heavier, but she will have more muscle mass, a higher metabolic rate and be on a higher calorie level where she can now start a productive deficit with the potential for long-term maintenance of those results. Her future health, body composition and, hopefully, relationship with her body will have all benefited.

You see, we all have a choice, in all my work as a personal trainer, weight loss coach and nutritionist, I have seen a wide range of clients all with differing struggles when it comes to achieving their weight loss goals. The fact of the matter is, when you boil it all down, anyone can lose weight. Our ability to lose weight is not actually the problem, it is the ability to maintain the weight we have lost—that is where things become harder. Everyone's journey is different, you may have an underlying medical condition like PCOS or hypothyroidism that might make it harder to lose weight, you might be experiencing peri-menopause or have an injury limiting your activity levels, again, making it harder to lose weight... BUT, not making it impossible. We like to blame things like our genetics or an underlying condition or big evil companies for why we aren't happy with our weight as this takes respon-sibility away from ourselves. But the truth is, we have a choice. Again, I'm not saying it's easy because there are many reasons, as hopefully you now understand, having read this book that makes it a lot harder, both from the psychology of our decision-making processes to the envi-ronment we now live in. BUT, to lose weight, we need to be in a calorie deficit... FACT. In order to maintain our weight loss, the changes we make while losing weight need to be permanent as well. I'm not saying the deficit has to be permanent, but if your lifestyle and diet don't align with your new weight, but rather with your previ-ous lifestyle that left you overweight and unhappy with your body, then prepare yourself for failure and disap-pointment. Remember, we are the product of our habits, there is no escaping this no matter how much you scream autophagy or how many ketones you think your body is producing. You didn't put on weight because of one bad meal, you didn't put on weight because you missed one workout or had one bad night of sleep, or because your girlfriend stressed you out (that bitch). You became over-weight because, essentially, your lifestyle was no longer balanced with your physiology, and this imbalance lasted long enough to produce a noticeable physical change. In order to correct this imbalance, we must adjust our life-style, but these adjustments will take time (no one got skinny from one day of exercise and eating salads), and they can't be temporary or the imbalance will just return. As Gabor Maté wrote, "If we gain the ability to look into ourselves with honesty, compassion and with unclouded vision, we can identify the ways we need to take care of ourselves". If we are unwilling to accept responsibility and learn from our mistakes, but rather look for the next thing to blame, then we will forever be trapped in a soci-ety where being overweight is the norm and the relatively simple issue of weight loss will only continue to become more confusing.

Let me leave you with this one last story (don't worry, not another Aesop fable). This is an old parable but I'm going to update the language a little because... well, fuck it, I don't need to explain myself. The story tells of a drunk man searching by a street light looking for his car keys because he has lost them. A police officer sees the drunken man searching the ground and asks him, "Oi, mate, what are you doing?" The drunk man replies with a slight slur, "Ah, mate, I've lost my fucking keyssss". The policeman, in a rare moment of sympathy, decides to help the man (I know, let's be honest, in this day and age, he's more likely to taser him and walk away, but just go with

350

it). The officer helps search for a few minutes to no avail. He asks the man, "Mate, you sure you lost them here?" To his surprise, the intoxicated man replies, "No, I lost the keys on the other side of the street!" The policeman, angered by the response, replies, "Don't get sarcastic with me, you cunt, I'm trying to help". "I'm not being sarcastic", replies the drunk man. "Then why the fuck are you looking over here then?" asks the rather frustrated and perplexed policeman. "Well, the light is better over here, so I thought I'd have a better chance of seeing them", he replied.

While this may sound like a bit of a daft story, I believe that through its absurdity, it actually reveals something pretty profound about human nature. It mirrors how the majority of people look at tackling their weight issues. There is this propensity for people to look for what they're searching for in the easiest places instead of in the places that are most likely to yield the results they're seeking. We do this even if we know that under the light isn't the best option. We see some people getting results on a certain diet and we convince ourselves that because we haven't yet tried that, maybe that's where we are going wrong. When this fails, we go back to the light and look again, picking the next option, only to fail again. We end up wasting time and creating conditions that make our situation worse.

If you can alter your focus, and rather than looking in the light (shit loads of cardio exercise and removing carbohydrates) and start working on long-term goals by improving your body fat set point (through the recommendations I have laid out in the last few chapters), then you will find your key a lot quicker.

Before I finish, I want to leave you with one last point that I think should be looked at when it comes to shifting our mindset. When we decide it's time for a change, there is a tendency to focus on setting some grandiose new goal. Take, for example, the old classic of signing up for a marathon because you are tired of feeling unfit and out of shape. While there is nothing wrong with this goal, it is not the act of running a marathon that changes your life and keeps it changed. What this means is the steps you put in place and the habits you form in order to move you forward towards the goal of running the marathon. For example, joining a running club and getting a running plan to gradually increase your distances, making friends to go running with, planning weekend training sessions and the changes you made to your diet as part of your marathon prep. All these changes along the way are what caused a change. So, it is important to remember—whatever your goal—that the endpoint should not represent the cessation of your new habits. For example, if you signed up for the marathon because you wanted to get fitter and healthier, you shouldn't hang up your running shoes after completing the marathon.

A focus on a single outcome can lead us to quit more easily when we struggle or run into any roadblocks. The thought of signing up for the marathon might be that spark of motivation you needed, but remember, motivation is a bit like a fart in the wind—it doesn't matter how strong it is, it won't hang around for long. This is why, over time, as we work towards our new goals, I suggest you check in with yourself. Visualise the person you want to be, ask yourself, "What am I doing to help me obtain this vision?" As we start to visualise and build on reaching our goals and our why, we can start to identify with this version of ourselves that we are hoping to become. Over time, our beliefs and priorities may shift so that now, rather than just wanting to be someone who can run a marathon, you are someone who enjoys health and fitness, you now do it because you identify with it rather than purely to complete the marathon. In fact, the goal of the marathon becomes almost irrelevant.

Many of my clients started out with the initial goal of weight loss, but when they were able to change their values and began to see themselves as someone who prioritised their health and the way it made them feel, they no longer defined their success with their scale weight and actually went on to improve their body composition and maintained their progress in the long term.

As you finish reading this book, think about the person you intend to be, turn those ideas into sustainable actions and you will align your habits to your values, sustaining your progress long after motivation and willpower have left the picture.

Good luck and thank you for reading.

TOP TIPS

Hopefully, if you have read this far, you now have a lot of knowledge and tools to improve your weight loss journey. That being said, I know how short our attention spans are and how shit most people's memories are as well, so I decided to add this little tip section to the end in order to give you some short, sharp, actionable steps. Some of these you may already be doing, some of them may not work for you, but even if you can find one or two from the different sections to start working on, you can start investing in your future success without having to drastically alter your life. It is important to note that these are just common-sense tips that work in line with your body and can help break down your overall goal into smaller, more manageable tasks. When people start to talk about "biohacking" or use terms like "metabolism boosters", politely nod and walk away because they are probably trying to sell you some nonsense. If you really believe putting butter in your coffee is going to help with weight loss, then I can probably get away with pissing on your face and telling you it's rain.

I have broken the tips down into four main sections—

sleep, nutrition, exercise and mindset. That being said, I will start with two that help frame the start of change.

- Create an action plan: Start by clearly defining your goals: SMARTER GOAL (example):

Specific – I would like to fit into a particular dress size by June next year.

Measurable – What dress size is this (size 8, for example – I'm currently a 12)?

Achievable – starting with two resistance sessions a week, increasing step count from 6k to 10k steps a day.

Relevant – Turning 30 next year, I want to enter my 30s in the right frame of body and mind.

Timed – Achieve the result by June as this is my friend's wedding, and I have picked out the dress for it.

Exciting – I am so ready for this. I have the dress picked out and my birthday holiday booked as well.

Recordable – I have taken my measurements and will continue to take them every Monday. By the end of my first month, I want to have dropped 2cms off my waist, and I want my current clothes to feel loose. After two months, I want to be able to fit into the size 10 dress.

- Goal journaling: Regularly defining clear and specific goals. We want to prime our brains for change. Here is what I suggest:

  Once a **week**, plan three short-term goals for that week (reach step count, calorie target and make sure you are in bed by 10).

  Once a **month**, plan three medium-term goals for that month (new PB on squats, lose 2cms off waist, increased average weekly step count).

  Every **six months**, plan three long-term goals for that period (complete a 10k run, get my first unassisted pull-up, achieve one dress size smaller).

This way, you are always working towards short-, medium- and long-term areas. You want your short-term goals to feed into the bigger picture but be achievable in the short term so you can celebrate wins along the way, keeping you motivated and moving forward. When we don't create our goals in this way, we can easily get side-tracked, overwhelmed or lose motivation and give up in the process.

Sleep:

- Shock horror, but I think if you are someone who struggles with sleep, it's time to say goodbye to the booze or at least limit it to certain occasions or just one day of the week. If you are normally someone who has a drink most days of the week, how about you start by limiting it to just one or two drinks on Friday evenings? That could be a goal for your first week (okay, I'm not going to give you examples of how you can make each point a goal, but you get the idea... make it an achievable and realistic target).

- The same can be said for caffeine. Enjoy that morning coffee, but after that, if you want another, switch to decaf. I think people misunderstand what half-life means. While the half-life of caffeine is around five hours, this means that after five hours, there is half that amount still in your system, so if you have a coffee around 1 o'clock (assuming it's about 95 mg of caffeine), then by about 6 o'clock, there is still around 47.5mg of caffeine in your system. Caffeine can easily impact your sleep, that is why, again, if you are someone who suffers from bad sleep, you need to really be cautious and limit your caffeine intake to mid-morning. I know so many people who complain about sleep yet are pounding coffees and energy drinks late into the day... that's like complaining about suffering from anxiety, yet I haven't stopped smashing cocaine up my nose every weekend (don't worry, I don't do this... just giving an example how people like to complain without actually doing anything to fix the problem).

- No surprise that with the introduction of a culture dominated by technology and screens and bright lights everywhere, our sleep has suffered. So, simply try to minimise your exposure to bright lights for at least two hours before going to bed. A darker room naturally activates sleeping hormones. This means keeping mobile devices, computers, tablets and laptops as far away from your bed as possible. This will help to avoid distractions like checking how many likes you have on your most recent attention-seeking selfie. You also want to cut out as much natural light as possible. Natural or artificial light can activate the awakening response, causing sleep disruption. So, investing in some good blackout curtains can help.

- While talking about investing, it is always worth investing in a good-quality mattress and pillows, which can make a big difference to your sleep quality. And for anyone sensitive to temperature (like peri-menopausal women), get yourself a cooling gel pad mattress topper— cooling pads can also be inserted inside your pillowcase—and use cotton sheets instead of man-made fibres or polycotton blends.

- You also want to try and keep the temperature of your bedroom cooler, so use lighter sheets, maybe get a fan (if, like me, you like a little bit of white noise and can't afford AC) or you can open a window if you aren't living in a noisy area. A hot shower (or bath if you are a weirdo) an hour before bed can also help you unwind, relax and the change in body temp can help with the onset of sleep.

- Shouldn't need to tell you this, but obviously, being more active during the day is usually associated with better sleep... that being said, strenuous exercise too close to bedtime can negatively impact sleep, so try and keep the workouts a few hours away from your bedtime.

- Oh, and with that being said, try and keep a regular bedtime. Our body likes consistency here, so try and not only have a set bedtime but a good bedtime routine. For example, wind down for about an hour before bed. Avoid staying awake in bed. Instead, try reading or putting on some relaxing music until you can fall asleep.

- Play a quiet sound app—calming background noises can drown out annoying intermittent sounds and can help relax you.

Nutrition: Obviously, when it comes to nutrition, if your goal is to lose weight, you need to create a calorie deficit. I could put "eat in a calorie deficit" as a tip but hopefully you already know that and, actually, as a "tip", it's not very helpful. So the tips in this section are about making it easier to stick to your deficit, improve your satiety, navigate cravings and any little tips and tricks I like to use with my clients. While having already mentioned the first one in the chapters above, I will start with it again just to remind you of its importance.

- Think protein first. Any meal, any snack, any time you open your mouth to eat something, make sure it contains protein. I always think that if you start by deciding which protein source that meal or snack will contain, you will immediately start to construct a more satiating and less calorie-dense meal. Don't get me wrong, you can still fuck it up, but it becomes harder. (Protein sources: chicken, egg, whey, turkey, fish (salmon, tuna, tilapia, cod, trout, halibut), cottage cheese, Greek yoghurt (plain), tofu, lean beef, pork loin, bison, beans and legumes).

- If you aren't thinking protein, then think fibre... or think protein then fibre. But again, by adding fibre into the meal before the other constituents, we are improving satiety of the meal, reducing caloric load and both protein and fibre help to reduce the glycaemic load of the meal, so it keeps any insulin zealots happy (think fruit and vegetables... obviously, green ones are usually lower in calories, so bulk out your meals with some extra green veg).

- I always get my clients to track their food, even for just one or two days, using something like MyFitness-Pal, as most of the general population have no idea what calories are in their foods or how much protein or fibre they usually eat. Doing this, even for a short period of time, can help highlight the problems with your current eating habits and help educate you on the changes you need to make.

- Trim the fat. Fat is the most calorie-dense of the macronutrients, making it easier to overconsume. Also, simply put, fat is easier to store as fat. I'm not for a second telling you to not eat fat, but for many people, reducing the fat content in their diet can help to reduce the immediate caloric load of their diet. When picking what fat to have in your diet, I would just focus on good sources of omega-3 fats (mackerel, salmon, herring, sardines... okay, you don't like seafood, then let's go for flaxseed, chia seeds, walnuts and eggs). If you are tracking, I would suggest a level of around 20% of calories coming from fats.

- Bulk up... again, similar to the think fibre point, but if you can add more fibrous foods or foods with a high-water content to your meals, you are increasing the volume of food eaten, which will help improve satiety while reducing caloric intake. For instance, replace half your usual portion of pasta or rice, with some different vegetables. We aren't telling you to remove the foods you may enjoy, we aren't decreasing your portion size, we are just reducing the calories while increasing the number of vitamins and minerals... WIN-WIN.

- Starting your meal with an appetiser of salad, whole fruit or soup can help to decrease the number of calories in your main meal by 15%.

- If you like snacks, then make sure to plan your snacks in advance. This way, we are less likely to get caught short, and we can make sure the snacks we do eat fit in with our calorie and macro targets.

- Don't ban foods, instead, budget for them. Banning foods only leads to you feeling more restricted in your diet and, eventually, giving up. If you aren't tracking and, therefore, you haven't got the knowledge of budgeting for that food you like in your daily life, then maybe allowing yourself to enjoy it once a week will be enough to not feel restricted yet will help to reduce your overall weekly calorie consumption.

- Slow down—try to sit and enjoy your meal. Chew your food more, put your fork down between mouthfuls, and savour your meal. Research shows that we eat about 15% fewer calories when we sit down and take our time to enjoy our food.

- Drink up. Water suppresses your appetite and naturally helps your body metabolise stored fat. This isn't a miracle and drinking more than two litres a day isn't going to make you suddenly skinny overnight, but staying hydrated is important for overall health, exercise performance and cognitive function, so you should be doing this even if your goal isn't weight loss.

- Limit the variety. If you are someone who tends to overeat or your portion size usually gets out of control, a reduction in variety can improve the satiety from a smaller portion of food. We also know that meal monotony helps reduce calorie intake, so can be a very useful tool for those of us looking to lose weight. It also makes it easier to track and adjust if we are consistent with our food choices.

- Enjoy your food. A diet shouldn't be painful because, if it is, it is more than likely you will never stick to it. Flexible control has been shown to increase long-term weight loss success. If you do enjoy something a little more calorie-dense, remember, guilt does not serve your weight loss goals. One bad day is not enough to make you fat. So, if you did have a day where you overindulged, recognise it, but then get back to your healthy eating habits. Beating yourself up and quitting is about as productive as me losing my car keys and deciding to throw away my wallet…

- Alcohol is not your friend. If you have to have a drink, try to stick to clear spirits and diet mixers, and make sure you dance like there is a swarm of wasps in your shirt... no, all jokes aside, a lot of weight gain surrounding alcohol intake is from the lack of exercise and poor food choices. If you enjoy a few drinks on Friday night, make sure to hit your step count on Saturday and Sunday (maybe even get a gym session in), and remember, water is your hangover friend, not sugar or fat or the combination of the two—no matter how much you want to tell yourself bacon sarnies doused in ketchup are the perfect hangover cure.

- Honestly, while lots of people like to demonise artificial sweeteners (despite there being no solid concrete evidence in humans that they are anything other than safe for human consumption), I personally think they are a great tool for anyone dieting. I have quite a sweet tooth, so I find things like diet drinks (Pepsi Max), sugar-free jellies, low-calorie ice cream and using flavour drops in things like plain Greek yoghurt or Total 0 Fage is a game-changer. It gives me that sweet taste without the accompanying calorie load.

- Finally, this is a trick I personally use... if you can find a protein powder (preferably a whey isolate that has virtually no carbs or fats) and you blend it with ice, frozen berries and whatever unsweetened nut milk or low-calorie milk you enjoy using and you make a big thick shake, it is a winning combination of low calories, high protein, some vitamins and antioxidants from the berries and you can make it taste a bit like a dessert (so, hopefully, scratching any itch you may have for something more indulgent), and if you make it big enough, it can really help satiate you. My top tip is to buy bananas and break them up into quarters and stick them in the freezer. Using a little bit of frozen banana in the shake makes it super creamy and doesn't add too many calories, so is still diet-friendly.

Exercise: Look, we should already understand that resistance training is king. By building and maintaining our muscle mass, we can remain active later in life, which will not only improve our quality of life but is the key to improving body composition. Let's be honest, exercise also improves sleep, gut health, mental health and so many other benefits. It always baffles me that I even have to suggest for you to start to exercise. That being said, let me give you a few little notes or tips to help:

- Yoga and Pilates are also very useful practices, so don't worry, I'm not saying you all have to start squatting twice your bodyweight.
- Don't undervalue step count, some of my clients who have made not only the most progress but maintained their progress almost effortlessly are the ones that were able to make walking more part of their lives (I think Covid and the lockdown helped push people to this, but it really is amazing what you can achieve just purely by increasing your step count). I'm not suggesting you go from 5,000 steps to 20,000 overnight, but increasing your step count per week or month is quite an easy target that can have dramatic effects in the long run.

- Exercise doesn't always have to be seen as punishment. Finding exercises and activities you enjoy will help you stick to the changes. For example, if you enjoy dance, Zumba or boxing, then make sure to make time for those activities. While I want you to try and prioritise resistance training, if you can only commit to 2x 30-minute sessions a week, that is a start, and that alongside your dance classes will go a long way in improving your overall strength and fitness.

- Change that mindset. Think of anyone who physically can't exercise for medical reasons, do you envy them? (The answer should be no… otherwise, what the actual fuck!?) The simple change in telling yourself, "I get to exercise", rather than, "I have to", should go a long way in changing your relationship with exercise. Celebrate your body and what it can do, and in doing so, it will reward you with increased strength and vitality (assuming you are eating, recovering and training correctly).

- If you are struggling with where to start, there is a plethora of free information online now (also, in part, thanks to Covid and the lockdowns), so go on YouTube, type in bodyweight home workouts if that's all you're willing to start with… BUT START. There are so many great apps out there (Harriet Harper or The HHF Method as it's called on the app store is second to none) that give you access to amazing training plans at low costs, and since every other person on Instagram is either a personal trainer, fitness influencer or reality TV star that has become a personal trainer, I don't think there is a shortage of choice.

- Commit to an achievable goal in your first week. If you are new to exercise, then maybe week one is booking in for a taster session at your local gym or a gym class. Maybe in week two, you book in for two sessions. Remember, even if you are motivated to make a fresh start, we don't need to throw the kitchen sink at our goals. Start small and build.

- Doing it with a friend (exercise, that is) can help motivate and keep you accountable. Tell your friends about your new goals and see if any of them want to join you. Signing up to do a 5k or a 10k with a friend can help make it more enjoyable and increase your adherence.

- Putting exercise appointments in your calendar (so booking the time off in advance) can help you stick to your plan, and sticking to a regular time every day can help.

- Set performance goals. Performance goals are one of the best tools in your weight loss belt, especially if you are someone who can become obsessive over scale weight and tracking their food. Remember, in times of a deficit, we can start to focus on our food intake even more, so while it may sound odd, by taking the focus off of you obsessing over scale weight and other metrics, and instead, focus on improving your training. For example, getting that first unassisted pull-up or getting your 5k time under 30 minutes. You can decrease the stress and rumination that can accompany you around this time, and instead, you can work to push yourself to train harder and focus on positives that are in your control. You may find that by focusing on performance-related goals, you end up improving in all areas as you reduce the stress and, actually, because you are no longer focusing purely on when and what you eat, that your food intake improves.

You have probably realised a lot of these sections are intertwined. For example, exercise can improve sleep and reduce stress. Improvements in sleep can improve diet adherence and your ability to stick to your exercise regime. So, this is why I mentioned trying to pick at least one thing from each section to work on. As we start to incorporate some of the tips, hopefully, it will have a synergistic effect on our overall health. I also mention this so I don't have to repeat myself by writing the tip, "Remember to exercise", under the stress section as we know exercise can help reduce stress.

Mindset/Stress: The tips included in this section are simple or simplified techniques, obviously therapies like cognitive behavioural therapy or dialectical behaviour therapy, while beneficial, are not only outside of the scope of this book, but also aren't really appropriate for the tip section, so I would suggest doing some further reading/investigating yourself if stress management is an area you want to learn more about. These tips are more a collection of useful quick tools to use in your day-to-day life.

• Journaling: Based on the literature, it appears that journaling can act as a coping mechanism for individuals who experience emotional distress. Journaling is also a very simple and effective strategy. When you write your thoughts by hand, you can slow your thoughts down and help reduce the mindset of overthinking. The main thing is consistency. Set a specific time each day or week to journal. Be specific and, over time, like with anything, as you practise this more, you will get better at not only your writing skills but also your communication skills. If you are struggling to know where to start, you can use these simple prompts. What am I grateful for today? How do I feel? What or who brings me the most joy in my life? What am I looking forward to? What is most important to me right now? What do I currently feel I am lacking in my life? What do I need less of right now? Okay, there are lots, and if you get stuck, just google journaling prompts—you can find lists of different prompts depending on what you want to work on with your journaling.

• Ice baths: Turns out cold water immersion isn't just something you see wanky fitness people doing online. The real benefit of cold-water immersion is improving mood (it can help release dopamine in the brain) and increasing your stress resilience. Dr. Andrew Huberman, who seems like the most trustworthy source of information when it comes to this kind of area, recommends doing deliberate cold exposure for 11 minutes per week. This is a total per week and not per session, so that means around two to four sessions lasting one to five minutes each distributed across the week.

- Box or square breathing is one of my favourite and easy-to-learn breathing techniques to help manage anxiety in the moment. Quick to learn the steps are relatively simple. Box breathing involves four basic steps, each lasting four seconds: 1) breathing in 2) holding the breath 3) breathing out 4) holding the breath. (See, not exactly complicated.) It can be highly effective in stressful situations. People with high stress jobs, such as soldiers and police officers, often use box breathing when their bodies are in fight-or-flight mode. I would, again, suggest practising this consistently so you can draw on this skill when you need it and become more proficient with it, rather than desperately trying to remember how to do it when you are on the cusp of a panic attack.

- Give someone a hug (assuming you have got consent first... given this day and age). A 20-second hug can help release the chemical, oxytocin, in your body. This is associated with happiness and a reduction in stress. This can also apply to having sex and getting a massage, but a hug is usually easier and cheaper and, hopefully, quicker, although, again, I don't want to presume.

- Listening to music (assuming it is music you like) or making music can also help release oxytocin and improve mood.

- Guided meditation can be a great tool to help manage stress and anxiety. There are lots of apps and resources out there to get you started.

- Pet a dog (again, assuming consent and you don't have some phobia of them). Research has shown that dogs and humans see an increase in oxytocin from physical contact, including patting and stroking. *"But, Chris, does this work with cats?"* Honestly, it might, but if you are choosing to pet a cat over a dog, then you probably have more things to worry about than your stress levels.

- Spend time imagining your future. When we create images of ourselves in the future, it becomes easier to make choices in the here and now that will bene-fit our future. In certain therapy practices, it can be helpful to consider not only the future you do want but the future you don't want as well. Exploring the pros and cons of both staying the same and work-ing hard to change. While change can be stressful and difficult, the changes you make may outweigh the price you pay for staying the same. Listing the pros and cons down can be a valuable exercise to come back to or draw on when you are feeling like you are getting off track and are questioning why you started in the first place.

- In moments of setbacks and difficulties, it is gener-ally wise to stick to the few things we know and do well to help re-establish our confidence. This can help us move forward even when it might feel like life is trying to drag us down. Rather than focusing on perfection, focus on the small wins you can control now. I'm good at hitting my step count, or I'm good at prepping breakfast and bringing my protein snacks with me to work. Remember, an all-or-nothing approach usually leaves you with the latter rather than the former.

I want to leave you with two quotes, the first is from Ricky Gervais. During one of his specials, he makes the quip, "People know that's what makes them fat... no one got fat behind their own back". As always, brutally honest and brilliant, he does highlight the reality—most people know why they have put on weight. No one gets fat from too much sleep, exercise and eating vegetables. Putting on weight doesn't happen overnight, you accumulate fat over time as you take in more energy than you burn. This is an indisputable FACT. While many are quick to blame factors outside of their control, the reality is, energy or calories in vs. energy or calories out is the heart of the matter. This governs our ability to lose or gain weight. What drives this, though, is our habits—any solution looking to control this equation needs to address our habits as an individual, otherwise, it will fail. As Sean Covey so elegantly put it, "We become what we repeatedly do".

SPECIAL THANKS

Having read many books over the last few years in my quest to become more learned and broaden my mind, I have come to find I rather enjoy reading the "Thank You" section that many authors write at the end of their books. When I first started reading these, I skimmed over them and didn't really take note, and I also didn't really understand why I was reading the authors' thanks to publishers or friends I don't know... what relevance was this to me, the reader? Now, having written my own book and having experienced the commitment needed to complete one, I have, through this experience, begun to understand more and more the need for a thank-you section at the end. Truth be told, I actually quite enjoy reading these sections now as I feel it brings you closer to understanding the author and who they have in their corner as it were helping them complete this undertaking. It also may give you insight into their inspiration or, again, their methodologies.

I will keep mine brief. As a recluse at heart, I don't feel like there is a long list of people I want to thank... and yet the ones in my corner are hopefully already aware of how grateful I am, but it seems only right to put it in writing.

To my loving mum and dad, thank you. I'm sure if someone had told you when I was 13 or even 18 that I would go on to write a book, you would have looked at that person like they were speaking Mandarin. A boy obsessed with both sports and his Gameboy (more specifically, Pokémon Blue on my Gameboy Colour), I can't imagine anyone putting money on me writing, let alone ever reading a book. Next to my sister, I may well have been illiterate. Well, we all know men mature later than women, and it just took me finding something I was interested in to actually push myself intellectually. That being said, your unwavering support in the face of it all (ignoring your disdain for my tattooed complexion), I will be forever grateful (and I guess thank you, Gigi, for setting a good example).

To my boss (Evgenia) of over six years now, thank you. You helped create an environment in which I have been able to work while furthering my education, and that is actually such an amazing thing that I know not enough people find, so thank you.

To Maurice and Alex, my business mentors and friends. I am really not sure where I would be now had you not turned up to the gym one day looking for someone to punch. Your knowledge, drive and ambition have inspired me and continue to inspire me to this day. I will forever be a student of yours.

To Sibbles, the only girl I like to say that ever rejected me (yes, this is now immortalised in print)... you gave me the idea to start my newsletter all those years ago, which helped foster my love for writing, so when I say,

"Without you, this book never would have been created", I really mean that (we can discuss your request for 10% commission over dinner... as friends... not letting you friend zone me again).

To Chloe, my dear friend with an above-average body (that I take credit for), having been there to proofread my first newsletters and give feedback and actually always asking the strangest questions, which have been a continued source of not only entertainment but ideas for articles... thank you. (I guess Anita should also get a special mention in the strange question department.... And no berries are not calorie-free even if they are frozen).

To Dr Emma and Dr Diba, your continued ability to challenge me psychologically, intellectually and emotionally, all while being equally ridiculous, has remained a source of much growth as I write this book, so I would be remiss if I left you out of the thank-you list.

To my ex, Clem... or I should really say, my friend, but from the context of what I'm about to say, it makes more sense to call you my ex. Despite me giving good reasons not to at times, you have always supported and believed in me, and I want you to know that your unwavering belief means the world to me, and really helped push me to get this book written. Thank you (and hopefully, none of the book has offended your woke ideals too much... come on, I had to get a little jab in there... I can't be too nice). Also, Clem is living proof that sugar does not suddenly make you fat as judging by your squashy intake, if it did, you would be morbidly obese by now.

To my... friend, Ginge. Thank you for helping me to understand the younger generation. Without your insights, I'm sure this book would have been a lot longer and contained even fewer pictures than it already does. No, honestly, thank you for your patience and belief and for putting up with my grumpy ass along the journey of writing this. Means a lot.

Finally, thank you to all the people in the health, fitness and nutrition space who continue to inspire me (yes, there are a few of those out there). Special thanks to Layne Norton, whose books and YouTube channel remain a continued source of unbiased education for me. TheFitnessChef, James Smith, Dr Andrew Jenkinson, Jack A. Bobo, and many others whose books helped motivate and sculpt this one.

And finally, to you, the reader, thanks for purchasing this book. I hope now the matter of your own weight loss is more on the simple side than the confusing one.

ENDNOTES

1 Obesity Energetics: Body Weight Regulation and the Effects of Diet Composition - PMC (nih.gov)

2 The Effect of Adherence to Dietary Tracking on Weight Loss: Using HLM to Model Weight Loss over Time - PMC (nih.gov)

3 What Matters in Weight Loss? An In-Depth Analysis of Self-Monitoring - PMC (nih.gov)

4 Dietary Self-Monitoring and Long-Term Success with Weight Management - PMC (nih.gov)

5 Effect of behavioural techniques and delivery mode on effectiveness of weight management: systematic review, meta-analysis and meta-regression - PMC (nih.gov)

6 Associations between self-monitoring and weight change in behavioral weight loss interventions - PubMed (nih.gov)

7 Comparing Self-Monitoring Strategies for Weight Loss in a Smartphone App: Randomized Controlled Trial - PubMed (nih.gov)

8 Successful weight loss maintainers use health-tracking smartphone applications more than a nationally representative sample: comparison of the National Weight Control Registry to Pew Tracking for Health - PubMed (nih.gov)

9 first-page-pdf (sciencedirect.com)

10 Long-term persistence of adaptive thermogenesis in subjects who have maintained a reduced body weight - PubMed (nih.gov)

11 Energy compensation and adiposity in humans - ScienceDirect

12 Biology's response to dieting: the impetus for weight regain - PMC (nih.gov)

13 Stephen, E.M.H. 1917. Nauru (or Pleasant Island): The Richest Island in the Pacific Ocean. The Rabaul Record, 1st September, 5–7.

14 Hodge, A.M., G.K. Dowse, P.Z. Zimmet and V.R. Collins 1995. Prevalence and secular

trends in obesity in Pacific and Indian Ocean island populations, Obesity Research 3/Supplement, 77s–87s.

15 Cohort profile: Cohort profile: the Dutch famine birth cohort (DFBC)— a prospective birth cohort study in the Netherlands - PMC (nih.gov)

16 Association of Intrauterine Exposure to Maternal Diabetes and Obesity With Type 2 Diabetes in Youth | Diabetes Care | American Diabetes Association (diabetesjournals.org)

17 Malnutrition in Obesity: Is It Possible? - PMC (nih.gov)

18 High consumption of ultra-processed foods is associated with increased risk of micronutrient inadequacy in children: The SENDO project | SpringerLink

19 https://www.nejm.org/doi/10.1056/NEJMoa012908?url_ver=Z39.88-2003&rfr_id=ori:rid:crossref.org&rfr_dat=cr_pub%20%200www.ncbi.nlm.nih.gov

20 https://www.nejm.org/doi/10.1056/NEJMoa1105816?url_ver=Z39.88-2003&rfr_id=ori:rid:crossref.org&rfr_dat=cr_pub%20%200www.ncbi.nlm.nih.gov

21 https://pubmed.ncbi.nlm.nih.gov/9202122/

22 https://pubmed.ncbi.nlm.nih.gov/8532024/

23 https://www.sciencedirect.com/science/article/pii/S0735109708024352

24 https://www.ncbi.nlm.nih.gov/pmc/articles/PMC3248304/

25 https://pubmed.ncbi.nlm.nih.gov/15111494/

26 https://pubmed.ncbi.nlm.nih.gov/8584938/

27 https://pubmed.ncbi.nlm.nih.gov/19017730/

28 https://www.ncbi.nlm.nih.gov/pmc/articles/PMC5519190/

29 https://www.ncbi.nlm.nih.gov/pmc/articles/PMC8959968/

30 https://pubmed.ncbi.nlm.nih.gov/18678372/

31 https://www.ncbi.nlm.nih.gov/pmc/articles/PMC3096111/

32 https://www.ncbi.nlm.nih.gov/pmc/articles/PMC4578152/

33 https://www.sciencedirect.com/science/article/pii/S075333222200066X

34 https://pubmed.ncbi.nlm.nih.gov/20808947/

35 FAB: Clayton & Rowbotham 2009 - How the mid-Victorians worked, ate and died (fabresearch.org)

36 Agriculture in the British Industrial Revolution - World History Encyclopedia

37 Effects of Soft Drink Consumption on Nutrition and Health: A Systematic Review and Meta-Analysis - PMC (nih.gov)

38 Relation between consumption of sugar-sweetened drinks and childhood obesity: a prospective, observational analysis - ScienceDirect

39 Effect of drinking soda sweetened with aspartame or high-fructose corn syrup on food intake and body weight - PubMed (nih.gov)

40 The effects of four hypocaloric diets containing different levels of sucrose or high fructose corn syrup on weight loss and related parameters - PMC (nih.gov)

41 (PDF) The Influence of Food Portion Size and Energy Density on Energy Intake: Implications for Weight Management (researchgate.net)

42 jbr20367_450_453_1602622700.97607.pdf – Patterns and food trends in portion sizes

43 https://www.rcplondon.ac.uk/news/health-inequalities-and-obesity

44 https://www.ncbi.nlm.nih.gov/pmc/articles/PMC3495296/

45 Heart and Mind in Conflict: The Interplay of Affect and Cognition in Consumer Decision Making | Journal of Consumer Research | Oxford Academic (oup.com)

46 Exploring the mechanism of within-meal variety and sensory-specific satiation - ScienceDirect

47 Sci-Hub | Sensory-specific Satiety. Nutrition Reviews, 44(3), 93–101 | 10.1111/j.1753-4887.1986.tb07593.x

48 Food Fortification: The Advantages, Disadvantages and Lessons from Sight and Life Programs - PMC (nih.gov)

49 Consumption of ultra-processed foods and health status: a systematic review and meta-analysis - PMC (nih.gov)

50 https://www.ncbi.nlm.nih.gov/pmc/articles/PMC7946062/

51 https://pubmed.ncbi.nlm.nih.gov/19748710/

52 https://www.ncbi.nlm.nih.gov/pmc/articles/PMC10260851/

53 https://www.ncbi.nlm.nih.gov/pmc/articles/PMC9310253/

54 https://academic.oup.com/jcr/article-abstract/9/2/200/1813242

55 https://pubmed.ncbi.nlm.nih.gov/18005487/

56 https://www.ncbi.nlm.nih.gov/pmc/articles/PMC2741065/

57 https://pubmed.ncbi.nlm.nih.gov/16723172/

58 https://onlinelibrary.wiley.com/doi/abs/10.1002/mar.10043

59 https://pubmed.ncbi.nlm.nih.gov/35023412/

60 https://www.sciencedirect.com/topics/psychology/confirmation-bias

61 https://www.livekindly.com/beyond-meat-having-global-influence-how-brands-merchandise-vegan-protein/

62 https://pubmed.ncbi.nlm.nih.gov/28853950/

63 https://pubmed.ncbi.nlm.nih.gov/29967839/

64 Merritt, A.C., Effron, D.A. and Monin, B. (2010), Moral Self-Licensing: When Being Good Frees Us to Be Bad. Social and Personality Psychology Compass, 4: 344-357.

65 https://www.sciencedirect.com/science/article/pii/S0195666319309092?via%3Dihub

66 Ken Heaton Award – Most Cited Paper 2013 - Rome Foundation (theromefoundation.org)

67 https://pubmed.ncbi.nlm.nih.gov/20227928/

68 Accentuate the positive: Counteracting psychogenic responses to media health messages in the age of the Internet (auckland.ac.nz)

69 https://www.ncbi.nlm.nih.gov/pmc/articles/PMC6164197/

70 https://www.ncbi.nlm.nih.gov/pmc/articles/PMC6545628/

71 https://www.ncbi.nlm.nih.gov/pmc/articles/PMC5788730/

72 Gabor Mate- When the body says no: The cost of hidden stress. Page 28

73 https://academic.oup.com/aje/article/165/7/828/158160

74 https://pubmed.ncbi.nlm.nih.gov/17537466/

75 https://www.ncbi.nlm.nih.gov/pmc/articles/PMC4289126/

76 https://pubmed.ncbi.nlm.nih.gov/23576047/

77 https://pubmed.ncbi.nlm.nih.gov/32946037/

78 https://pubmed.ncbi.nlm.nih.gov/16519909/

79 https://www.sciencedirect.com/science/article/pii/S0925443913001919

80 The Carbohydrate-Insulin Model of Obesity: Beyond "Calories In, Calories Out" - PubMed (nih.gov)

81 De novo lipogenesis in humans: metabolic and regulatory aspects - PubMed (nih.gov)

82 Obesity Energetics: Body Weight Regulation and the Effects of Diet Composition - PubMed (nih.gov)

83 Calorie for calorie, dietary fat restriction results in more body fat loss than carbohydrate restriction in people with obesity - PMC (nih.gov)

84 Metabolic and behavioral effects of a high-sucrose diet during weight loss - PubMed (nih.gov)

85 Treatment of massive obesity with rice/reduction diet program. An analysis of 106 patients with at least a 45-kg weight loss - PubMed (nih.gov)

86 The Effects of Overfeeding on Body Composition: The Role of Macronutrient Composition – A Narrative Review - PMC (nih.gov)

87 The Australian paradox: a substantial decline in sugars intake over the same timeframe that overweight and obesity have increased - PubMed (nih.gov)

88 Once-Weekly Semaglutide in Adults with Overweight or Obesity - PubMed (nih.gov)

89 Ad Libitum Energy Intake Differences Between a Plant-Based, Low-Fat and an Animal-Based, Low-Carbohydrate Diet: An Inpatient Randomized Crossover Study - PMC (nih.gov)

90 Postprandial Administration of Intranasal Insulin Intensifies Satiety and Reduces Intake of Palatable Snacks in Women - PMC (nih.gov)

91 Insulin infusion during a nocturnal fast suppresses the subsequent day-time intake - PubMed (nih.gov)

92 An insulin index of foods: the insulin demand generated by 1000-kJ portions of common foods - ScienceDirect

93 Dietary protein impact on glycemic control during weight loss - PubMed (nih.gov)

94 A moderate-protein diet produces sustained weight loss and long-term changes in body composition and blood lipids in obese adults - PubMed (nih.gov)

95 Importance of maintaining a low omega–6/omega–3 ratio for reducing inflammation - PMC (nih.gov)

96 Dietary linoleic acid intake and blood inflammatory markers: a systematic review and meta-analysis of randomized controlled trials - PubMed (nih.gov)

97 Omega-6 fatty acids and inflammation - PubMed (nih.gov)

98 Biomarkers of Dietary Omega-6 Fatty Acids and Incident Cardiovascular Disease and Mortality - PubMed (nih.gov)

99 Impact of Obesity-Induced Inflammation on Cardiovascular Diseases (CVD) - PMC (nih.gov)

100 Associations Between Linoleic Acid Intake and Incident Type 2 Diabetes Among US Men and Women | Diabetes Care | American Diabetes Association (diabetesjournals.org)

101 Linoleic-acid-enriched diet: long-term effects on serum lipoprotein and apolipoprotein concentrations and insulin sensitivity in noninsulin-dependent diabetic patients - PubMed (nih.gov)

102 Effects of Saturated Fat, Polyunsaturated Fat, Monounsaturated Fat, and Carbohydrate on Glucose-Insulin Homeostasis: A Systematic Review and Meta-analysis of Randomised Controlled Feeding Trials - PubMed (nih.gov)

103 Why we eat too much- Dr Andrew Jenkinson- The new science of appetite.

104 Daily energy expenditure through the human life course | Science

105 Nonexercise movement in elderly compared with young people - PubMed (nih.gov)

106 Obese Japanese adults with type 2 diabetes have higher basal metabolic rates than non-diabetic adults - PubMed (nih.gov)

107 Increased BMR in overweight and obese patients with type 2 diabetes may result from an increased fat-free mass - PubMed (nih.gov)

108 https://www.ncbi.nlm.nih.gov/pmc/articles/PMC3319208/#B72

109 The effect of exercise interventions on resting metabolic rate: A systematic review and meta-analysis - PubMed (nih.gov)

110 Exercise reduces appetite and traffics excess nutrients away from energetically efficient pathways of lipid deposition during the early stages of weight regain - PubMed (nih.gov)

111 Biology's response to dieting: the impetus for weight regain - PubMed (nih.gov)

112 https://www.nature.com/articles/s41598-022-12048-0

113 https://www.ncbi.nlm.nih.gov/pmc/articles/PMC8338757/

114 https://www.hopkinsmedicine.org/health/wellness-and-prevention/exercising-for-better-sleep

115 A systematic review of dietary protein during caloric restriction in resistance trained lean athletes: a case for higher intakes - PubMed (nih.gov)

116 Pathways to obesity - PubMed (nih.gov)

117 Protein, weight management, and satiety - PubMed (nih.gov)

118 https://www.sciencedirect.com/science/article/pii/S0002916523029404?via%3Dihub

119 https://pubmed.ncbi.nlm.nih.gov/16002798/

120 https://pubmed.ncbi.nlm.nih.gov/14557793/

121 https://pubmed.ncbi.nlm.nih.gov/10722779/

122 https://www.ncbi.nlm.nih.gov/books/NBK224634/

123 https://pubmed.ncbi.nlm.nih.gov/8114857/

124 https://pubmed.ncbi.nlm.nih.gov/8400605/

125 https://pubmed.ncbi.nlm.nih.gov/15001604/

126 What is the role of portion control in weight management? - PMC (nih.gov)

127 https://www.ncbi.nlm.nih.gov/pmc/articles/PMC9031614/

128 https://www.ahajournals.org/doi/abs/10.1161/circ.125.
suppl_10.amp030

129 Matthew Walker- Why we sleep – The new science of sleep
and Dreams

130 https://pubmed.ncbi.nlm.nih.gov/23908148/

131 https://pubmed.ncbi.nlm.nih.gov/20921542/

132 https://www.ncbi.nlm.nih.gov/pmc/articles/PMC4861065/

133 https://www.ncbi.nlm.nih.gov/pmc/articles/PMC4338356/

134 https://www.ncbi.nlm.nih.gov/pmc/articles/PMC5878366/

135 (PDF) Why Choosing Healthy Foods is Hard, and How
to Help: Presenting the 4Ps Framework for Behavior Change
(researchgate.net)

136 Effect of effort on meal selection and meal acceptability in
a student cafeteria. (apa.org)

137 Promoting routine stair use: evaluating the impact of a stair
prompt across buildings - PubMed (nih.gov)

138 https://www.jstor.org/stable/40263846

139 Preordering school lunch encourages better food choices by
children - PubMed (nih.gov)

140 Rational snacking: Young children's decision-making on the
marshmallow task is moderated by beliefs about environmental
reliability - ScienceDirect

141 The Ant and the Grasshopper - Collection at Bartleby.com

Printed in Great Britain
by Amazon